# Information Technology Essentials

# Information Technology
## Essentials

Ethan Harvey

www.statesacademicpress.com

Published by States Academic Press,
109 South 5th Street,
Brooklyn, NY 11249, USA

ISBN: 978-1-63989-289-1

**Cataloging-in-Publication Data**

Information technology essentials / Ethan Harvey.
     p. cm.
Includes bibliographical references and index.
ISBN 978-1-63989-289-1
1. Information technology. 2. Computer systems. 3. Information superhighway.
I. Harvey, Ethan.
T58.5 .I54 2022
004--dc23

For information on all States Academic Press publications
visit our website at www.statesacademicpress.com

# Contents

**Permissions**

**Index**

# Preface

The use of computers for the purpose of storage, retrieval, transmission and manipulation of data is known as information technology. It is a sub-discipline of information and communication technology which is concerned with the commercial use of computers. Some of the important innovations of information technology are television and radio equipment, performance management software, and video conferencing equipment. The software studied under this domain can be categorized into system software and application software. System software can be broadly classified into operating systems, basic input/output systems, boot programs, assemblers and device drivers. Information technology is an upcoming field of science that has undergone rapid development over the past few decades. The topics included in this book on information technology are of utmost significance and bound to provide incredible insights to readers. It will serve as a valuable source of information for those interested in this field.

Given below is the chapter wise description of the book:

Chapter 1- Information technology is the branch of science which makes use of computers to store, retrieve, transmit and manipulate information or data. Some of the important topics studied under information technology are information security, network security, cyber attacks, cryptography, cipher models, etc. This chapter serves as an introduction to information technology and explains the subject matter in a simple manner.

Chapter 2- Computer network is an interconnection of multiple devices that use a set of common communication protocols to share their resources, data and applications. Science and technology have undergone rapid developments in the past decade which has resulted in the discovery of significant tools and techniques in the field of computer networks which have been extensively detailed in this chapter.

Chapter 3- Communication in computer networks can take place through wired or wireless channels. Some of the important topics associated with this domain are bandwidth and data rates, network topology, EM spectrum, Wi-Fi standards, Network layer services, etc. All these diverse principles of communications in computer networks have been carefully analyzed in this chapter.

Chapter 4- The practice of transferring data into small pieces to various networks is known as packet switching. Packet networks make use of circuit networks for the transmission of a formatted unit of data. The chapter closely examines the key concepts of packet switching to provide an extensive understanding of the subject.

Chapter 5- Information management is the branch of information technology that deals with the infrastructure used to control the accumulation and transmission of information. A few of the significant topics studied in relation to information management are data modeling, computer data storage, ontology, knowledge organizations, etc. These topics are crucial for a complete understanding of the subject.

At the end, I would like to thank all those who dedicated their time and efforts for the successful completion of this book. I also wish to convey my gratitude towards my friends and family who supported me at every step.

**Ethan Harvey**

# Introduction to Information Technology and Security

Information technology is the branch of science which makes use of computers to store, retrieve, transmit and manipulate information or data. Some of the important topics studied under information technology are information security, network security, cyber attacks, cryptography, cipher models, etc. This chapter serves as an introduction to information technology and explains the subject matter in a simple manner.

## Information Technology

Information technology (IT) is the use of any computers, storage, networking and other physical devices, infrastructure and processes to create, process, store, secure and exchange all forms of electronic data.

### IT Software and Hardware

IT includes several layers of physical equipment (hardware), virtualization and management or automation tools, operating systems and applications (software) used to perform essential functions. User devices, peripherals and software, such as laptops, smartphones or even recording equipment, can be included in the IT domain. IT can also refer to the architectures, methodologies and regulations governing the use and storage of data.

Business applications include databases like SQL Server, transactional systems such as real-time order entry, email servers like Exchange, Web servers like Apache, customer relationship management and enterprise resource planning systems. These applications execute programmed instructions to manipulate, consolidate, disperse or otherwise affect data for a business purpose.

Computer servers run business applications. Servers interact with client users and other servers across one or more business networks. Storage is any kind of technology that holds information as data. Information can take any form including file data, multimedia, telephony data and Web data, data from sensors or future formats. Storage includes volatile random access memory (RAM) as well as non-volatile tape, hard disk and solid-state flash drives.

IT architectures have evolved to include virtualization and cloud computing, where physical resources are abstracted and pooled in different configurations to meet application requirements. Clouds may be distributed across locations and shared with other IT users, or contained within a corporate data center, or some combination of both deployments.

## Advantages and Disadvantages of Information Technology

### Advantages

- Communication: With help of information technologies the instant messaging, emails, voice and video calls becomes quicker, cheaper and much efficient.

- Globalization and cultural gap: By implementing information systems we can bring down the linguistic, geographical and some cultural boundaries. Sharing the information, knowledge, communication and relationships between different countries, languages and cultures becomes much easier.

- Availability: An Information system has made it possible for businesses to be open 24×7 all over the globe. This means that a business can be open anytime anywhere, making purchases from different countries easier and more convenient. It also means that you can have your goods delivered right to your doorstep with having to move a single muscle.

- Creation of new types of jobs: One of the best advantages of information systems is the creation of new and interesting jobs. Computer programmers, Systems analyzers, Hardware and Software developers and Web designers are just some of the many new employment opportunities created with the help of IT.

- Cost effectiveness and productivity: The IS application promotes more efficient operation of the company and also improves the supply of information to decision-makers; applying such systems can also play an important role in helping companies to put greater emphasis on information technology in order to gain a competitive advantage. IS has a positive impact on productivity, however there are some frustrations can be faced by systems users which are directly linked to lack of training and poor systems performance because of system spread.

### Disadvantages

- Unemployment and lack of job security: Implementing the information systems can save a great deal of time during the completion of tasks and some labor mechanic works. Most paperwork's can be processed immediately, financial transactions are automatically calculated, etc. As technology improves, tasks that were formerly performed by human employees are now carried out by computer systems. For example, automated telephone answering systems have replaced live receptionists in many organizations or online and personal assistants can be good example also. Industry experts believe that the internet has made job security a big issue as since technology keeps on changing with each day. This means that one has to be in a constant learning mode, if he or she wishes for their job to be secure.

- Dominant culture: While information technology may have made the world a global village, it has also contributed to one culture dominating another weaker one. For example it is now argued that US influences how most young teenagers all over the world now act, dress and behave. Languages too have become overshadowed, with English becoming the primary mode of communication for business and everything else.

- Security issues: Thieves and hackers get access to identities and corporate saboteurs target sensitive company data. Such data can include vendor information, bank records, intellectual property and personal data on company management. The hackers distribute the information over the Internet, sell it to rival companies or use it to damage the company's image. For example, several retail chains were targeted recently by hackers who stole cus-tomer information from their information systems and distributed Social Security num-bers and credit card data over the Internet.

- Implementation expenses: To integrate the information system it require pretty good amount of cost in a case of software, hardware and people. Software, hardware and some other services should be rented, bought and supported. Employees need to be trained with unfamiliar information technology and software.

Information systems contribute to the efficient running of organizations. Information systems are showing the exponential growth in each decades. Today's information technology has tremendously improved quality of life. Modern medicine has benefited the most with better information system using the latest information technology. By understanding and learning what advantages and disadvantages it can bring, we have to try, believe and put an effort with our best to make that existing advantage much better and navigate the disadvantages to have a less impact on organizations and society.

## Categories of Computer

There are 4 types of computer:

- Supercomputer.
- Mainframe.
- Personal Computer.
- Embedded Computer.

## Supercomputer

The fastest, most powerful and most expensive computer. Capable of processing more than one quadrillion instructions in a single second. Supercomputers generally run one program at a time, as fast as possible. Applications requiring complex, sophisticated mathematical calculations use supercomputers.

Example: Large-scale simulations and applications in medicine, aerospace, automotive design, online banking, weather forecasting, nuclear energy research, and petroleum exploration.

## Mainframe

A large, expensive, powerful computer that can handle hundreds or thousands of connected user simultaneously. Second largest computers after supercomputers, Capable of great processing speeds and data storage.

With mainframes, enterprises are able to bill millions of customers, prepare payroll for thousands of employees, and manage thousands of items in inventory.

Example: Mainframe is used in large organizations such as hospitals, universities, large businesses, banks or insurance companies that need to manage large amount of centralized data.

## Personal Computer

A personal computer is a computer that can perform all of its input, processing, output, and storage activities by itself. A personal computer contains a processor, memory, and one or more input, output, and storage devices. Personal computers also often contain a communications device. Two types of personal computers are desktop computers and notebook computers.

## Mobile Computers and Mobile Devices

A mobile computer is a personal computer you can carry from place to place. Similarly, a mobile device is a computing device small enough to hold in your hand.

## Mobile Computers

- Notebook Computers: A notebook computer, also called a laptop computer, is a portable, personal computer often designed to fit on your lap. Notebook computers are thin and lightweight, yet they can be as powerful as the average desktop computer.

- A net book: Smaller, lighter, and often not as powerful as a traditional notebook computer. Most net books cost less than traditional notebook computers, usually only a few hundred dollars.

- Tablet PCs: Tablet PC is a special type of notebook computer that allows you to write or draw on the screen using a digital pen. Tablet PCs are useful especially for taking notes in lectures, at meetings, conferences, and other forums where the standard notebook computer is not practical.

## Mobile Devices

Some mobile devices are Internet-enabled, meaning they can connect to the Internet wirelessly. Five popular types of mobile devices are smart phones, PDAs, handheld computers, portable media players, and digital cameras.

## Smart Phones

Internet-enabled phone provides personal information management function such as a calendar, an appointment book, an address book, a calculator, and a notepad. Send and receive e-mail messages and access the web. Include built-in digital cameras.

### PDAs (Personal Digital Assistant)

Provides personal information management functions such as a calendar, an appointment book, an address book, a calculator and a notepad. Most PDAs also offer a variety of other application software such as word processing, spread sheet, personal finance, and games.

### Handheld Computers

Small enough to fit in one hand communicate wirelessly with other devices or computers and also include a digital pen or stylus for input. Industry-specific and serve the needs of mobile employees, such as meter readers and parcel delivery people , whose jobs require them to move from place to place.

### Portable Media Players

A mobile device can store, organize, and play digital media. Can listen to music; watch videos, movies, and television shows; and view photos on the device's screen.

### Digital Cameras

Device that allows users to take pictures and store the photographed images digitally, instead of, on traditional film while many digital cameras look like a traditional camera, some are built into smart phones and other mobile devices.

### Embedded Computers

Special purpose computer that functions as a component in a larger product embedded computers are everywhere : at home, in your car, and at work Perform various functions, depending on the requirements of the product in which they reside.

# Information and Communication Technology

Information and Communication Technology can simply be defined in its simplest form as an electronic medium for creating, storing, manipulating receiving and sending information from one place to another. It makes message delivery faster, more convenient, easy to access, understand and interpret. It uses gadgets such as cell phones, the Internet, wireless network, computer, radio, television, Satellites, base stations etc. These resources are used to create, store, communicate, transmit and manage information.

## The Scope of Information and Communication Technology (ICT)

Information and Communication Technology is a field that has a wide coverage. It extensively deals with communication technology and how it impacts on other fields of human endeavour. It is the fastest growing academic field of study and a viable source of livelihood. It is the convergence of telephone and computer networking through a single cabling system with ease of data storage, manipulation, management, and retrieval. It is concerned with database management, computer programming, and software development. Web designing, mobile application development, project management, security, networking analysis, media equipment, computer engineering, computer studies, the internet, intranet, internet protocol (IP), system software, application software, signal technology, base station management etc.

## Information and Communication Technology as a Field of Study

Information technology inclusion in most high school's curriculum is relatively new. However, it has gain prominence as some institutions have made it a compulsory subject. This is as a result of the understanding that it cut across every facet of human endeavor most especially the education sector. More so, it is the fastest growing industry in the 21st century. It is commonplace to hear e-learning, e-commerce, e-banking etc. It is, therefore incumbent on education curriculum developers to place ICT as a hub around which other disciplines revolve at least for the fact that it is a platform on which modern learning takes place. Needless to say that there is a paradigm shift with respect to popular opinion on how knowledge is acquired and dispensed.

Those who were hitherto conservative in this regard in the past seem to be winning the race ahead of those who merely believe and talk about it but with no evidence of commitment especially in the education sector. It is expected that in no distance future, textbooks may to a high extent be faced out in schools to be replaced with a soft copy accessible globally. This is not a news to the developed World as they are already far ahead. So been ICT compliant is a necessary tool for any meaningful learning in this dispensation.

Information and Communication Technology as a field of study is a challenging one in the light of the foregoing. Unlike the old perception, it is not all comers affair without proper training and re-training. Although the demand for professionals is growing in this regard, the need to build a career in it through proper training in a well-defined curriculum to be undertaken in institutions of learning cannot be overemphasized.

## Importance of Information and Communication Technology (ICT)

- It creates an analytical mind of students that help them study and proffer solutions to problems emanating from all related fields that employ it as a learning tool.

- Being an emerging academic field of study, it helps students to be innovative and develop new ways of solving problems scientifically.

- It makes information storage and retrieval easy.

- It enhances computer networking globally known today as internet and intranet.

- It accelerates economic development nationally as it is a virile source of national income for all nations that have fully embraced its usefulness.

- It creates gainful employment, hence a viable source of livelihood.

- It makes comprehension of other subjects easy. Virtually all fields of learning are amenable to ICT such as the application of projector for teaching in the classroom.

- It creates an avenue for the exchange of ideas and inventions among information technology scholars locally and internationally.

- It is the basis for e-learning and online library. Hence information dissemination is easier than ever.

- It is pivotal to globalization in its entire ramification and the realization of the Millennium development goals as agreed by the United Nations in the year 2000.

- It is used at various offices for proper documentation of official activities and administration.

## Challenges of Information and Communication Technology

Information and Communication Technology is confronted by a number of challenges which is characteristic of an emerging field. The following are some of the challenges:

- Expensive ICT materials: The requisite materials for practical knowledge of ICT especially at the advanced level are costly e.g Computer, projector, Internet machine e.t.c.

- Highly technical and practical driven: It is technically driven. It requires a great deal of logic and analytical reasoning for in-depth understanding and application.

- Poor orientation about the concept: The first challenge in embracing ICT as a field of study for students who have no prior orientation from their foundation education is that of speedy assimilation.

- Underdevelopment: ICT is a global concept and in order vape shop have an up-to-date knowledge on the subject there must necessarily be technological development nationally at least well established global information link on the subject. Many nations are yet to attain this.

- Universal acceptability as a compulsory field of study: The subject is yet to be fully embraced by all institutions of learning from the cradle globally. Although it is now compulsory at the high school level in some countries. Unless there are solid foundation and love for the subject, compliance for all may still take a time to attain in line with the global millennial goals.

- Hijack by unscrupulous persons: ICT is being used by some persons for evil purposes such as cybercrime and malicious programs that can cause severe damage to computers and similar gadgets.

# Information Security

Information Security is not only about securing information from unauthorized access. Information Security is basically the practice of preventing unauthorized access, use, disclosure, disruption, modification, inspection, recording or destruction of information. Information can be physical or electronic one. Information can be anything like Your details or we can say your profile on social media, your data in mobile phone, your biometrics etc. Thus Information Security spans so many research areas like Cryptography, Mobile Computing, Cyber Forensics, Online Social Media etc.

During First World War, Multi-tier Classification System was developed keeping in mind sensitivity of information. With the beginning of Second World War formal alignment of Classification System was done. Alan Turing was the one who successfully decrypted Enigma Machine which was used by Germans to encrypt warfare data. Information Security programs are built around 3 objectives, commonly known as CIA – Confidentiality, Integrity, Availability.

- Confidentiality: Means information is not disclosed to unauthorized individuals, entities and process. For example if we say I have a password for my Email account but someone saw while I was doing a login into Email account. In that case my password has been compromised and Confidentiality has been breached.

- Integrity: Means maintaining accuracy and completeness of data. This means data cannot be edited in an unauthorized way. For example if an employee leaves an organisation then in that case data for that employee in all departments like accounts, should be updated to reflect status to JOB LEFT so that data is complete and accurate and in addition to this only authorized person should be allowed to edit employee data.

- Availability: Means information must be available when needed. For example if one needs to access information of a particular employee to check whether employee has outstanded the number of leaves, in that case it requires collaboration from different organizational teams like network operations, development operations, incident response and policy/change management. Denial of service attack is one of the factor that can hamper the availability of information.

Apart from this there is one more principle that governs information security programs. This is Non repudiation.

- Non repudiation: Means one party cannot deny receiving a message or a transaction nor can the other party deny sending a message or a transaction. For example in cryptography it is sufficient to show that message matches the digital signature signed with sender's private key and that sender could have a sent a message and nobody else could have altered it in transit. Data Integrity and Authenticity are pre-requisites for Non repudiation.

- Authenticity: Means verifying that users are who they say they are and that each input arriving at destination is from a trusted source. This principle if followed guarantees the valid and genuine message received from a trusted source through a valid transmission. For example if take above example sender sends the message along with digital signature which was generated using the hash value of message and private key. Now at the receiver side this digital signature is decrypted using the public key generating a hash value and message is again hashed to generate the hash value. If the 2 value matches then it is known as valid transmission with the authentic or we say genuine message received at the recipient side.

- Accountability: Means that it should be possible to trace actions of an entity uniquely to that entity. For example as we discussed in Integrity section Not every employee should be allowed to do changes in other employees data. For this there is a separate department in an organization that is responsible for making such changes and when they receive request for a change then that letter must be signed by higher authority for example Director of college and person that is allotted that change will be able to do change after verifying his bio metrics, thus timestamp with the user (doing changes) details get recorded. Thus we can say if a change goes like this then it will be possible to trace the actions uniquely to an entity.

At the core of Information Security is Information Assurance, which means the act of maintaining CIA of information, ensuring that information is not compromised in any way when critical issues arise. These issues are not limited to natural disasters, computer/server malfunctions etc.

Thus, the field of information security has grown and evolved significantly in recent years. It offers many areas for specialization, including securing networks and allied infrastructure, securing applications and databases, security testing, information systems auditing, business continuity planning etc.

## Network Security

Network security is the security provided to a network from unauthorized access and risks. It is the duty of network administrators to adopt preventive measures to protect their networks from potential security threats. Computer networks that are involved in regular transactions and communication within the government, individuals, or business require security. The most common and simple way of protecting a network resource is by assigning it a unique name and a corresponding password.

## Types of Network Security Devices

- Active Devices: These security devices block the surplus traffic. Firewalls, antivirus scanning devices, and content filtering devices are the examples of such devices.

- Passive Devices: These devices identify and report on unwanted traffic, for example, intrusion detection appliances.

- Preventative Devices: These devices scan the networks and identify potential security problems. For example: penetration testing devices and vulnerability assessment appliances.

- Unified Threat Management (UTM): These devices serve as all-in-one security devices. Examples include firewalls, content filtering, web caching, etc.

## Firewalls

A firewall is a network security system that manages and regulates the network traffic based on some protocols. A firewall establishes a barrier between a trusted internal network and the internet. Firewalls exist both as software that run on a hardware and as hardware appliances. Firewalls that are hardware-based also provide other functions like acting as a DHCP server for that network.

Most personal computers use software-based firewalls to secure data from threats from the internet. Many routers that pass data between networks contain firewall components and conversely, many firewalls can perform basic routing functions.

Firewalls are commonly used in private networks or *intranets* to prevent unauthorized access from the internet. Every message entering or leaving the intranet goes through the firewall to be examined for security measures. An ideal firewall configuration consists of both hardware and software based devices. A firewall also helps in providing remote access to a private network through secure authentication certificates and logins.

## Hardware and Software Firewalls

Hardware firewalls are standalone products. These are also found in broadband routers. Most hardware firewalls provide a minimum of four network ports to connect other computers. For larger networks – e.g., for business purpose – business networking firewall solutions are available. Software firewalls are installed on your computers. A software firewall protects your computer from internet threats.

## Antivirus

An antivirus is a tool that is used to detect and remove malicious software. It was originally designed to detect and remove viruses from computers.

Modern antivirus software provide protection not only from virus, but also from worms, Trojan-horses, adwares, spywares, keyloggers, etc. Some products also provide protection from malicious URLs, spam, phishing attacks, botnets, DDoS attacks, etc.

## Content Filtering

Content filtering devices screen unpleasant and offensive emails or webpages. These are used as a part of firewalls in corporations as well as in personal computers. These devices generate the message "Access Denied" when someone tries to access any unauthorized web page or email. Content is usually screened for pornographic content and also for violence- or hate-oriented content. Organizations also exclude shopping and job related contents.

Content filtering can be divided into the following categories:

- Web filtering.

- Screening of Web sites or pages.

- E-mail filtering.

- Screening of e-mail for spam.

- Other objectionable content.

## Intrusion Detection Systems

Intrusion Detection Systems, also known as Intrusion Detection and Prevention Systems, are the appliances that monitor malicious activities in a network, log information about such activities, take steps to stop them, and finally report them.

Intrusion detection systems help in sending an alarm against any malicious activity in the network, drop the packets, and reset the connection to save the IP address from any blockage. Intrusion detection systems can also perform the following actions:

- Correct Cyclic Redundancy Check (CRC) errors.

- Prevent TCP sequencing issues.

- Clean up unwanted transport and network layer options.

## Cyber Attacks

A cyber attack is any type of offensive action that targets computer information systems, infrastructures, computer networks or personal computer devices, using various methods to steal, alter or destroy data or information systems.

### Types of Cyber Attacks

- Denial-of-service (DoS) and distributed denial-of-service (DDoS) attacks.

A denial-of-service attack overwhelms a system's resources so that it cannot respond to service requests. A DDoS attack is also an attack on system's resources, but it is launched from a large number of other host machines that are infected by malicious software controlled by the attacker.

Unlike attacks that are designed to enable the attacker to gain or increase access, denial-of-service doesn't provide direct benefits for attackers. For some of them, it's enough to have the satisfaction of service denial. However, if the attacked resource belongs to a business competitor, then the benefit to the attacker may be real enough. Another purpose of a DoS attack can be to take a system offline so that a different kind of attack can be launched. One common example is session hijacking.

There are different types of DoS and DDoS attacks; the most common are TCP SYN flood attack, teardrop attack, smurf attack, ping-of-death attack and botnets.

## TCP SYN Flood Attack

In this attack, an attacker exploits the use of the buffer space during a Transmission Control Protocol (TCP) session initialization handshake. The attacker's device floods the target system's small in-process queue with connection requests, but it does not respond when the target system replies to those requests. This causes the target system to time out while waiting for the response from the attacker's device, which makes the system crash or become unusable when the connection queue fills up.

There are a few countermeasures to a TCP SYN flood attack:

- Place servers behind a firewall configured to stop inbound SYN packets.

- Increase the size of the connection queue and decrease the timeout on open connections.

## Teardrop Attack

This attack causes the length and fragmentation offset fields in sequential Internet Protocol (IP) packets to overlap one another on the attacked host; the attacked system attempts to reconstruct packets during the process but fails. The target system then becomes confused and crashes. If users don't have patches to protect against this DoS attack, disable SMBv2 and block ports 139 and 445.

## Smurf Attack

This attack involves using IP spoofing and the ICMP to saturate a target network with traffic. This attack method uses ICMP echo requests targeted at broadcast IP addresses. These ICMP requests originate from a spoofed "victim" address. For instance, if the intended victim address is 10.0.0.10, the attacker would spoof an ICMP echo request from 10.0.0.10 to the broadcast address 10.255.255.255. This request would go to all IPs in the range, with all the responses going back to 10.0.0.10, overwhelming the network. This process is repeatable, and can be automated to generate huge amounts of network congestion.

To protect your devices from this attack, you need to disable IP-directed broadcasts at the routers. This will prevent the ICMP echo broadcast request at the network devices. Another option would be to configure the end systems to keep them from responding to ICMP packets from broadcast addresses.

## Ping of Death Attack

This type of attack uses IP packets to 'ping a target system with an IP size over the maximum of 65,535 bytes. IP packets of this size are not allowed, so attacker fragments the IP packet. Once the target system reassembles the packet, it can experience buffer overflows and other crashes. Ping of death attacks can be blocked by using a firewall that will check fragmented IP packets for maximum size.

## Botnets

Botnets are the millions of systems infected with malware under hacker control in order to carry out DDoS attacks. These bots or zombie systems are used to carry out attacks against the target systems, often overwhelming the target system's bandwidth and processing capabilities. These DDoS attacks are difficult to trace because botnets are located in differing geographic locations.

Botnets can be mitigated by:

- RFC3704 filtering, which will deny traffic from spoofed addresses and help ensure that traffic is traceable to its correct source network. For example, RFC3704 filtering will drop packets from bogon list addresses.

- Black hole filtering, which drops undesirable traffic before it enters a protected network. When a DDoS attack is detected, the BGP (Border Gateway Protocol) host should send routing updates to ISP routers so that they route all traffic heading to victim servers to a nullo interface at the next hop.

## Man-in-the-Middle (MitM) Attack

A MitM attack occurs when a hacker inserts itself between the communications of a client and a server. Here are some common types of man-in-the-middle attacks:

## Session Hijacking

In this type of MitM attack, an attacker hijacks a session between a trusted client and network server. The attacking computer substitutes its IP address for the trusted client while the server continues the session, believing it is communicating with the client. For instance, the attack might unfold like this:

- A client connects to a server.

- The attacker's computer gains control of the client.

- The attacker's computer disconnects the client from the server.

- The attacker's computer replaces the client's IP address with its own IP address and spoofs the client's sequence numbers.

- The attacker's computer continues dialog with the server and the server believes it is still communicating with the client.

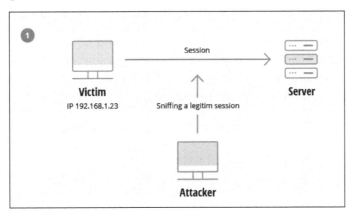

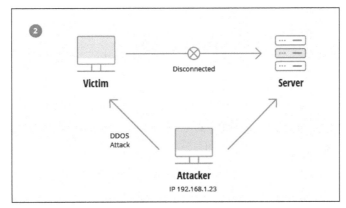

## IP Spoofing

IP spoofing is used by an attacker to convince a system that it is communicating with a known, trusted entity and provide the attacker with access to the system. The attacker sends a packet with the IP source address of a known, trusted host instead of its own IP source address to a target host. The target host might accept the packet and act upon it.

## Replay

A replay attack occurs when an attacker intercepts and saves old messages and then tries to send them later, impersonating one of the participants. This type can be easily countered with session timestamps or nonce (a random number or a string that changes with time).

Currently, there is no single technology or configuration to prevent all MitM attacks. Generally, encryption and digital certificates provide an effective safeguard against MitM attacks, assuring both the confidentiality and integrity of communications. But a man-in-the-middle attack can be injected into the middle of communications in such a way that encryption will not help : for example, attacker "A" intercepts public key of person "P" and substitute it with his own public key. Then, anyone wanting to send an encrypted message to P using P's public key is unknowingly using A's public key. Therefore, A can read the message intended for P and then send the message to P, encrypted in P's real public key, and P will never notice that the message was compromised. In addition, A could also modify the message before resending it to P. As you can see, P is using encryption and thinks that his information is protected but it is not, because of the MitM attack.

So, how can you make sure that P's public key belongs to P and not to A? Certificate authorities and hash functions were created to solve this problem. When person 2 (P2) wants to send a message to P, and P wants to be sure that A will not read or modify the message and that the message actually came from P2, the following method must be used:

- P2 creates a symmetric key and encrypts it with P's public key.

- P2 sends the encrypted symmetric key to P.

- P2 computes a hash function of the message and digitally signs it.

- P2 encrypts his message and the message's signed hash using the symmetric key and sends the entire thing to P.

- P is able to receive the symmetric key from P2 because only he has the private key to decrypt the encryption.

- P, and only P, can decrypt the symmetrically encrypted message and signed hash because he has the symmetric key.

- He is able to verify that the message has not been altered because he can compute the hash of received message and compare it with digitally signed one.

- P is also able to prove to himself that P2 was the sender because only P2 can sign the hash so that it is verified with P2 public key.

## Phishing and Spear Phishing Attacks

Phishing attack is the practice of sending emails that appear to be from trusted sources with the goal of gaining personal information or influencing users to do something. It combines social engineering and technical trickery. It could involve an attachment to an email that loads malware onto your computer. It could also be a link to an illegitimate website that can trick you into downloading malware or handing over your personal information.

Spear phishing is a much targeted type of phishing activity. Attackers take the time to conduct research into targets and create messages that are personal and relevant. Because of this, spear phishing can be very hard to identify and even harder to defend against. One of the simplest ways that a hacker can conduct a spear phishing attack is email spoofing, which is when the information in the "From" section of the email is falsified, making it appear as if it is coming from someone you know, such as your management or your partner company. Another technique that scammers use to add credibility to their story is website cloning : they copy legitimate websites to fool you into entering personally identifiable information (PII) or login credentials.

To reduce the risk of being phished, you can use these techniques:

- Critical thinking: Do not accept that an email is the real deal just because you're busy or stressed or you have 150 other unread messages in your inbox. Stop for a minute and analyze the email.

- Hovering over the links: Move your mouse over the link, but do not click it! Just let your mouse cursor h over the link and see where would actually take you. Apply critical thinking to decipher the URL.

- Analysing email headers: Email headers define how an email got to your address. The "Reply-to" and "Return-Path" parameters should lead to the same domain as is stated in the email.

- Sandboxing: You can test email content in a sandbox environment, logging activity from opening the attachment or clicking the links inside the email.

## Drive-by Attack

Drive-by download attacks are a common method of spreading malware. Hackers look for insecure websites and plant a malicious script into HTTP or PHP code on one of the pages. This script might install malware directly onto the computer of someone who visits the site, or it might re-direct the victim to a site controlled by the hackers. Drive-by downloads can happen when visiting a website or viewing an email message or a pop-up window. Unlike many other types of cyber security attacks, a drive-by doesn't rely on a user to do anything to actively enable the attack : you don't have to click a download button or open a malicious email attachment to become infected. A drive-by download can take advantage of an app, operating system or web browser that contains security flaws due to unsuccessful updates or lack of updates. To protect yourself from drive-by attacks, you need to keep your browsers and operating systems up to date and avoid websites that might contain malicious code. Stick to the sites you normally use. Although keep in mind that even these sites can be hacked. Don't keep too many unnecessary programs and apps on your device. The more plug-ins you have, the more vulnerabilities there are that can be exploited by drive-by attacks.

## Password Attack

Because passwords are the most commonly used mechanism to authenticate users to an information system, obtaining passwords is a common and effective attack approach. Access to a person's password can be obtained by looking around the person's desk, "sniffing" the connection to the network to acquire unencrypted passwords, using social engineering, gaining access to a password database or outright guessing. The last approach can be done in either a random or systematic manner:

- Brute-force password guessing means using a random approach by trying different passwords and hoping that one work some logic can be applied by trying passwords related to the person's name, job title, hobbies or similar items.

- In a dictionary attack, a dictionary of common passwords is used to attempt to gain access to a user's computer and network. One approach is to copy an encrypted file that contains the passwords, apply the same encryption to a dictionary of commonly used passwords, and compare the results.

In order to protect yourself from dictionary or brute-force attacks, you need to implement an account lockout policy that will lock the account after a few invalid password attempts.

## SQL Injection Attack

SQL injection has become a common issue with database-driven websites. It occurs when a malefactor executes a SQL query to the database via the input data from the client to server. SQL commands are inserted into data-plane input (for example, instead of the login or password) in order to run predefined SQL commands. A successful SQL injection exploit can read sensitive data from the database, modify (insert, update or delete) database data, execute administration operations (such as shutdown) on the database, recover the content of a given file, and, in some cases, issue commands to the operating system.

For example, a web form on a website might request a user's account name and then send it to the database in order to pull up the associated account information using dynamic SQL like this:

"SELECT * FROM users WHERE account = '"+ userProvidedAccountNumber +"';"

While this works for users who are properly entering their account number, it leaves a hole for attackers. For example, if someone decided to provide an account number of "' *or* '1' = '1'", that would result in a query string of:

"SELECT * FROM users WHERE account = '' or '1' = '1';"

Because '1' = '1' always evaluates to TRUE, the database will return the data for all users instead of just a single user.

The vulnerability to this type of cyber security attack depends on the fact that SQL makes no real distinction between the control and data planes. Therefore, SQL injections work mostly if a website uses dynamic SQL. Additionally, SQL injection is very common with PHP and ASP applications due to the prevalence of older functional interfaces. J2EE and ASP.NET applications are less likely to have easily exploited SQL injections because of the nature of the programmatic interfaces available.

In order to protect yourself from a SQL injection attacks, apply leastoprivilege model of permissions in your databases. Stick to stored procedures (make sure that these procedures don't include any dynamic SQL) and prepared statements (parameterized queries). The code that is executed against the database must be strong enough to prevent injection attacks. In addition, validate input data against a white list at the application level.

## Cross-site Scripting (XSS) Attack

XSS attacks use third-party web resources to run scripts in the victim's web browser or scriptable application. Specifically, the attacker injects a payload with malicious JavaScript into a website's database. When the victim requests a page from the website, the website transmits the page, with the attacker's payload as part of the HTML body, to the victim's browser, which executes the malicious script. For example, it might send the victim's cookie to the attacker's server, and the attacker can extract it and use it for session hijacking. The most dangerous consequences occur when XSS is used to exploit additional vulnerabilities. These vulnerabilities can enable an attacker to not only steal cookies, but also log key strokes, capture screenshots, discover and collect network information, and remotely access and control the victim's machine.

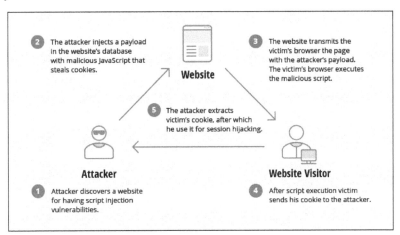

While XSS can be taken advantage of within VBScript, ActiveX and flash, the most widely abused is JavaScript primarily because JavaScript is supported widely on the web. To defend against XSS attacks, developers can sanitize data input by users in an HTTP request before reflecting it back. Make sure all data is validated, filtered or escaped before echoing anything back to the user, such as the values of query parameters during searches. Convert special characters such as ?, &, /, <, > and spaces to their respective HTML or URL encoded equivalents. Give users the option to disable client-side scripts.

## Eavesdropping Attack

Eavesdropping attacks occur through the interception of network traffic. By eavesdropping, an attacker can obtain passwords, credit card numbers and other confidential information that a user might be sending over the network. Eavesdropping can be passive or active:

- Passive eavesdropping: A hacker detects the information by listening to the message transmission in the network.

- Active eavesdropping: A hacker actively grabs the information by disguising himself as friendly unit and by sending queries to transmitters. This is called probing, scanning or tampering.

Detecting passive eavesdropping attacks is often more important than spotting active ones, since active attacks requires the attacker to gain knowledge of the friendly units by conducting passive eavesdropping before. Data encryption is the best countermeasure for eavesdropping.

## Birthday Attack

Birthday attacks are made against hash algorithms that are used to verify the integrity of a message, software or digital signature. A message processed by a hash function produces a message digest (MD) of fixed length, independent of the length of the input message; this MD uniquely characterizes the message. The birthday attack refers to the probability of finding two random messages that generate the same MD when processed by a hash function. If an attacker calculates same MD for his message as the user has, he can safely replace the user's message with his, and the receiver will not be able to detect the replacement even if he compares MDs.

## Malware Attack

Malicious software can be described as unwanted software that is installed in your system without your consent. It can attach itself to legitimate code and propagate; it can lurk in useful applications or replicate itself across the Internet. Here are some of the most common types of malware:

- Macro viruses: These viruses infect applications such as Microsoft Word or Excel. Macro viruses attach to an application's initialization sequence. When the application is opened, the virus executes instructions before transferring control to the application. The virus replicates itself and attaches to other code in the computer system.

- File infectors: File infector viruses usually attach themselves to executable code, such as .exe files. The virus is installed when the code is loaded. Another version of a file infector associates itself with a file by creating a virus file with the same name, but an .exe extension. Therefore, when the file is opened, the virus code will execute.

- System or boot-record infectors: A boot-record virus attaches to the master boot record on hard disks. When the system is started, it will look at the boot sector and load the virus into memory, where it can propagate to other disks and computers.

- Polymorphic viruses: These viruses conceal themselves through varying cycles of encryption and decryption. The encrypted virus and an associated mutation engine are initially decrypted by a decryption program. The virus proceeds to infect an area of code. The mutation engine then develops a new decryption routine and the virus encrypts the mutation engine and a copy of the virus with an algorithm corresponding to the new decryption routine. The encrypted package of mutation engine and virus is attached to new code, and the process repeats. Such viruses are difficult to detect but have a high level of entropy because of the many modifications of their source code. Anti-virus software or free tools like Process Hacker can use this feature to detect them.

- Stealth viruses: Stealth viruses take over system functions to conceal themselves. They do this by compromising malware detection software so that the software will report an infected area as being uninfected. These viruses conceal any increase in the size of an infected file or changes to the file's date and time of last modification.

- Trojans: A Trojan or a Trojan horse is a program that hides in a useful program and usually has a malicious function. A major difference between viruses and Trojans is that Trojans do not self-replicate. In addition to launching attacks on a system, a Trojan can establish a back door that can be exploited by attackers. For example, a Trojan can be programmed to open a high-numbered port so the hacker can use it to listen and then perform an attack.

- Logic bombs: A logic bomb is a type of malicious software that is appended to an application and is triggered by a specific occurrence, such as a logical condition or a specific date and time.

- Worms: Worms differ from viruses in that they do not attach to a host file, but are self-contained programs that propagate across networks and computers. Worms are commonly spread through email attachments; opening the attachment activates the worm program. A typical worm exploit involves the worm sending a copy of itself to every contact in an infected computer's email address In addition to conducting malicious activities, a worm spreading across the internet and overloading email servers can result in denial-of-service attacks against nodes on the network.

- Droppers: A dropper is a program used to install viruses on computers. In many instances, the dropper is not infected with malicious code and, therefore might not be detected by virus-scanning software. A dropper can also connect to the internet and download updates to virus software that is resident on a compromised system.

- Ransom ware: Ransomware is a type of malware that blocks access to the victim's data and threatens to publish or delete it unless a ransom is paid. While some simple computer ransomware can lock the system in a way that is not difficult for a knowledgeable person to reverse, more advanced malware uses a technique called cryptoviral extortion, which encrypts the victim's files in a way that makes them nearly impossible to recover without the decryption key.

- Adware: Adware is a software application used by companies for marketing purposes; advertising banners are displayed while any program is running. Adware can be automatically downloaded to your system while browsing any website and can be viewed through pop-up windows or through a bar that appears on the computer screen automatically.

- Spyware: Spyware is a type of program that is installed to collect information about users, their computers or their browsing habits. It tracks everything you do without your knowledge and sends the data to a remote user. It also can download and install other malicious programs from the internet. Spyware works like adware but is usually a separate program that is installed unknowingly when you install another freeware application.

## Cryptography

Cryptography is the study and practice of techniques for secure communication in the presence of third parties called adversaries. It deals with developing and analyzing protocols which prevents malicious third parties from retrieving information being shared between two entities thereby following the various aspects of information security.

Secure Communication refers to the scenario where the message or data shared between two parties can't be accessed by an adversary. In Cryptography, an Adversary is a malicious entity, which aims to retrieve precious information or data thereby undermining the principles of information security.

Data Confidentiality, Data Integrity, Authentication and Non-repudiation are core principles of modern-day cryptography.

- Confidentiality refers to certain rules and guidelines usually executed under confidentiality agreements which ensure that the information is restricted to certain people or places.

- Data integrity refers to maintaining and making sure that the data stays accurate and consistent over its entire life cycle.

- Authentication is the process of making sure that the piece of data being claimed by the user belongs to it.

- Non-repudiation refers to ability to make sure that a person or a party associated with a contract or a communication cannot deny the authenticity of their signature over their document or the sending of a message.

Consider two parties Alice and Bob. Now, Alice wants to send a message m to Bob over a secure channel. So, what happens is as follows:

The sender's message or sometimes called the Plaintext, is converted into an unreadable form using a Key k. The resultant text obtained is called the Ciphertext. This process is known as Encryption. At the time of receival, the Ciphertext is converted back into the plaintext using the same Key k, so that it can be read by the receiver. This process is known as Decryption.

```
Alice (Sender)        Bob (Receiver)

C = E (m, k)   ---->    m = D (C, k)
```

Here, C refers to the Ciphertext while E and D are the Encryption and Decryption algorithms respectively.

Let's consider the case of Caesar Cipher or Shift Cipher as an example.

As the name suggests, in Caesar Cipher each character in a word is replaced by another character under some defined rules. Thus, if A is replaced by D, B by E and so on. Then, each character in the word would be shifted by a position of 3. For example:

```
Plaintext : Geeksforgeeks

Ciphertext : Jhhnvirujhhnv
```

Even if the adversary knows that the cipher is based on Caesar Cipher, it cannot predict the plain-text as it doesn't have the key in this case which is to shift the characters back by three places.

Cryptography is an important aspect when we deal with network security. 'Crypto' means secret or hidden. Cryptography is the science of secret writing with the intention of keeping the data secret. Cryptanalysis, on the other hand, is the science or sometimes the art of breaking cryptosystems. These both terms are a subset of what is called as Cryptology.

## Classification

The flowchart depicts that cryptology is only one of the factors involved in securing networks.

Cryptology refers to study of codes, which involves both writing (cryptography) and solving (crypt-analysis) them. Below is a classification of the crypto-terminologies and their various types.

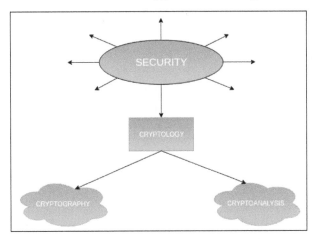

Cryptography is classified into symmetric cryptography, asymmetric cryptography and hashing. Below are the description of these types.

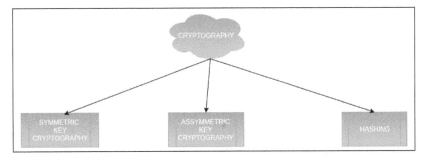

## Symmetric Key Cryptography

It involves usage of one secret key along with encryption and decryption algorithms which help in securing the contents of the message. The strength of symmetric key cryptography depends upon the number of key bits. It is relatively faster than asymmetric key cryptography. There arises a key distribution problem as the key has to be transferred from the sender to receiver through a secure channel.

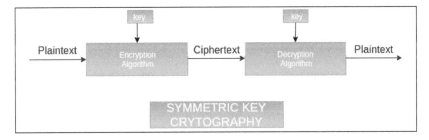

## Assymetric Key Cryptography

It is also known as public key cryptography because it involves usage of a public key along with secret key. It solves the problem of key distribution as both parties uses different keys for encryption/decryption. It is not feasible to use for decrypting bulk messages as it is very slow compared to symmetric key cryptography.

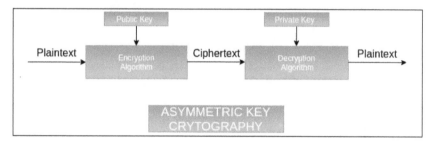

## Hashing

It involves taking the plain-text and converting it to a hash value of fixed size by a hash function. This process ensures integrity of the message as the hash value on both, sender\'s and receiver\'s side should match if the message is unaltered.

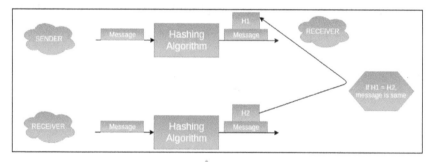

## Cryptanalysis

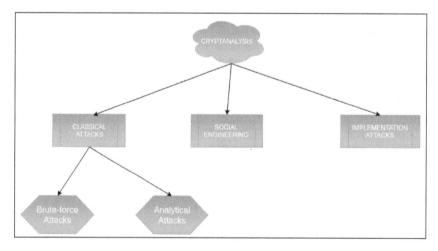

- Classical Attacks: It can be divided into Mathematical analysis and Brute-force attacks. Brute-force attacks run the encryption algorithm for all possible cases of the keys until a match is found. Encryption algorithm is treated as a black box. Analytical attacks are those attacks which focus on breaking the cryptosystem by analysing the internal structure of the encryption algorithm.

- Social Engineering Attack: It is something which is dependent on the human factor. Tricking someone to reveal their passwords to the attacker or allowing access to the restricted area comes under this attack. People should be cautious when revealing their passwords to any third party which is not trusted.

- Implementation Attacks: Implementation attacks such as side-channel analysis can be used to obtain a secret key. They are relevant in cases where the attacker can obtain physical access to the cryptosystem.

# Cipher Models

The process of covering from plaintext to ciphertext is called Encryption, restoring the plaintext from ciphertext is known as Decryption.

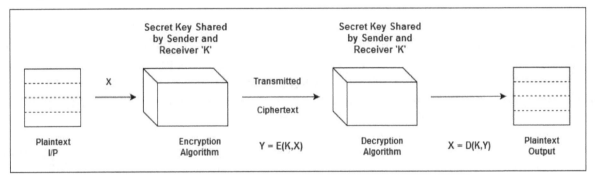

Symmetric Cipher Model uses a single secret key for both encryption & decryption.

Where,

    K= Secret Key

    X = Plaintext/Message

    Ciphertext Y = E(X, K)

    Decrypted/Plaintext X = D(Y, K)

A symmetric encryption scheme has five components:

- Plaintext: This is the original intelligible message or data that is fed into the algorithm as input.

- Encryption algorithm: The encryption algorithm performs various substitutions and transformations on the plaintext.

- Secret key: The secret key is also input to the encryption algorithm.The key is a value independent of the plaintext and of the algorithm. The algorithm will produce a different output depending on the specific key being used at the time.The exact substitutions and transformations performed by the algorithm depend on the key.

- Ciphertext: This is the scrambled message produced as output. It depends on the plaintext and the secret key. For a given message, two different keys will produce two different ciphertexts. The ciphertext is an apparently random stream of data and, as it stands, is unintelligible.

- Decryption algorithm: This is essentially the encryption algorithm run in reverse. It takes the ciphertext and the secret key and produces the original plaintext.

E.g.: Original text X → plain text e.g. CNS

Encryption Algorithm = replacing each letter of the alphabet with the letter standing three places further down the alphabet. i.e. $(X + 3)$ so,

> Coded text Y → Cipher text for CNS is *Fqv*

> Decryption Algorithm = reverse of encryption i,e $(Y - 3)$

> Here key = 3.

Symmetric ciphers use symmetric algorithms to encrypt and decrypt data. These ciphers are used in symmetric key cryptography. A symmetric algorithm uses the same key to encrypt data as it does to decrypt data. For example, a symmetric algorithm will use key kk to encrypt some plaintext information like a password into a ciphertext. Then, it uses kk again to take that ciphertext and turn it back into the password.

Symmetric ciphers are the opposite of asymmetric ciphers, like those used in public-key cryptography. These ciphers use asymmetric algorithms which use one key to encrypt data and a different key to decrypt ciphers. Typically, those two keys are called public and private keys, as is the case with RSA encryption. The public key is used to encrypt data, and the private key is used to decrypt data.

Symmetric ciphers have many important advantages, like speed. But they lack in other areas like security and key management. Due to these pros, however, there are a number of important symmetric ciphers in production today. The most popular of these is Advanced Encryption Standard (AES). Because of its security concerns, however, it is often used on a single machine for encryption and decryption. This eliminates the need to share the secret key. Symmetric ciphers are a good place to get started when learning cryptography as they were the first widespread systems used in modern computing. Like all forms of cryptography, the general process of symmetric key cryptography is to first encrypt a message. This encryption algorithm will turn any plaintext data into ciphertext, an unreadable code. Then, that ciphertext is transmitted to another party who decrypts it to find the original message.

This process uses some sort of key in the encryption and decryption algorithms. Typically this key is only a series of bits, representing some number. What the key is exactly depends on the encryption being used. For symmetric ciphers, the same key is used in both the encryption and decryption algorithm. So, the algorithm functions for encryption and decryption look like this:

> encrypt(plaintext, key)=ciphertext,

> decrypt(ciphertext, key)=plaintext.

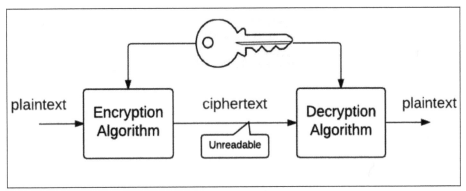

The symmetric encryption process.

Symmetric key cryptography is much simpler than public-key cryptography. Imagine that you want to exchange secret messages with your online friend. You want to be as careful as possible, but you unfortunately don't know what they look like. You decide to set up the following system:

- You buy a locker at the train station and a padlock with only 1 key.

- When it's your turn to send a message, you go down to station, leave a message, and lock it.

- You pick a time and place to meet with your online friend.

- You give them the key when you see them (however, you can't see their face).

- Your friend can then go to the locker, open it, and read your message.

- To send a message back to you, your friend must go through the same process.

Unfortunately, this protocol is very insecure.

## Simple Symmetric Ciphers

## Caeser Cipher

Simple symmetric are the oldest forms of cryptography, dating back to the Caesar cipher, a cipher used by Julius Caesar to communicate in secret. This cipher, a type of substitution cipher, took any message that Caesar might write to someone, and shifted each character in that message by a certain amount. For example, the message "hello" shifted by a value of 5 would result in "mjqqt". This cipher is symmetric because the same key, in this case 5, is used to encrypt and decrypt the message.

Caesar's cipher is especially prone to attacks like frequency analysis. Words and characters in lanaguage are not random. If an attacker intercepts enough messages, they might learn that they letter j shows up a lot in the cipher text codes. Now the attacker has a clue that j is Caesar cipher code for a common letter, probably an s or an a. definitely not a z. repeating this process enough can break this code.

## One-time Pad

The one-time pad is another famous symmetric cipher. It's famous for its reported use by KGB and

American spies during the Cold War. Let's say one spy wanted to get another spy a message, and for simplicity that message is in binary format. The two spies have already met up beforehand and decided on a key of `10110` for this one message. This key is usually decided at random to heighten security. The first spy, Alice, wants to send the message `01101` to Bob, the second spy. To encrypt Alice's message, she creates a new cipher text that has a `0` if the corresponding bit is the same between the original message and the key. Otherwise, it has a `1`. This is also called an XOR in boolean logic.

Now, Alice's encrypted message is `11011`. To decrypt this message, Bob does the exact same process. Two XOR operations result in a null operation in boolean logic. So,

$$11011 \oplus 10110 = 01101$$

where $\oplus$ is the mathematical symbol for XOR.

There is a problem with the one-time pad (apart from other general problems with symmetric ciphers). The key needs to be exactly as long as the message itself. Alice and Bob can get around this issue by simply looping around to the beginning of the key when they reach the end. However, this will make the code much easier to break by opposing spies using brute force or statistical analysis. However, one-time pads are perfectly secret in theory. This means that an attacker cannot know anything about a particular cipher text if they intercept it. In practice, however, it's insecure to distribute and exchange keys.

## Types of Symmetric Ciphers

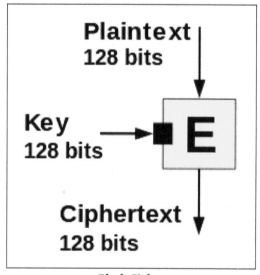

Block Cipher.

Modern symmetric key ciphers can be one of two types. The block cipher take in n bits of plaintext and n bits of key to produce n bits of ciphertext. The are known as block ciphers because they operate on blocks of n x n bits at a time. The block cipher is used in many current symmetric cryptosystems.

There a few important issues with basic block ciphers. They are malleable, which means the message they convey is subject to change by an attacker. If you encrypt a certain message, mm, to enc(m), an attacker can intercept that and change it to enc($m_0$). The attacker then sends it along, and you're recipient decrypts your message to find $m_0$, not mm. For example, an attacker could intercept a message that decrypts to "Meet me at 10PM" and change it to "Meet me at 11PM". Further, messages that are longer than one block long need to be split up into smaller messages, a process known as Electronic Code Book (ECB). Cipher Block Chaining (CBC) fixes some of these issues by introducing some elements of randomness into the process, however it has a terrible effect on performance.

The stream cipher is similar to the one-time pad in that is uses the XOR function on the plaintext with a pseudo-random sequence. So, instead of a secret key that it static like `01011` from the TIY problem above, it constantly is changing and is always pseudo-random. The input plaintext is encrypted incrementally, often one byte at a time. A random sequence is not possible because distributing it to the receiver is inherently unsafe. So, a pseudo-random sequence is used. These pseudo-random sequences are the outputs of a generator, given an initial seed. A seed is simply a number used to initialize a pseudo-random number generator.

Stream ciphers are also malleable and often generate ciphertexts that are statistically correlated with their input plaintext. This is especially true if the randomness of the algorithm is poorly implemented. Often, sections of the key are thrown out completely. Even with popular stream ciphers like RC4, the few first kilobytes of the key are often discarded.

## Advantages and Disadvantages

Choosing between symmetric and asymmetric (often called public-key) cryptography is very important because the choice will have severe impact on the entire system. Symmetric ciphers and systems are beneficial for performance because they operate at around 1000 times faster than a public-key cryptosystem. Plus symmetric ciphers are simpler and easier to implement. So, symmetric systems are used for bulk encryption, especially when security is not as big of a concern.

Some symmetric ciphers can be broken through a brute-force attack, lowering their overall security. If you decided to use Caesar's cipher to encrypt your data, you could be hacked immediately because breaking them with brute is trivial with current computers. Typically these attacks simply try every possible key until the correct one is found. Even with more advanced symmetric ciphers, this is still a problem that must be handled using key changes and randomness.

Symmetric ciphers are disadvantageous because they require a secret channel to exchange the key. This channel is inherently insecure, and so an attacker might steal the key, rendering the system vulnerable. Further, key management becomes an issue in large settings with symmetric keys. Say you have a company with 100 employees. If you used RSA encryption, you would only need 200 total keys (a public and private key for each person). However, if you used symmetric keys, you would need $\frac{100*99}{2*1} = 4950$! that's because each pair of people would need their own symmetric key.

Example:

Let's analyze our example to see how our system matches up with these pros and cons.

- Alice and Bob have a very simple system that was easy to implement. They only had to make one key (as opposed to 4, a public and private key for each person), and the whole thing was up and running quickly.

- A brute force attack (where the attacker tries every single possible secret key to find the correct one) could break down this system faster than if they needed 4 keys to do this, but that's not the main concern.

- If Alice and Bob wanted to scale their system up to more people, where each pair of people had their own locker for secure communication, they would need to buy $\dfrac{n(n-1)}{2}$ keys, where $n$ is the number of people in the system.

- The biggest concern with this system is the sharing of the key. They need to meet every time to hand it off. They don't know each other by sight, so Alice could give the key to the wrong person. Even if they did know each other by sight, someone could still come and take the key away from them *while* they are trading it. Both of these attacks (impersonation and man-in-the-middle attacks) happen all the time.

## Hill Cipher

Invented by Lester S. Hill in 1929, the Hill cipher is a polygraphic substitution cipher based on linear algebra. Hill used matrices and matrix multiplication to mix up the plaintext. To counter charges that his system was too complicated for day to day use, Hill constructed a cipher machine for his system using a series of geared wheels and chains. However, the machine never really sold. Hill's major contribution was the use of mathematics to design and analyse cryptosystems.

This example will rely on some linear algebra and some number theory. The key for a hill cipher is a matrix e.g.

$$\begin{bmatrix} 2 & 4 & 5 \\ 9 & 2 & 1 \\ 3 & 17 & 7 \end{bmatrix}$$

In the above case, we have taken the size to be 3×3, however it can be any size (as long as it is square). Assume we want to encipher the message ATTACK AT DAWN. To encipher this, we need to break the message into chunks of 3. We now take the first 3 characters from plaintext, ATT and create a vector that corresponds to the letters (replace A with 0, B with 1 ... Z with 25 etc.) to get: [0 19 19] (this is [‹A› ‹T› ‹T›]).

To get ciphertext we perform a matrix multiplication,

$$\begin{bmatrix} 2 & 4 & 5 \\ 9 & 2 & 1 \\ 3 & 17 & 7 \end{bmatrix}\begin{bmatrix} 0 \\ 19 \\ 19 \end{bmatrix} = \begin{bmatrix} 171 \\ 57 \\ 456 \end{bmatrix}(\bmod\ 26) = \begin{bmatrix} 15 \\ 5 \\ 14 \end{bmatrix} = \text{'PFO'}$$

This process is performed for all 3 letter blocks in the plaintext. The plaintext may have to be padded with some extra letters to make sure that there is a whole number of blocks.

We need to find an inverse matrix modulo 26 to use as 'decryption key'. i.e. we want something that will take 'PFO' back to 'ATT'. If 3 by 3 key matrix is called K, decryption key will be the 3 by 3 matrix $K^{-1}$, which is the inverse of K.

$$K^{-1} \begin{bmatrix} 15 \\ 5 \\ 14 \end{bmatrix} (\bmod\ 26) = \begin{bmatrix} 0 \\ 19 \\ 19 \end{bmatrix} = \text{'ATT'}$$

To find $K^{-1}$ we have to use a bit of maths. It turns out that $K^{-1}$ above can be calculated from key. A lengthy discussion will not be included here, but we will give a short example.

Let K be the key matrix. Let d be the determinant of K. We wish to find $K^{-1}$ (the inverse of K), such that $K \times K^{-1} = I$ (mod 26), where I is the identity matrix. The following formula tells us how to find $K^{-1}$ given K:

$$K^{-1} = d^{-1} \times \text{adj}(K)$$

Where $d \times d^{-1} = 1 (\bmod\ 26)$, and adj(K) is the adjugate matrix of K.

d (the determinant) is calculated normally for K (for the example above, it is 489 = 21 (mod 26)). The inverse, $d^{-1}$, is found by finding a number such that $d \times d^{-1} = 1$ (mod 26) (this is 5 for the example above since 5*21 = 105 = 1 (mod 26)). The simplest way of doing this is to loop through the numbers 1..25 and find the one such that the equation is satisfied. There is no solution (i.e. choose a different key) if gcd(d,26) ≠ 1 (this means d and 26 share factors, if this is the case K cannot be inverted, this means the key you have chosen will not work, so choose another one).

That is it. Once $K^{-1}$ is found, decryption can be performed.

## Cryptanalysis of the Hill Cipher

### 2 by 2 Case

Because the Hill cipher is linear, we only need to find 2 bigram correspondences to determine the key matrix. For example, if we knew that 'th' was encrypted to 'gk' and 'er' was encrypted to 'bd', we could solve a set of simultaneous equations and find the encryption key matrix. We will capitalise on this fact to break the cipher. Imagine we have a ciphertext:

```
fupcmtgzkyukbqfjhuktzkkixtta
```

and we know that "of the" occurs somewhere in the message. This means one of the following cases is correct (remember the Hill cipher enciphers pairs of characters):

```
fu pc mt gz ky uk bq fj hu kt zk ki xt ta
-------------------------------------------
of th e.  ..  ..  ..  ..  ..  ..  ..  ..  ..  ..  ..
.o ft he  ..  ..  ..  ..  ..  ..  ..  ..  ..  ..  ..
```

```
.. of th e. .. .. .. .. .. .. .. .. .. ..
.. .o ft he .. .. .. .. .. .. .. .. .. ..
.. .. of th e. .. .. .. .. .. .. .. .. ..
.. .. .o ft he .. .. .. .. .. .. .. .. ..
...
```

and so forth. If the second line were correct, we would have the following: PC -> FT i.e. the letters PC are deciphered to FT, and MT -> HE. We can now set up an equation (replacing A with 0, B with 1, O with 14 etc.) which captures this information:

$$D\begin{bmatrix}P\\C\end{bmatrix}=\begin{bmatrix}F\\T\end{bmatrix}\Rightarrow D\begin{bmatrix}15\\2\end{bmatrix}=\begin{bmatrix}5\\19\end{bmatrix}(\text{mod }26)$$

As well as the following equation:

$$D\begin{bmatrix}M\\T\end{bmatrix}=\begin{bmatrix}H\\E\end{bmatrix}\Rightarrow D\begin{bmatrix}12\\19\end{bmatrix}=\begin{bmatrix}7\\4\end{bmatrix}(\text{mod }26)$$

And we want to determine the matrix D which is the decryption key. We first combine the two equations above into one equation:

$$D\begin{bmatrix}15 & 12\\2 & 19\end{bmatrix}=\begin{bmatrix}5 & 7\\19 & 4\end{bmatrix}(\text{mod }26)$$

Now we can rearrange the equation to find the numbers we want:

$$D\begin{bmatrix}5 & 7\\19 & 4\end{bmatrix}=\left(\begin{bmatrix}15 & 12\\2 & 19\end{bmatrix}\right)^{-1}(\text{mod }26)$$

Now we need to invert a matrix (mod 26).

Let P be the matrix we want to invert. Let d be the determinant of P. We wish to find P⁻¹ (the inverse of P), such that P × P⁻¹ = I (mod 26), where I is the identity matrix. The following formula tells us how to find P⁻¹ given P:

$$P^{-1}=d^{-1}\times\text{adj}(P)$$

Where d × d⁻¹ = 1 (mod 26), and adj(P) is the adjugate matrix of P. The determinant of the matrix we are inverting is ac - bd (mod 26) = 15*19 - 12*2 = 261 = 1 (mod 26). We also need to find the inverse of the determinant (1), which luckily in this case is 1 because 1 is its own inverse. The adjugate matrix is the following:

$$\text{adj}\left(\begin{bmatrix}15 & 12\\9 & 19\end{bmatrix}\right)=\begin{bmatrix}19 & -12\\-2 & 15\end{bmatrix}$$

Now we can calculate the inverse:

$$P^{-1} = 1^{-1} \times \text{adj}\left(\begin{bmatrix} 15 & 12 \\ 2 & 19 \end{bmatrix}\right) = 1 \times \begin{bmatrix} 19 & -12 \\ -2 & 15 \end{bmatrix} = \begin{bmatrix} 19 & 14 \\ 24 & 15 \end{bmatrix}$$

Now we need to go back up to earlier equation to determine D. We have,

$$D = \begin{bmatrix} 5 & 7 \\ 19 & 4 \end{bmatrix}\left(\begin{bmatrix} 15 & 12 \\ 2 & 19 \end{bmatrix}\right)^{-1} = \begin{bmatrix} 5 & 7 \\ 19 & 4 \end{bmatrix}\begin{bmatrix} 19 & 14 \\ 24 & 15 \end{bmatrix}$$

$$= \begin{bmatrix} 263 & 175 \\ 457 & 326 \end{bmatrix} = \begin{bmatrix} 3 & 19 \\ 15 & 14 \end{bmatrix} (\text{mod } 26)$$

So now we have decryption key! BUT, if we try to decrypt sentence with it, we get:

`frfthezyssqyvfetlvbafvaconfz`

Which is obviously not the correct answer? So what went wrong? It means one of initial assumptions was wrong, the assumption being that crib 'of the' began at the second position. To determine the actual key we need to try dragging 'of the' across each position until we get english at the output. If we had used an offset of 18, matching KT -> FT and ZK -> HE and repeated the procedure above we would get the matrix:

$$D = \begin{bmatrix} 17 & 5 \\ 18 & 23 \end{bmatrix}$$

Now when we try to decrypt ciphertext, we get:

`defendtheeastwallofthecastle`

This is just what we wanted. The technique we have used here is called 'crib dragging', which can be very tiresome if performed by hand. It is much easier to write a computer program to do it for you.

## Polyalphabetic Substitution Ciphers

Each plaintext character is replaced by another letter. A way of substitution is changed cyclically and it depends on a current position of the modified letter.

## Usage

Polyalphabetic substitution ciphers were invented by an artist, philosopher and scientist Leon Battista Alberti. In 1467 he presented a device called the cipher disk. It provides polyalphabetic substitutions with mixed alphabets.

## Description

In polyalphabetic substitution ciphers one should define a few possible combinations of substitutions of all alphabet letters by other letters. Then, one should use the substitutions cyclically, one after the other, changing the replacement after each new letter. To use this cipher, one should choose, remember and deliver to all parties some substitutions of all alphabet letters. Then, the substitutions should be used in a specific order. To decrypt the message, one should use corresponding substitutions in the same order but the letters should be changed in the other side. The strongest version of a polyalphabetic substitution cipher is to define all its transformations randomly. Such a method was preferred by Alberti himself.

On the other hand, due to the large amount of data to remember, some easy to remember and easy to hand over to another person substitutions were invented and widely used. The Vigenère cipher is an example of such an approach.

## Security of Polyalphabetic Substitution Ciphers

A properly implemented polyalphabetic substitution cipher is quite difficult to break. Its strength is based on many possible combinations of changing alphabet letters. Some effective methods of attacking such ciphers were discovered in the nineteenth century. They are about to guess a secret key's length in a first step. After that, one can examine the ciphertext using frequency analysis methods.

## Vigenère Cipher

The vigenere cipher is an algorithm that is used to encrypting and decrypting the text. The vigenere cipher is an algorithm of encrypting an alphabetic text that uses a series of interwoven caesar ciphers. It is based on a keyword's letters. It is an example of a polyalphabetic substitution cipher. This algorithm is easy to understand and implement. This algorithm was first described in 1553 by Giovan Battista Bellaso. It uses a Vigenere table or Vigenere square for encryption and decryption of the text. The vigenere table is also called the tabula recta.

## Two Methods Perform the Vigenère Cipher

## Method 1

When the vigenere table is given, the encryption and decryption are done using the vigenere table (26 * 26 matrix) in this method.

Example: The plaintext is "JAVATPOINT", and the key is "BEST".

To generate a new key, the given key is repeated in a circular manner, as long as the length of the plain text does not equal to the new key.

| J | A | V | A | T | P | O | I | N | T |
|---|---|---|---|---|---|---|---|---|---|
| B | E | S | T | B | E | S | T | B | E |

## Encryption

The first letter of the plaintext is combined with the first letter of the key. The column of plain text "J" and row of key "B" intersects the alphabet of "K" in the vigenere table, so the first letter of ciphertext is "K".

Similarly, the second letter of the plaintext is combined with the second letter of the key. The column of plain text "A" and row of key "E" intersects the alphabet of "E" in the vigenere table, so the second letter of ciphertext is "E".

This process continues continuously until the plaintext is finished.

Ciphertext = KENTUTGBOX

## Decryption

Decryption is done by the row of keys in the vigenere table. First, select the row of the key letter, find the ciphertext letter's position in that row, and then select the column label of the corresponding ciphertext as the plaintext.

| K | E | N | T | U | T | G | B | O | X |
|---|---|---|---|---|---|---|---|---|---|
| B | E | S | T | B | E | S | T | B | E |

For example, in the row of the key is "B" and the ciphertext is "K" and this ciphertext letter appears in the column "J", that means the first plaintext letter is "J".

Next, in the row of the key is "E" and the ciphertext is "E" and this ciphertext letter appears in the column "A", that means the second plaintext letter is "A". This process continues continuously until the ciphertext is finished.

Plaintext = JAVATPOINT

## Method 2

When the Vigenère table is not given, the encryption and decryption are done by Vigenère algebraically formula in this method (convert the letters (A-Z) into the numbers (0-25)).

Formula of encryption is,

$$E_i = (P_i + K_i) \bmod 26$$

Formula of decryption is,

$$D_i = (E_i - K_i) \bmod 26$$

If any case $(D_i)$ value becomes negative (-ve), in this case, we will add 26 in the negative value.

Where,

E denotes the encryption.

D denotes the decryption.

P denotes the plaintext.

K denotes the key.

"i" denotes the offset of the ith number of the letters, as shown in the table below:

| A | B | C | D | E | F | G | H | I | J | K | L | M | N | O | P | Q | R | S | T | U | V | W | X | Y | Z |
|----|----|----|----|----|----|----|----|----|----|----|----|----|----|----|----|----|----|----|----|----|----|----|----|----|----|
| 00 | 01 | 02 | 03 | 04 | 05 | 06 | 07 | 08 | 09 | 10 | 11 | 12 | 13 | 14 | 15 | 16 | 17 | 18 | 19 | 20 | 21 | 22 | 23 | 24 | 25 |

Example: The plaintext is "JAVATPOINT", and the key is "BEST".

Encryption: $E_i = (P_i + K_i) \bmod 26$

| Plaintext | J | A | V | A | T | P | O | I | N | T |
|-----------|----|----|----|----|----|----|----|----|----|----|
| Plaintext value (P) | 09 | 00 | 21 | 00 | 19 | 15 | 14 | 08 | 13 | 19 |
| Key | B | E | S | T | B | E | S | T | B | E |
| Key value (K) | 01 | 04 | 18 | 19 | 01 | 04 | 18 | 19 | 01 | 04 |
| Ciphertext value (E) | 10 | 04 | 13 | 19 | 20 | 19 | 06 | 01 | 14 | 23 |
| Ciphertext | K | E | N | T | U | T | G | B | O | X |

Decryption:

$$D_i = (E_i - K_i) \bmod 26$$

If any case $(D_i)$ value becomes negative (-ve), in this case, we will add 26 in the negative value. Like, the third letter of the ciphertext;

N = 13 and S = 18

$D_i = (E_i - K_i) \bmod 26$

$D_i = (13 - 18) \bmod 26$

$D_i = -5 \bmod 26$

$D_i = (-5 + 26) \bmod 26$

$D_i = 21$

| Ciphertext | K | E | N | T | U | T | G | B | O | X |
|---|---|---|---|---|---|---|---|---|---|---|
| Ciphertext value (E) | 10 | 04 | 13 | 19 | 20 | 19 | 06 | 01 | 14 | 23 |
| Key | B | E | S | T | B | E | S | T | B | E |
| Key value (K) | 01 | 04 | 18 | 19 | 01 | 04 | 18 | 19 | 01 | 04 |
| Plaintext value (P) | 09 | 00 | 21 | 00 | 19 | 15 | 14 | 08 | 13 | 19 |
| Plaintext | J | A | V | A | T | P | O | I | N | T |

## Program

C language

```c
#include <iostream>

#include <string>

using namespace std;


int main()

{

    Vigenere cipher("VIGENERECIPHER");

    string original = "I AM INDIAN";

    string encrypted = cipher.encrypt(original);

    string decrypted = cipher.decrypt(encrypted);


    cout << original << endl;

    cout << "Encrypted: " << encrypted << endl;

    cout << "Decrypted: " << decrypted << endl;

}


class Vigenere

{

    public:

        string key;


        Vigenere(string key)

        {
```

```
    for (int i = 0; i < key.size(); ++i)
    {
        if (key[i] >= 'A' && key[i] <= 'Z')
            this -> key += key[i];
        else if (key[i] >= 'a' && key[i] <= 'z')
            this -> key += key[i] + 'A' - 'a';
    }
}


string encrypt(string text)
{
    string out;
    for (int i = 0, j = 0; i < text.length(); ++i)
    {
        char c = text[i];
        if (c >= 'a' && c <= 'z')
            c += 'A' - 'a';
        else if (c < 'A' || c > 'Z')
            continue;
        out += (c + key[j] - 2 * 'A') % 26 + 'A';
        j = (j + 1) % key.length();
    }
    return out;
}


string decrypt(string text)
{
    string out;
    for (int i = 0, j = 0; i < text.length(); ++i)
    {
```

```
        char c = text[i];

        if (c >= 'a' && c <= 'z')

            c += 'A' - 'a';

        else if (c < 'A' || c > 'Z')

            continue;

        out += (c - key[j] + 26) % 26 + 'A';

        j = (j + 1) % key.length();

    }

    return out;

    }

};
```

Output

I AM INDIAN

Encrypted: SDERFGTUJ

Decrypted: IAMINDIAN

## Stream Ciphers and Block Ciphers

## Stream Ciphers

- Stream cipher takes one bit or one byte at a time from digital data and encrypts.

- Vernam cipher is an example of stream cipher.

- $p_i$ = ith digit from binary form of plaintext, $K_i$ = ith digit from binary form of key, $c_i$ = ith digit from binary form of ciphertext, $\oplus$ = exclusive – or (XOR) operation.

- $p_i = c_i \oplus ki$

## Block Cipher

- Block of plaintext is taken at a time and ciphertext block is produced.

- The block is of 64 bits or 128 bits.

- The block cipher processes n bits from the plaintext block to produce n bits of a ciphertext block.

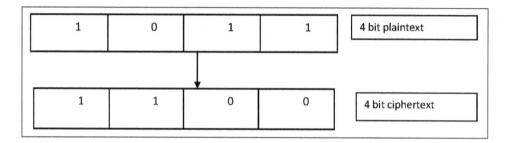

## Block Cipher – Block Size 2, $2^n$ Possible Plaintext

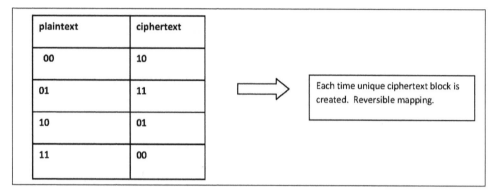

| plaintext | ciphertext |
|-----------|------------|
| 00 | 10 |
| 01 | 11 |
| 10 | 01 |
| 11 | 00 |

Each time unique ciphertext block is created. Reversible mapping.

| plaintext | ciphertext |
|-----------|------------|
| 00 | 11 |
| 01 | 11 |
| 10 | 01 |
| 11 | 10 |

For 00 and 01, same ciphertext is generated. So irreversible mapping

## Feistel - Ideal Block Cipher

| | |
|------|------|
| 0000 | 1111 |
| 0001 | 1100 |
| 0010 | 1010 |
| 0011 | 1000 |
| 0100 | 0110 |
| 0101 | 0100 |
| 0110 | 0010 |
| 0111 | 0000 |
| 1000 | 1101 |
| 1001 | 1011 |
| 1010 | 1001 |

| | |
|---|---|
| 1011 | 0111 |
| 1100 | 0101 |
| 1101 | 0011 |
| 1111 | 0001 |

4 bit input. 16 possible inputs are mapped with 16 possible outputs, represented by 4 ciphertext bits.

This type of block is referred as Ideal Block Cipher. Because it allows plaintext-ciphertext mapping for all possible

## Problem with Feistel - Ideal Block Cipher

- Ideal block cipher is like substitution cipher.

- As the block size is small, Vulnerable to statistical analysis.

- For large block size , ideal block building implementation and ideal block storing is infeasible.

- For 4 bits, 16 rows are needed. Required length of key is 64 bits (4 bits of16 rows). For n bits, $n \times 2^n$ bits.

- To prevent statistical attacks, block length must be 64 bits. So requires $64 \times 2^{64}$ bits.

## Feistel Cipher

- Block cipher having k bits in key and n bits in a block. So $2^k$ possible transformations not $2^n$ !.

- Feistel suggested to use substitution and permutation alternatively to produce ciphertext.

  ○ Substitution: Each plaintext element is replaced by a corresponding element. Replacement is unique.

  ○ Permutation: The order of plaintext element is changed.

Feistel cipher suggests confusion and diffusion. – To suppress statistical cryptanalysis.

## Diffusion

One plaintext digit affects in deriving the value of several ciphertext digit.

Message $M = m_1 m_2 m_3 \ldots$ k consecutive letters are added to derive the letter of ciphertext $y_n$

$$y_n = \left( \sum_{i=1}^{k} m_{n+i} \right) \mod 26$$

Statistical relation between plaintext and ciphertext is intricate and it is tricky to derive key.

## Confusion

The statistical relationship between ciphertext and encryption key is so complex that it is difficult to derive key. Confusion is created by applying substitution algorithm in complex way.

## Feistel Cipher Structure

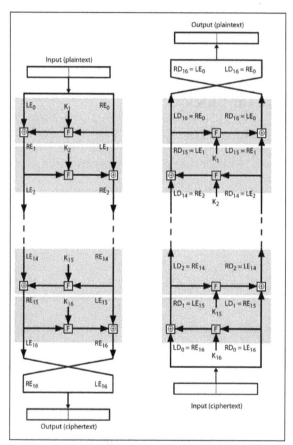

Input: Plaintext block (2w bits length), Key K.

## Procedure

- Divide Plaintext block to create two blocks of equal length, $LE_0$ and $RE_0$.

- Perform n rounds, to get the ciphertext block.

    Each round is denoted by I having inputs $LE_{i-1}$ and $RE_{i-1}$ generated by the preceding round.

    Subkey $K_i$ is derived from overall K.

Round function F is applied to the right half $RE_{i-1}$, take output and exclusive – OR with left half and substitute for the right half of $RE_i$. $LE_i$ will be substituted with $RE_{i-1}$.

$$LE_i = RE_{i-1}$$
$$RE_i = LE_{i-1} \oplus F(RE_{i-1}, K_i)$$

- Output of the nth round $LE_n \ || \ RE_n$.

- Permutation is performed by interchanging two halves of the data and combined. $RE_n \ || \ LE_n$.

## Strength of Feistel Network

Strength depends on following parameters:

- Block size – Larger block more security.

- Key size – Larger key size more security.

- Number of rounds – More rounds more security.

- Subkey generation algorithm – Complex algorithm- difficult for cryptanalysis to generate key.

- Round function F – Complex function, greater resistance to cryptanalysis.

## Feistel Cipher Structure – Decryption

Input: Ciphertext block of length 2w bits.

Key: Subkey $K_i$ in reverse order.

Assuming 16 rounds are performed.

$$LD_i = RD_{i-1}$$
$$RD_i = LD_{i-1} \oplus F(RD_{i-1}, K_i)$$

## Design of Block Cipher

- Number of Rounds: More number of rounds, difficult for cryptanalytic attack. Even if function F is easy to break, more number of rounds make cipher strength high.

- Function F design: F adds confusion. F must be difficult to evaluate through linear equations. F must produce avalanche effect. One bit change produces change in several bits. F must follow bit independence criteria. Bit i is flipped for any i, j, k then output bit j and k should be changed independently.

- Key generation: Generate one subkey for each round. Subkeys should be derived in such way that individual subkeys cannnot be determined.

From the subkey, one should not be able to derive main key.

# Encryption Standards

## Data Encryption Standard

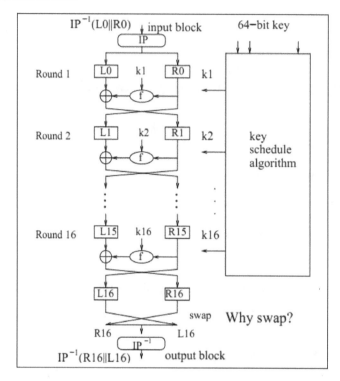

- Plainext is broken into blocks of length 64 bits. Encryption is blockwise.

- A message block is first gone through an initial permutation IP, then divided into two parts $L_0$, where $L_0$ is the left part of 32 bits and $R_0$ is the right part of the 32 bits.

- Round i has input $L_{i-1}, R_{i-1}$ and output $L_i, R_i$.

$$L_i = R_{i-1}, R_i = L_{i-1} \oplus f(R_{i-1}, K_i)$$

and $K_i$ is the subkey for the 'i'th where $1 \leq i \leq 16$

$$L_1 = R_0, \quad R_1 = L_0 \oplus f(R_0, K_1)$$
$$L_2 = R_1, \quad R_2 = L_1 \oplus f(R_1, K_2)$$
$$L_3 = R_2, \quad R_3 = L_2 \oplus f(R_2, K_3)$$

............... .......................

............... .......................

............... .......................

$$L_{16} = R_{15}, \quad R_{16} = L_{15} \oplus f(R_{15}, K_{16})$$

- After round 16, $L_{16}$ and $R_{16}$ are swapped, so that the decryption algorithm has the same structure as the encrption algorithm.

- Finally, the block is gone through the inverse the permutation $IP^{-1}$ and then output.

- One round of DES in very simple way during encryption.

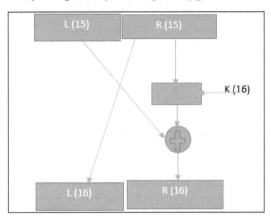

## DES Decryption

- Observation: In encryption, we have,

$$L_i = R_{i-1}, R_i = R_i = L_{i-1} \oplus f(R_{i-1}, K_i)$$

and $K_i$ is the subkey for the 'i'th round. Hence,

$$R_{i-1} = L_i, L_{i-1} = R_i \oplus f(L_i, K_i) \text{ for each 'i'}$$

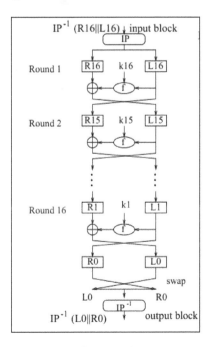

- Due to swap operation after the 16th round encryption, the output of encryption is $IP^{-1}(R_{16}, L_{16})$.

- Equation as follows:

$$R_{15} = L_{16}, \quad L_{15} = R_{16} \oplus f\left(L_{16}, K_{16}\right)$$
$$R_{14} = L_{15}, \quad L_{14} = R_{15} \oplus f\left(L_{15}, K_{15}\right)$$
$$R_{13} = L_{14}, \quad L_{13} = R_{14} \oplus f\left(L_{14}, K_{14}\right)$$
$$\ldots\ldots\ldots\ldots \quad \ldots\ldots\ldots\ldots\ldots\ldots$$
$$\ldots\ldots\ldots\ldots \quad \ldots\ldots\ldots\ldots\ldots\ldots$$
$$\ldots\ldots\ldots\ldots \quad \ldots\ldots\ldots\ldots\ldots\ldots$$
$$R_{1} = L_{2}, \quad L_{1} = R_{2} \oplus f(L_{2}, K_{2})$$

- If we give $IP^{-1}(R_{16}, L_{16})$ as the input for the same algorithm with round subkeys $(K_{16}, K_{15}, \ldots\ldots K_{1})$, then the output is $IP^{-1}(L_{0}, R_{0})$, the original message block.

- Decryption is performed using the same algorithm, except the $K_{16}$ is used as the first round, $K_{15}$ in the second, and so on, with $K_{1}$ used in the 16th round.

- One round of DES in very simple way during decryption.

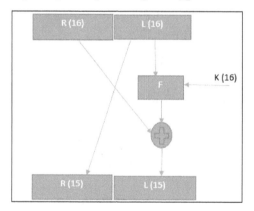

## Difference between Encryption and Decryption

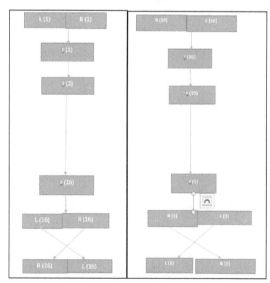

## Initial Permutations

- DES has an initial permutation and final permutation after 16 rounds.

- These permutations are inverse of each other and operate on 64 bits.

- They have no cryptographic significance.

- The designers did not disclose their purpose.

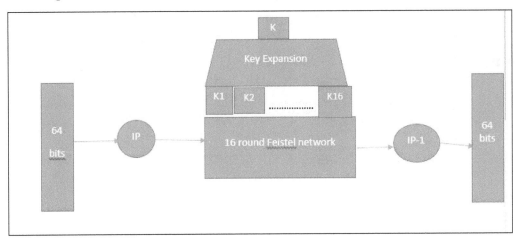

- The initial permutation will look like this:

  ○ Input and Output of the permutation layer:

$$\left(X_1, X_2, \ldots\ldots, X_{64}\right)------>\left(X_{IP(1)}, X_{IP(2)}, --------->, X_{IP(64)}\right)$$

### The Initial Permutation: IP

| 58 | 50 | 42 | 34 | 26 | 18 | 10 | 2 |
|----|----|----|----|----|----|----|---|
| 60 | 52 | 44 | 36 | 28 | 20 | 12 | 4 |
| 62 | 54 | 46 | 38 | 30 | 22 | 14 | 6 |
| 64 | 56 | 48 | 40 | 32 | 24 | 16 | 8 |
| 57 | 49 | 41 | 33 | 25 | 17 | 9 | 1 |
| 59 | 51 | 43 | 35 | 27 | 19 | 11 | 3 |
| 61 | 53 | 45 | 37 | 29 | 21 | 13 | 5 |
| 63 | 55 | 47 | 39 | 31 | 23 | 15 | 7 |

- The final permutation will look like this:

$$\left(X_1, X_2, \ldots\ldots, X_{64}\right)------>\left(X_{IP(1)^{-1}}, X_{IP(2)^{-1}}, --------->, X_{IP(64)^{-1}}\right)$$

| 40 | 8 | 48 | 16 | 56 | 24 | 64 | 32 |
|---|---|---|---|---|---|---|---|
| 39 | 7 | 47 | 15 | 55 | 23 | 63 | 31 |
| 38 | 6 | 46 | 14 | 54 | 22 | 62 | 30 |
| 37 | 5 | 45 | 13 | 53 | 21 | 61 | 29 |
| 36 | 4 | 44 | 12 | 52 | 20 | 60 | 28 |
| 35 | 3 | 43 | 11 | 51 | 19 | 59 | 27 |
| 34 | 2 | 42 | 10 | 50 | 18 | 58 | 26 |
| 33 | 1 | 41 | 9 | 49 | 17 | 57 | 25 |

## One Round of the DES

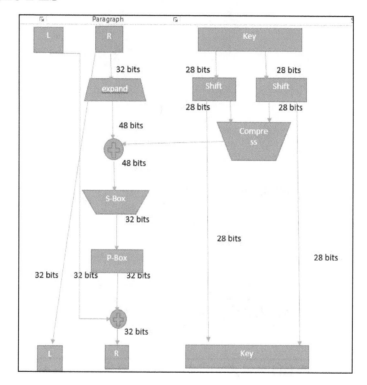

## DES Expansion

- Input 32 bits:

| 0 | 1 | 2 | 3 | 4 | 5 | 6 | 7 | 8 | 9 |
|---|---|---|---|---|---|---|---|---|---|
| 10 | 11 | 12 | 13 | 14 | 15 | 16 | 17 | 18 | 19 |
| 20 | 21 | 22 | 23 | 24 | 25 | 26 | 27 | 28 | 29 |
| 31 | 32 | | | | | | | | |

- Output 48 bits:

| 31 | 0 | 1 | 2 | 3 | 4 | 5 | 6 | 7 | 8 |
|---|---|---|---|---|---|---|---|---|---|
| 7 | 8 | 9 | 10 | 11 | 12 | 11 | 12 | 13 | 14 |
| 15 | 16 | 15 | 16 | 17 | 18 | 19 | 20 | 19 | 20 |
| 21 | 22 | 23 | 24 | 23 | 25 | 26 | 27 | 28 | 27 |
| 28 | 29 | 30 | 31 | 0 | | | | | |

## DES S-Box (Substitution Box)

- 8 "Substitution boxes" or S-boxes.

- Each S-box maps 6 bits to 4 bits.

| 14 | 4 | 13 | 1 | 2 | 15 | 11 | 8 | 3 | 10 | 6 | 12 | 5 | 9 | 0 | 7 |
|----|----|----|----|----|----|----|----|----|----|----|----|----|----|----|----|
| 0 | 15 | 7 | 4 | 14 | 2 | 13 | 1 | 10 | 6 | 12 | 11 | 9 | 5 | 3 | 8 |
| 4 | 1 | 14 | 8 | 13 | 6 | 2 | 11 | 15 | 12 | 9 | 7 | 3 | 10 | 5 | 0 |
| 15 | 12 | 8 | 2 | 4 | 9 | 1 | 7 | 5 | 11 | 3 | 14 | 10 | 0 | 6 | 13 |

S-Box (1)

- Row Index: The combination of first and last bit gives the row number.

- Column Index: Remaining 4 bits gives the column number.

- What is the output if input is 101000?

    Row = 10 = 2, Column = 0100 = 4:

- We have to look at 2nd row and 4th column, then Output is 13.

- Here you can feel the importance of S-box. It takes 6 bits as input and gives 4 bits as output.

## Properties of the S-box

- The rows are permutations.

- The outputs are a non-linear combination of the inputs.

- Change one bit of the input, and half of the output bits change(Avanlanche Effect).

- Each output bit is dependent on all the input bits.

## The Function f(x, k)

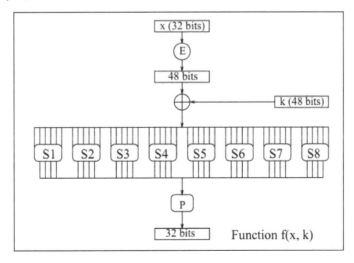

Function f(x, k)

- This is called fiestal function or round function.

- Function f is nothing but mixing of X and K.

## DES P-box (Permutation Box)

- Input 32 bits.

| 0 | 1 | 2 | 3 | 4 | 5 | 6 | 7 | 8 | 9 | 10 | 11 | 12 | 13 | 14 | 15 |
|---|---|---|---|---|---|---|---|---|---|----|----|----|----|----|----|
| 16 | 17 | 18 | 19 | 20 | 21 | 22 | 23 | 24 | 25 | 26 | 27 | 28 | 29 | 30 | 31 |

- Output 32 bits.
- The output bits are just Transposition of bits.

| 15 | 6 | 19 | 20 | 28 | 11 | 27 | 16 | 0 | 14 | 22 | 25 | 4 | 17 | 30 | 9 |
|----|---|----|----|----|----|----|----|---|----|----|----|---|----|----|---|
| 1 | 7 | 23 | 13 | 31 | 26 | 2 | 8 | 18 | 12 | 29 | 5 | 21 | 10 | 3 | 24 |

## DES Subkey

- Input Key size: 64 bits, of which 8 are parity bits.
- 56 bit DES key,0,1,2,........55.

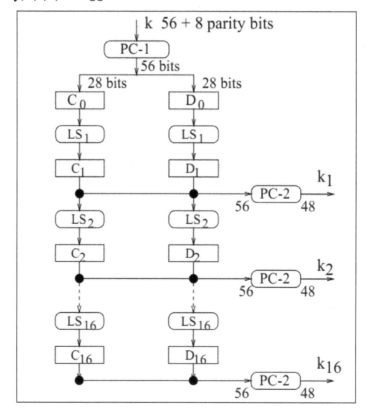

## Parity Check Bits for Error Detection

For any binary string $a_1 a_2 .........a_n$, append another bit $a_{n+1} = a_1 \oplus a_2 ........ \oplus a_n$, obtaining $a_1 a_2 ........ a_n a_{n+1}$. This new sequence can detect one error.

$$8 \left\{ \begin{array}{cccccccc} * & * & * & * & * & * & * & p_1 \\ * & * & * & * & * & * & * & p_2 \\ * & * & * & * & * & * & * & p_3 \\ * & * & * & * & * & * & * & p_4 \\ * & * & * & * & * & * & * & p_5 \\ * & * & * & * & * & * & * & p_6 \\ * & * & * & * & * & * & * & p_7 \\ * & * & * & * & * & * & * & p_8 \end{array} \right\}$$

Adding 8 parity check bits in DES key.

Each $P_i$ in position 8i is the parity check bit of the previous 7 bits.

## Permuted Choice 1

PC-1: The permutation PC-1(permuted choice1) discards the parity bits and transposes the remaining 56 bits as below:

| | | | | | | | |
|---|---|---|---|---|---|---|---|
| 57 | 49 | 41 | 33 | 25 | 17 | 9 | F |
| 1 | 58 | 50 | 42 | 34 | 26 | 18 | F |
| 10 | 2 | 59 | 51 | 43 | 35 | 27 | F |
| 19 | 11 | 3 | 60 | 52 | 44 | 36 | F |
| 63 | 55 | 47 | 39 | 31 | 23 | 15 | F |
| 7 | 62 | 54 | 46 | 38 | 30 | 22 | F |
| 14 | 6 | 61 | 53 | 45 | 37 | 29 | F |
| 21 | 13 | 5 | 28 | 20 | 12 | 4 | F |

Key Permutation PC-1.

- Without positions 8,16,24,32,40,48,56,64 marked with "F".

- Simply given as PC-1 is a permutation of {1,2,3......,64}-{8,16,24,32,40,48,56,64}.

## Left Shift Operation

LSi: Each $LS_i$ is a circular shift of some positions. The number of shifted positions is given below:

| 1 | 2 | 3 | 4 | 5 | 6 | 7 | 8 | 9 | 10 | 11 | 12 | 13 | 14 | 15 | 16 |
|---|---|---|---|---|---|---|---|---|----|----|----|----|----|----|----|
| 1 | 1 | 2 | 2 | 2 | 2 | 2 | 2 | 1 | 2 | 2 | 2 | 2 | 2 | 2 | 1 |

- For rounds 1,2,9 and 16 the shifts is 1,and for the remaining all the rounds shifts are 2.

- PC-2: Permuted choice 2 selects 48 bits from the 56 bit input.

| 14 | 17 | 11 | 24 | 1  | 5  |
|----|----|----|----|----|----|
| 3  | 28 | 15 | 6  | 21 | 10 |
| 23 | 19 | 12 | 4  | 26 | 8  |
| 16 | 7  | 27 | 20 | 13 | 2  |
| 41 | 52 | 31 | 37 | 47 | 55 |
| 30 | 40 | 51 | 45 | 33 | 48 |
| 44 | 49 | 39 | 56 | 34 | 53 |
| 46 | 42 | 50 | 36 | 29 | 32 |

PC-2

- Final 48 bits obtained after the permuted choice is the Key.

## Advanced Encryption Standard

The more popular and widely adopted symmetric encryption algorithm likely to be encountered nowadays is the Advanced Encryption Standard (AES). It is found at least six time faster than triple DES. A replacement for DES was needed as its key size was too small. With increasing computing power, it was considered vulnerable against exhaustive key search attack. Triple DES was designed to overcome this drawback but it was found slow.

The features of AES are as follows:

- Symmetric key symmetric block cipher.

- 128-bit data, 128/192/256-bit keys.

- Stronger and faster than Triple-DES.

- Provide full specification and design details.

- Software implementable in C and Java.

## Operation of AES

AES is an iterative rather than Feistel cipher. It is based on 'substitution–permutation network'. It comprises of a series of linked operations, some of which involve replacing inputs by specific outputs (substitutions) and others involve shuffling bits around (permutations). AES performs all its computations on bytes rather than bits. Hence, AES treats the 128 bits of a plaintext block as 16 bytes. These 16 bytes are arranged in four columns and four rows for processing as a matrix.

Unlike DES, the number of rounds in AES is variable and depends on the length of the key. AES uses 10 rounds for 128-bit keys, 12 rounds for 192-bit keys and 14 rounds for 256-bit keys. Each of these rounds uses a different 128-bit round key, which is calculated from the original AES key.

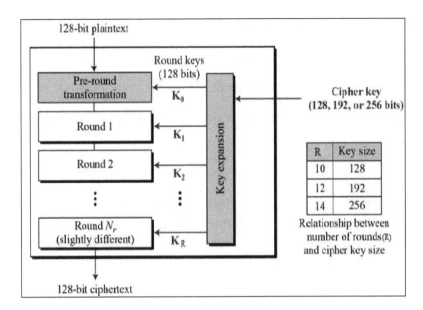

## Encryption Process

Here, we restrict to description of a typical round of AES encryption. Each round comprise of four sub-processes. The first round process is depicted below:

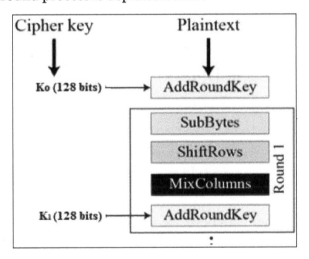

## Byte Substitution (SubBytes)

The 16 input bytes are substituted by looking up a fixed table (S-box) given in design. The result is in a matrix of four rows and four columns.

## Shift Rows

Each of the four rows of the matrix is shifted to the left. Any entries that 'fall off' are re-inserted on the right side of row. Shift is carried out as follows:

- First row is not shifted.

- Second row is shifted one (byte) position to the left.

- Third row is shifted two positions to the left.

- Fourth row is shifted three positions to the left.

- The result is a new matrix consisting of the same 16 bytes but shifted with respect to each other.

## Mix Columns

Each column of four bytes is now transformed using a special mathematical function. This function takes as input the four bytes of one column and outputs four completely new bytes, which replace the original column. The result is another new matrix consisting of 16 new bytes. It should be noted that this step is not performed in the last round.

## Add Roundkey

The 16 bytes of the matrix are now considered as 128 bits and are XORed to the 128 bits of the round key. If this is the last round then the output is the ciphertext. Otherwise, the resulting 128 bits are interpreted as 16 bytes and we begin another similar round.

## Decryption Process

The process of decryption of an AES ciphertext is similar to the encryption process in the reverse order. Each round consists of the four processes conducted in the reverse order:

- Add round key.

- Mix columns.

- Shift rows.

- Byte substitution.

Since sub-processes in each round are in reverse manner, unlike for a Feistel Cipher, the encryption and decryption algorithms needs to be separately implemented, although they are very closely related.

## AES Analysis

In present day cryptography, AES is widely adopted and supported in both hardware and software. Till date, no practical cryptanalytic attack against AES has been discovered. Additionally, AES has built-in flexibility of key length, which allows a degree of 'future-proofing' against progress in the ability to perform exhaustive key searches. However, just as for DES, the AES security is assured only if it is correctly implemented and good key management is employed.

## Difference between AES and DES

AES and DES are both examples of symmetric block ciphers but have certain dissimilarities.

| AES | DES |
|---|---|
| AES stands for Advanced Encryption Standard. | DES stands for Data Encryption Standard. |
| The date of creation is 1999. | The date of creation is 1976. |
| Key length can be 128-bits, 192-bits, and 256-bits. | The keyThe number length is 56 bits in DES. |
| Number of rounds depends on key length: 10(128-bits), 12(192-bits), or 14(256-bits). | DES involves 16 rounds of identical operations. |
| The structure is based on a substitution-permutation network. | The structure is based on a feistal network. |
| The design rational for AES is open. | The design rational for DES is closed. |
| The selection process for this is secret but accepted open public comment. | The selection process for this is secret. |
| AES is more secure than the DES cipher and is the de facto world standard. | DES can be broken easily as it has known vulnerabilities. 3DES(Triple DES) is a variation of DES which is secure than the usual DES. |
| The rounds in AES are: Byte Substitution, Shift Row, Mix Column and Key Addition. | The rounds in DES are: Expansion, XOR operation with round key, Substitution and Permutation. |
| AES can encrypt 128 bits of plaintext. | DES can encrypt 64 bits of plaintext. |
| AES cipher is derived from square cipher. | DES cipher is derived from Lucifer cipher. |
| AES was designed by Vincent Rijmen and Joan Daemen. | DES was designed by IBM. |
| No known crypt-analytical attacks against AES but side channel attacks against AES implementations possible. Biclique attack have better complexity than brute-force but still ineffective. | Known attacks against DES include : Brute-force, Linear crypt-analysis and Differential crypt-analysis. |

# Hashing in Cryptography

Hashing, or a hashing algorithm, is a one-way process that converts your input data of any size into fixed-length enciphered data. At the center of the process is where you'll find the hash function. Basically, you can take either a short sentence or an entire stream of data, run it through a hash function, and wind up with a string of data of a specific length. It's a way to hide your original data to make it as challenging as possible to reverse engineer. In a more technical sense, it's a technique that uses a mathematical operation to shrink a random quantity of input data (called a hash key) into a fixed-length string of bits in a way that's too impractical to reverse with modern computers. So, the definition of a hash function would be something that takes input data and uses it to create a fixed-length output value that's unique and virtually irreversible.

The output values returned by a hash function are called by a few different names:

- Hash values,

- Digests,

- Hash codes,

- Hashes.

For every input, you get a unique hash output. Once you create a hash, the only way to get the same exact hash is to input the same text. If you change even just one character, the hash value will change as well.

## Hashing Vs. Encryption

Hashing and encryption are two separate cryptographic processes. Encryption is something you can use to convert plaintext (readable) data into something indecipherable using algorithms and a key. However, you can decrypt that data either by using the same (symmetric encryption) or a mathematically-different-but-related cryptographic key (asymmetric encryption).

A cryptographic hash function is different. Once you hash data, you can't restore it to its original format because it's a one-way process. But what do hash functions look like and how do they work?

## Examples of Cryptographic Hash Functions

Here's a simplified illustration to show you what we mean:

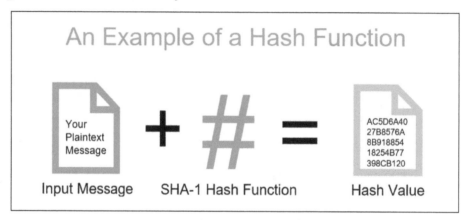

The length of the output or hash depends on the hashing algorithm you use. Hash values can be 160 bits for SHA-1 hashes, or 256 bits, 384 bits, or 512 bits for the SHA-2 family of hashes. They're typically displayed in hexadecimal characters. The input data's quantity and size can be varied, but the output value always remains the same in terms of size. For example, let's consider the following hash inputs and outputs:

| Example Input Texts | Hash Values Using SHA-1 |
|---|---|
| Hello | D364965C90C53DBF14064B9AF4BAAB-CA72196E2E |
| Hello! You are reading an article about the cryptographic hash function! | B26BACAB73C46D844CABEC26CE32B-030FED1164F |

In this example, you can see that the hash value's length remains the same whether the input value is just a small word or a complete sentence. (For example, a 160-bit hash value has 40 hexadecimal characters, whereas a 256-bit hash digest has 64 hex characters.) Hash functions are used in several different ways. However, we're going to focus mainly on a few of the ways that they're useful:

- Ensuring data integrity.

- Creating and verify digital signatures (which are encrypted hashes).

- Facilitating secure password storage.

## Types of Cryptographic Hash Algorithms

There are many cryptographic hash algorithms out there that businesses and organizations use. Some of the most popular hashing algorithms include:

- The SHA family (SHA-1, SHA-2 [including SHA-256 and SHA-512], and SHA-3).

- The MD family (MD).

- Whirlpool.

- Tiger.

- NTLM.

- LanMan (LM hash).

Now, not all of these are considered secure algorithms for every type of application or purpose. Some hash functions are fast, while others are slow. When it comes to using cryptographic hash functions for password hashing, for example, you'll want to use a slow hash function rather than a fast one (the slower the better).

## Cryptographic Hash Properties

- Determinism: Regardless of the size of the input or the key value, the operation should always result in the same consistent length output or hash value.

- Computational Speed: The speed of a hash function is important and should vary based on how it's being used. For example, in some cases, you need a fast hash function, whereas in others it's better to use a slow hash function.

- Image Resistance: Hashes should be extremely impractical to reverse (i.e., it should serve as a one-way function for all intents and purposes). The hash function should be so difficult and make the data so obscure that it would be improbable for someone to reverse engineer the hash to determine its original key value. Even one tiny change to the original input should result in an entirely different hash value.

## Characteristics of a Hash Function in Cryptography

These are the two prominent qualities of cryptographic hash functions:

## A Hash Function is Practically Irreversible

Hashing is often considered a type of one-way function. That's because it's highly infeasible (technically possible, though) to reverse it because of the amount of time and computational resources that would be involved in doing so. That means you can't figure out the original data based on the hash value without an impractical amount of resources at your disposal.

In other words, if the hash function is $h$, and the input value is $x$, the hash value will be $h(x)$. If you have access to $h(x)$ and know the value of hash function $h$, it's (*almost*) impossible to figure out the value of $x$.

## Hash Values are Unique

No two different input data should (ideally) generate the same hash value. If they do match, it causes what's known as a collision, which means the algorithm isn't safe to use and is vulnerable to what are known as birthday attacks. Collision resistance is something that improves the strength of your hash and helps to keep the data more secure. That's because a cybercriminal would not only have to crack not only the hash value but the salt value, too.

So, if the hash function is $h$, and there are two different input data sets $x$ and $y$, the hash value of $h(x)$ should always be different than $h(y)$. Hence, $h(x) \neq h(y)$. What this means is that if you make the slightest change in the original data, its hash value changes. Hence, no data tampering goes unnoticed.

## How Does Hashing Work?

First of all, the hashing algorithm divides the large input data into blocks of equal size. The algorithm then applies the hashing process to each data block separately. Although one block is hashed individually, all of the blocks are interrelated. The hash value of the first data block is considered an input value and is added to the second data block. In the same way, the hashed output of the second block is lumped with the third block, and the combined input value is hashed again. And so on and so on, the cycle continues until you get the final has output, which is the combined value of all the blocks that were involved.

That means if any block's data is tampered with, its hash value changes. And because its hash value is fed as an input into the blocks that follow, all of the hash values alter. This is how even the smallest change in the input data is detectable as it changes the entire hash value.

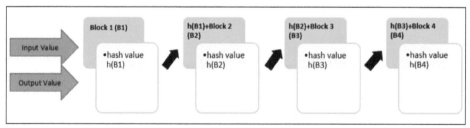

The process involved with a hash function in cryptography.

In the graphic, the input value of data block-1 is (B1), and the hash value is h(B1). The next block 2's input value B2 is combined with the previous hash value h(B1) to produce the hash value h(B2). This process of combining one block's output value with the next block's input value continues down the line through all of the blocks.

## Main Features of a Hash Function in Cryptography

### It Enables Users to Identify Whether Data has been Tampered with

When generated using a unique and random number, all hash values are different. So, if an attacker tries to modify, alter, or remove any part of the original input data (text data, software, application, email content, and even the media file), its hash value changes. As soon as the hash value changes, the users are notified about it. Users will immediately know that a message's content or a software application is not in the same condition as it was sent or created by the original sender/developer.

Hence, if a hacker inserts malicious code into a software program, for example, the user gets a warning not to download or install it because it's been altered. Likewise, if an attacker changes the content of an email to trick recipients into sharing their confidential information, transfer funds, or download a malicious attachment, users will know that the message was modified. Therefore, they should not take any actions suggested in the message.

## A Hash Function Prevents your Data from Being Reverse Engineered

Once you apply a hash function to data, you're left with an incomprehensible output. So, even if an intruder manages to get their hands on the data's hashed values through a leaky database or by stealing it through a cyber-attack, they can't easily interpret or guess the original (input) data.

Because the hash value can't be reversed easily using modern resources, it's improbably for hackers to decipher the hash value even if they know which hash function (algorithm) has been used to hash the data. It's just infeasible due to the amount of resources and time such a process would require at scale. Hence, cryptographic hash serves as a means of data protection while data is traveling or at-rest.

## You can't Retrieve the Data because it doesn't Exist

Because the hashing has non-reversible nature, you can't retrieve the original data from the hashed value. Now, this is a good thing when your intention is to keep hackers from accessing your plaintext data. But when you're the one who needs to recover the data for some reason, a hash function in cryptography can be an issue.

For example, with regard to password storage, if you have hashed the passwords to store it, you can't recover it if you or users forget it. The only option you or your users have at your disposal is to reset the password. At the same time, you just send the hash value of a file, the recipient can know the integrity of it, but they can't actually convert the hash value into plaintext. For that, you need to send the encrypted version of the file along with its hash value.

## Applications of Cryptographic Hash Functions

A hash function in cryptography is used to map data integrity. Hashing protects data from leakage, compares the large chunks of data, and detects the data tampering, if any. Some of the uses of hashing include:

- Digital signatures,
- Biometrics,
- Password storage,

- SSL/TLS certificates,

- Code signing certificates,

- Document signing certificates,

- Email signing certificates.

When you have to compare a large piece of data or software, you can't check each code and word of it. But if you hash it, it converts big data into small, fixed-length hash values, which you can check and compare a lot more easily.

## Hashing in Code Signing

Let's take a few moments to understand how code signing certificates utilize the cryptographic hash function. Say, you're a software publisher or developer who uses code signing certificates to digitally sign your downloadable software, scripts, applications, and executable. This certificate enables you to assure your users, clients, and their operating systems about your identity (i.e., that you're you) and that your product is legitimate. It also uses a hash function that warns them if it's been tampered with since you originally signed it.

Once you have a final version of your code ready to go, you can put the code signing certificate to work. This means that the code signing certificate hashes the entire software, and the hash gets encrypted, which creates the publisher or developer's digital signature.

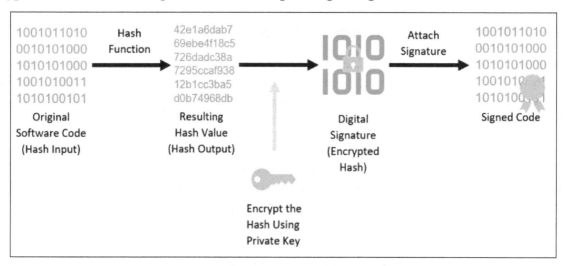

So, when a user downloads your software, their OS generates a hash value to see whether it matches the original hash value of your software. If it does, that's great and means they can proceed safely with that knowledge in mind. But if someone tries to pull a sleight of hand and change your software or your digital signature, the hash value they generate will no longer match your original hash, and the user will be notified about the compromise.

This means that an unmodified hash value vouches for the integrity of your software. So, in this case, the cryptographic hash function ensures that no one can modify your software without someone noticing.

## Hashing in Password Storage

When a user stores their password on your site (i.e., on your server), there's a process that takes place that applies a hash function to their plaintext password (hash input). This creates a hash digest that your server stores within its password list or database.

There isn't a list of your users' original plaintext passwords anywhere on your server that your employees (or any cybercriminals) could get their hands on. The hashing process takes place within the server, and there's no "original file" of plaintext data for them to exploit. This is different from encryption, which involves the use of an encryption key to encrypt data and decryption key that can decrypt it. Remember, with hashing, the goal is for the data to *not* be reverted to its original plaintext format (i.e., to only be a one-way function). With encryption, on the other hand, the goal is for the encrypted data to be decryptable with the right key (i.e., a two-way function).

However, that doesn't necessarily mean that passwords are entirely secure (even when hashed). This is where something called salting comes into play —But first, let's consider an example of how hashing works.

## A Hypothetical Example

Alice is a vendor whose business supplies stationery to Bob's office on credit. After a month, she sends Bob an invoice with an inventory list, billing amount, and her bank account details. She applies her digital signature to the document and hashes it before sending it to Bob. However, Todd, a hacker, intercepts the document while it's in transit and replaces Alice's bank account details with his.

Upon receiving the letter, Bob's computer calculates the hash value of the document and notices that it's different than the original hash value. Bob's computer immediately notifies him that there's something fishy about the document and that it's not trustworthy. Without a hashed document, Bob would have easily trusted the document's content because he knew Alice and the transaction details in the document were legitimate. But because the hash values didn't match, Bob became aware of the alteration. Now, he contacts Alice by phone and shares with her the information in the document he received. Alice confirms that her bank account is different than what is written in the document. This is how a hashing function saves Alice and Bob from financial fraud.

## Salting and its use with Password Hash Functions

Salting means adding randomly generated characters to the input values before hashing them. It's a technique that's used in password hashing. It makes the hashing values unique and more difficult to crack.

Suppose Bob and Alice has the same password ("Sunshine") for a social media site. The site is using SHA-2 to store the passwords. Because the input value is same, their hash values are going to be the same "8BB0CF6EB9B17D0F7D22B456F121257DC1254E-1F01665370476383EA776DF414."

Now, let's suppose a hacker manages to discover Bob's password (input value) using malware, brute force attacks, or by using other advanced hash cracking tools. They can bypass the authentication mechanism of all other accounts that have the same password "Sunshine." They just need to see the table of hash values and find the user IDs having the same hash value in their password column.

This is where salting comes in handy. Here, some random alphanumeric characters are added to the input values. So, suppose the salt "ABC123" is added to Bob's password, and "ABC567" is added to Alice's password. When the system stores the password, it stores the hash value for the inputs "SunshineABC123" and "SunshineABC567". Now, even if both the original passwords are the same, their hash values are different because of the salts that were added. And the hacker can't access Alice's account even if they have managed to steal Bob's password.

This is the big difference between encryption and hashing. While encryption is also a process that converts plaintext data into incomprehensible format using a key, you can use the same or another key to decrypt it. With hashing, on the other hand, it uses a hash function to map your input data to a fixed-length output. This is something that you can't restore because it essentially serves as a one-way process.

### Hash Function Weaknesses

Just like other technologies and processes, hash functions in cryptography aren't perfect, either. There are a few key issues that are worth mentioning:

- In the past, there were incidences where popular algorithms like MD5 and SHA-1 were producing the same hash value for different data. Hence, the quality of collision-resistance was compromised.

- There is a technology named "rainbow tables" that hackers use to try to crack unsalted hash values. This is why salting before hashing is so crucial to secure password storage.

- There are some software services and hardware tools (called "hash cracking rigs") that attackers, security researchers, or even government agencies use to crack the hashed passwords.

- Some types of brute force attacks can crack the hashed data.

## Public Key Algorithm

### The Modulus

- Let a be an integer and n a positive integer. a mod n gives the remainder when a is divided by n.

- n is called modulus.

- $a = qn + r$ $0 <= r < n$; $q = \lfloor a/n \rfloor$ .

- $a= \lfloor a/n \rfloor xn + (a \bmod n)$.

## Congruent Modulo n

- if (a mod n) = ( b mod n) then $a \equiv b \pmod n$.

- $73 \equiv 4 \pmod{23}$ as:

  73 mod 23 = 4 and

  4 mod 23 = 4

- Is $21 \equiv -9 \pmod{10}$ ?

  21 mod 10 =1.

- −9 mod 10.

  −9 = 10 x−1 + 1.

  so −9 mod 10 = 1.

- So It is true that $21 \equiv -9 \pmod{10}$.

## Modular Arithmetic

| + | 0 | 1 | 2 |
|---|---|---|---|
| 0 | 0 | 1 | 2 |
| 1 | 1 | 2 | 0 |
| 2 | 2 | 0 | 1 |

| x | 0 | 1 | 2 |
|---|---|---|---|
| 0 | 0 | 0 | 0 |
| 1 | 0 | 1 | 2 |
| 2 | 0 | 2 | 1 |

## Additive and Multiplicative Inverse

| w | -w | $W^{-1}$ |
|---|---|---|
| 0 | 0 | – |
| 1 | 2 | 1 |
| 2 | 1 | 2 |

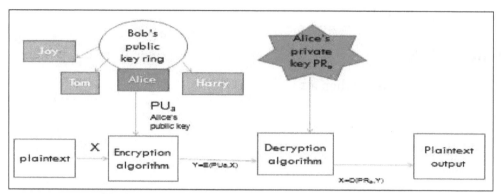

Public key cryptosystems (Bob wants to send message to Alice).

## Practical Public Key Cryptosystem – Suitable Trap Door One Way Function

- $Y = f_k(X)$ easy if k and X are known.

- $X = f_k^{-1}(Y)$ easy, if k and Y are known.

- $X = f_k^{-1}(Y)$ infeaible, if Y is known but k is not known.

## RSA Algorithm

- p, q two prime numbers.

- n = pq.

- Encryption key e, with GCD($\Phi$(n),e) =1; 1<e< $\Phi$(n), $\Phi$(n) is called totient function.

- $d = e^{-1}$ (mod $\Phi$(n)).

- $C = M^e$ mod n, M is the message to be transmitted. C is the ciphertext.

- $M = C^d$ mod n.

Private key consist of [d, n] and public key consist of [e, n].

## Greatest Common Divisor and Relatively Prime Numbers

- GCD (a, b) of a and b is the largest number that divides a, b. GCD(16,12) = 4.

- When no common factors (except 1), then numbers are relatively prime GCD(8,15) = 1.

- Hence 8 & 15 are relatively prime.

## $\Phi$(n) Totient Function

- $\Phi$(n) is number of positive integers less than n and relatively prime to n.

- $\Phi$(1) = 1.

- To calculate $\Phi$(24) , take all the positive integers less than 24 that are relatively prime to 24.

- 1,5,7,11,13,17,19,23.

There are 8 numbers so $\Phi(24) = 8$.

Euclidean Algorithm to Find GCD(Greatest Common Divisor) - uses Theorem that: GCD(a, b) = GCD(b, a mod b).

EUCLID(a, b):

- A = a; B = b.

- if B = 0 return A = gcd(a, b).

- R = A mod B.

- A = B.

- B = R.

- goto 2.

## Example GCD (576,132)

$$576 = 132 \text{ x } 2 + 48 \qquad GCD(576,132)$$

$$132 = 48 \text{ x } 2 + 36 \qquad GCD(132,48)$$

$$48 = 36 \text{x} 1 + 12 \qquad GCD(48,36)$$

$$36 = 12 \text{x} 3 + 0 \quad GCD(36,12)$$

$$GCD(576,132) = 12$$

To Find Multiplicative Inverse $b^{-1} \bmod m$ EXTENDED EUCLID (m, b):

- (A1, A2, A3) = (1, 0, m).

  (B1, B2, B3) = (0, 1, b).

- if B3 = 0:

  return A3 = gcd(m, b); no inverse.

- if B3 = 1:

  return B3 = gcd(m, b); B2 = $b^{-1} \bmod m$.

- Q = A3 div B3.

- (T1, T2, T3)=(A1 − Q B1, A2 − Q B2, A3 − Q B3).

- (A1, A2, A3)=(B1, B2, B3).

- (B1, B2, B3)=(T1, T2, T3).

- goto 2.

## Inverse of 550 mod 1759

| Q | A1 | A2 | A3 | B1 | B2 | B3 |
|---|-----|------|------|------|------|-----|
| – | 1 | 0 | 1759 | 0 | 1 | 550 |
| 3 | 0 | 1 | 550 | 1 | −3 | 109 |
| 5 | 1 | −3 | 109 | −5 | 16 | 5 |
| 21 | −5 | 16 | 5 | 106 | −339 | 4 |
| 1 | 106 | −339 | 4 | −111 | 355 | 1 |

## RSA Algorithm

- p, q two prime numbers.

- n = pq.

- Encryption key e, with GCD($\Phi(n)$,e) =1; 1<e< $\Phi(n)$, $\Phi(n)$ is called totient function.

- d = $e^{-1}$ (mod $\Phi(n)$).

- C = $M_e$ mod n, M is the message to be transmitted called plaintext. C is the ciphertext. M<n.

- M = $C^d$ mod n.

Private key consist of [d, n] and public key consist of [e, n] .

Example:

- Select two primes, p = 17 and q = 11.

- Calculate n = pq = 17 × 11 = 187.

- Calculate $\Phi(n)$ = (p-1)(q-1) = 16x10=160.

- Select e such that e is relatively prime to $\Phi(n)$=160 and less than $\Phi(n)$. Suppose e=7.

- Determined such that de ≡ 1 (mod 160) and d<160. d=23 because 23 × 7 = 161 = (1 × 160)+1.

Use extended Euclid's algorithm to calculate d.

PU = [7,187] PR = [23,187]

M = 88 C = ?

C=$88^7$ mod 187

## Exponentiation in Modular Arithmetic

- $a^{16}$ =axaxaxaxaxaxaxaxaxaxaxaxaxaxaxa

- $a^{16}$ can be achieved by repeatedly squaring each partial result($a^2$, $a^4$, $a^8$, $a^{16}$)

- To calculate $a^{11}$ = (a) $(a^2)(a^8)$. Calculate a mod n, $a^2$ mod n, $a^4$ mod n, $a^8$ mod n. Then calculate [(a mod n) x ($a^2$ mod n) x ($a^8$ mod n)] mod n.

For $a^b$ Mod n – a, b, n Positive Integers:

- b expressed as binary number $b_k b_{k-1}...b_0$

- $\sum_{bi \neq 0} 2^i$

$$a^b \bmod n = \left[ \prod_{bi \neq 0} a\left(2^i\right) \right]$$

Algorithm Computing $a^b$ Mod n. b is Expressed as $b_k b_{k-1}..b_0$:

- $C \leftarrow 0, f \leftarrow 1$

- For $i \leftarrow k$ down to 0

  do $c \leftarrow 2xc$

  $f \leftarrow (fxf) \bmod n$

  if bi = 1

  then $c \leftarrow c+1$

  $f \leftarrow (fxa) \bmod n$

  return f

  $a^b$ mod n where a = 7 b = 560 = 1000110000 n = 561

| i | 9 | 8 | 7 | 6 | 5 | 4 | 3 | 2 | 1 | 0 |
|---|---|---|---|---|---|---|---|---|---|---|
| Bi | 1 | 0 | 0 | 0 | 1 | 1 | 0 | 0 | 0 | 0 |
| c | 1 | 2 | 4 | 8 | 17 | 35 | 70 | 140 | 280 | 560 |
| f | 7 | 49 | 157 | 526 | 160 | 241 | 298 | 166 | 67 | 1 |

## Encryption – Decryption through RSA

C=$88^7$ mod 187

C=11

For decryption, M = $11^{23}$ mod 187 = 88

## The Security of RSA

- Brute force: trying all possible keys.

- Mathematical attack: factoring the product of two primes.

- Timing attacks: depends on running time of decryption algorithm.

- Hardware fault based attack: hardware fault in processor.

- Chosen ciphertext attack.

## Distribution of Public Keys

- Public announcement.

- Publicly available directory.

- Public key authority.

- Public key certificates.

## Public Announcement

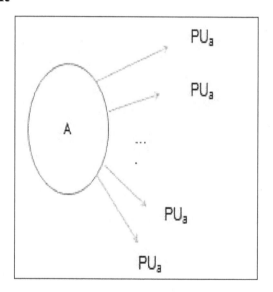

## Publicly Available Directory

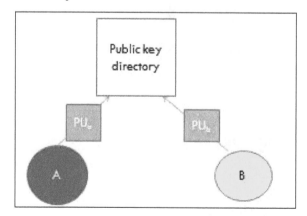

- The authority maintains a directory with a [name, public key] entry for each participant.

- Each participant registers a public key with the directory authority. Participants could access the directory electronically.

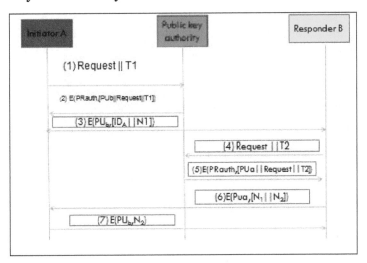

## Public Key Certificates

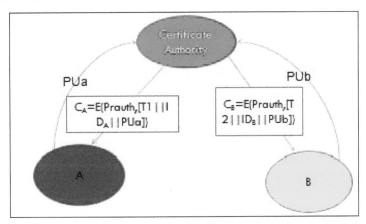

## Exchanging Certificates

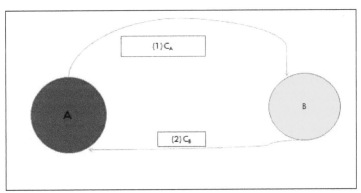

# References

- Introduction-to-information-technology: sites.google.com, Retrieved 11, July 2020

- Information-and-communication-technology-meaning-important: youniversitytv.com, Retrieved 21, January 2020

- Network-security, information-security-cyber-law: tutorialspoint.com, Retrieved 14, August 2020

- Cryptography-introduction: geeksforgeeks.org, Retrieved 10, May 2020

- Introduction-to-crypto-terminologies: geeksforgeeks.org, Retrieved 04, March 2020

- Cryptanalysis-hill-cipher, stochastic-searching: practicalcryptography.com, Retrieved 28, June 2020

- Polyalphabetic-substitution-ciphers: crypto-it.net, Retrieved 24, February 2020

- Difference-between-aes-and-des-ciphers: geeksforgeeks.org, Retrieved 19, June 2020

- Hash-function-in-cryptography-how-does-it-work: sectigostore.com, Retrieved 12, April 2020

# 2

# Computer Networks

Computer network is an interconnection of multiple devices that use a set of common communication protocols to share their resources, data and applications. Science and technology have undergone rapid developments in the past decade which has resulted in the discovery of significant tools and techniques in the field of computer networks which have been extensively detailed in this chapter.

A computer network is a group of computers that use a set of common communication protocols over digital interconnections for the purpose of sharing resources located on or provided by the network nodes. We need to generate and disseminate information. Following are some of the daily objects of information exchange of user community:

- Music files,

- Emails,

- Phone Calls,

- Blogs,

- Remote Database Servers,

- Facebook Posts,

- Skype Calls, audio, and Video.

Consider the services or a few other similar services that you may think of yourself. You will find one common thread that binds all of them together - the network; either a local network or the Internet the resources are being shared and the network is the media for sharing.

## Layers

One of the most common strategies to solve a problem is "Divide and Conquer". Computer networks follow this strategy. The entire networking problem is solved in pieces. These solution pieces are independent to a large extent. More importantly, they can evolve independently of each other without much trouble. Each piece, in networking parlance, is known as a layer. Layers are arranged in hierarchical order, lower layer provides a service to a layer above and that layer provides service another layer above it and so on. There are some reasons for designing networks in form of hierarchical components; i.e. the layers. Here is the list:

- A component's work is clearly defined. For example, a layer known as network layer is assigned a job of deciding where to send the outgoing packet. Irrespective of what others do and how others do their job, the network layer continues to make decisions about sending packets on their right route. Similar is the case with other layers.

- When each layer is working independently, it becomes easier to replace that layer by another, more suitable for changed situation or faster or smarter version. For example, IPv4, a typical network layer used by the Internet is being replaced by IPv6. Both are network layer protocols. If you want your computer to start using IPv6 and replace IPv4, nothing on the computer needs to change, neither your FTP program, nor your Ethernet or Wi-Fi card.

- Each layer is designed to take a specific service or providing a service or both. That means, each layer's functions and interfaces are clearly defined. Different vendors competing for designing products get a fair market and thus can produce best products at reasonable prices.

- These layers help the designers divide the service into small manageable components and thus, help them evolve independently. A company researching on Gigabit Ethernet and Terabit Ethernet does not need to bother about what IETF (Internet Engineering Task Force, a standardization body for Internet) is doing for Internet standards. The Ethernet card technically works at lower two layers, popularly known as Physical and Data Link Layers and do not need to worry about network, transport and application layers where IETF works (standardizes). Similarly, other companies which design clients and servers are operating at the application layer, they have nothing to do with Ethernet and other cards however their data, in bits are carried by those cards to the other end.

- Layering enables standardization of specific layers and thus makes sure that companies who design their products can interoperate. For example, if we design a new browser and we have followed IETF guidelines for developing a browser, our browser can communicate with any web server of this world.

- If a component is to be replaced, for example, I bought a new 10Gb Ethernet card for my laptop, do I need to upgrade my browser? Should I reinstall my TCP/IP software? Nothing else needs to be changed. It is because when the interface is standardized, replacing a component with another, providing identical service but otherwise different component, is easy and even seamless in most cases.

- This layering and standardization together provide one more advantage. When I develop a browser, and my users start using it, I do not need to compel them to use a specific card or operating system. They can use any brand they like.

However, Layering has some disadvantages as well. Let us look at few major ones:

- The first disadvantage of layering architecture is that it is inefficient when applied to small problems. It is like dividing a small work into pieces. That usually adds to and not reduces the overall work.

- The second problem is to synchronize and regulate the function of all the layers. When synchronization overhead is not acceptable, layering should not be called for. Demand for synchronization reduces the speed too. For example, a data link layer has many incoming packets which it passes on to a network layer. However fast the data link layer works, it cannot work faster than the network layer consumes the data it produces. Another way round, if a transport layer provides data to a network layer for sending it to another network, and the network is congested (there is a traffic jam), the network layer cannot work as fast as the transport layer expects it to and thus it has to slow down.

- Each layer has some speed of processing and the overall speed of the system is equal to the slowest component, i.e. the layer which processes data in the slowest manner.

- When inter-layer communication is minimized to preserve the independence of layers, it becomes more time consuming for a layer to judge the environment.

- The memory usage, in the layered architecture, is more than a normal. In a multilayered architecture, different stages of a process running at different layers (for example, on the Internet, the applications like SMTP, FTP, Telnet, etc. run at the application layer; at the same point of time, the TCP and UDP run at the transport layer and IP runs at the network layer) have to be stored and retrieved repeatedly as and when a particular process running at a specific layer starts, stops, and resumes their operation. Therefore, the system requires more storage space (memory) to execute a large number of processes. When the memory, as well as the processing power, is limited, layering is not a good solution. IoT devices like car sensors, implantable medical devices like insulin pumps, garage door sensors, etc. have very small amount of memory and thus they do not prefer to have layers like conventional networks.

## Two Models, OSI and TCP/IP

There are two ways described in the literature, the first one being used for pedagogy but never used in practice and another is normally used but one has to retrofit like the first one to study it.

The OSI layering mechanism was designed by Open System Interconnection group from ISO, hence the name OSI. The OSI model employed a seven-layer scheme which was heavily influenced by a model known as SNA (System Network Architecture) from IBM. The TCP-IP model is a retrofit to a practical solution provided by the Internet community. The OSI model is almost non-existent in terms of its implementation.

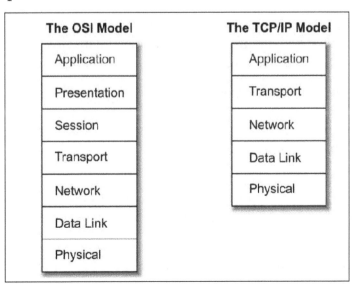

## The OSI Model

This model was designed by International Standards Organization in 1983. Some of the leading companies at that time and some of the governments thought of having a standard solution for the network and the services provided. The layering mechanism of OSI model contained seven layers. It contains two extra layers as compared to the TCP/IP model, i.e., the presentation layer and the session layer. One may like to have them, though having other things are much more important.

The presentation layer is designed to check minor differences in the way the data is presented by the sender and the receiver. For example, the sender and the receiver may have different ways of storing integer values in the memory. Some machines store an integer starting with the most significant bit to the least significant bit, while other machines store it starting from the least significant bit to the most significant bit. The role of presentation layer is to convert the data to ensure that it is presented according to the native representation scheme of the sender or the receiver machines.

The session layer is designed to manage sessions between the sender and the receiver. Both the functionalities (of the presentation and session layers) are too small to deserve a layer. The TCP/IP model does not have either of them. Additionally, the TCP/IP model does not even mention anything about the data link or the physical layer (which exists in OSI model), but all the network cards used for networking have them, so they are mentioned here.

## The TCP/IP Model

This model is used by the networks that we use and the internet that we access. That means it is the real world network. TCP/IP network is based on an approach known as connection oriented service over a connectionless delivery model.

The connection-oriented service demands connection to be established before any communication can begin. The opposite called connectionless, works in a way that does not require to establish a connection before any data transfer.

The connection-oriented mechanism's best example is the telephone system. When we call somebody, the call is established first and then the communication begins. The line remains occupied during the call, irrespective of the case that we use the line or otherwise.

The best example of the connectionless system is sending SMS. The sender and receiver do not need to remain sync, the connection is not established, before sender starts sending, the connection is not required to be terminated once the SMS is sent, the receiver might receive multiple SMS sent by the sender in some other order than it is sent.

The TCP/IP model combines the connectionless and connection-oriented approaches in its design. Applications like Telnet, FTP, Web browsing uses a model where connection oriented service is provided by TCP/IP model over a delivery design which is connectionless.

Sender's TCP layer (transport layer in OSI Parlance), wants to communicate with receiver's TCP layer. This happens in most of the applications that we use daily. The process demands the establishment of the connection beforehand and terminating the connection afterward. Interestingly, the TCP gets the job done by instructing a layer below, the IP layer. IP layer, unlike TCP, does not establish a connection but just sends the packet to next router, next router sends it further to next to next router and so on till the receiver accepts the same. Like SMS messages, the receiver might receive the message in any order, might not receive the message without sender learning about the failure and so on. Thus, the IP is said to deploy connectionless delivery mechanism. The combined work of these two protocols, TCP and IP, describes the connection-oriented service over the connectionless delivery system. In fact, the TCP/IP model also provides an option to have Connectionless service over the connectionless delivery system, deployed using UDP/IP protocol. The TCP/IP and OSI models differ in many ways, the major difference, though, is the one which we described above, the connection-oriented service over connectionless delivery system. OSI did not do that.

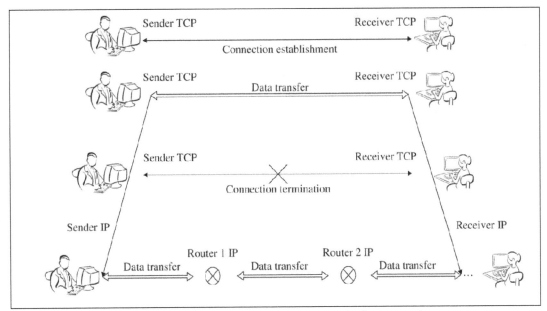

Connection oriented service over a connectionless network.

## Functions of each Layer

Now let us look at each of the layers, from the bottommost physical layer to the topmost application layer. Let us begin with the physical layer.

## The Physical Layer

The job of the physical layer is to carry bits from one end to another using the communication medium available, i.e., a wired or a wireless connection to transfer the bits to the other end. It is interesting to note that there is more than one mechanism to transfer the bits from one end to another using the same medium. The study of physical layer describes different ways of transferring bits from one end to another and their pros and cons.

There are two basic methods of transferring bits across, first is using analog (curved) waves, popularly known as antilog signalling and another using digital (square) signaling. The digital signals are of two different types when discrete voltage levels represent zeros and ones, it is known as digital signalling. As zeros and one are at different levels, when one draws a graph, it draws square figures and thus known as square signals. This layer determines how 1 and 0 are represented when sent across. This layer also manages how the job is done when multiple senders are sending and multiple receivers are receiving. Look at figure. The data link layer passes bits to the physical layer, physical layer converts that to signals and send the signals to the recipient. The receiving physical layer converts the signal back to bits. There are two basic modes of transmission, wired and wireless. In wired communication, the physical layer manages to send data over the wire while the wireless case, the data is transmitted over the air. There are two types of cables used in practice. A copper cable (a series of cat-3, cat-5, cat-6 and cat-7 cables), or a fiber optic cable is usually the choice when wired communication is done.

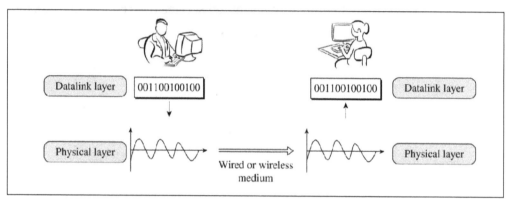

The work of physical layer.

In a wireless mechanism, there are many methods used to transmit. A common method called Direct Sequence Spread Spectrum uses multiple bits to send a single bit. Another method called Orthogonal Frequency Division Multiplexing is also commonly used. However, all these methods use some frequency to transmit the bits over. The transmission technically is, always in form of electromechanical signals. Copper cables send electrons over the media while fiber optic cables are made up of glass and send photons across.

## The Data Link Layer

The data link layer's job is to send the bits using the physical layer. Additionally, it provides quality control measures by ensuring the bits sent and the bits received remain identical. This is important as there is every chance of the data getting corrupted in the transit. The data link layer provides ways for the sender and the receiver to recognize erroneous or unintended data. To ensure error-free transmission, the data link layer adds additional bits to the data using some algorithm. These additional bits are calculated from the data itself. The calculation procedure is designed in a way such that the additional bits are different for different data. The same algorithm is also applied to the data at the other end and the results are compared. If the results match, then the data is accepted; otherwise, it is rejected. This is known as the error-detection mechanism. In some cases, the bits added are designed to not only detect the errors but also to correct them.

Correcting errors is also possible to a limited extent. When the redundant bits are possible to point to the exact place where the error has changed the bit, it is possible for the receiver to change the bit value to the original position. That process is known as error correction.

To perform these actions, the data link layer encapsulates the packet given by network layer into a frame. That means the data unit at data link layer is known as a frame. The frame contains many fields including senders and receivers unique address. Those addresses help the system to determine who the recipient of the frame is and route the frame to that node. On the other hand, the sender address enables the receiver to understand who has sent this frame and so can respond back if need be. Another important part of the frame is collection of fields which can help detect or correct errors.

It is also possible that the receiving data link layer sends back the confirmation in form of some type of acknowledgment. An acknowledgment (or ack for short) indicates that frame is received properly at the other end. Many Data link layers have explicit mechanisms to provide sending and receiving acks and taking appropriate actions based on that. Look at figure. The data coming from network layer is divided into multiple chunks. The data link layer generates the frame out of it. The frame contains some header as well as the trailer.

Another critical issue is the mismatch in the speeds of the sender and the receiver. The sender might send faster than the receiver can process and thus it is possible that some data is lost due to this problem. Data link layer deploys some mechanisms by which it can request the sender to slow down. That mechanism is popularly known as flow control.

## The Network Layer

The network layer's job is to look at the packet, decide where it is heading to (i.e. what is the value in the recipient's address field of the packet), decide the best path to that destination requires it to forward it to which neighbour. That means, the network layer's job is to find next immediate destination based on final destination.

In fact, this requirement demands two distinct jobs to be done. First, every router must know where every other network in the world is, and how to reach to each and every network. Once the router learns that, it can always judge the nearest next immediate neighbour for any destination. The routers store that information in a tabular form, popularly known as a routing table and this process, therefore, is known as routing. The algorithm deployed by the router is known as the routing algorithm. Another job that the network layer is designed to do is called forwarding; i.e. forward the incoming packet to the right neighbour based on its destination address and information available in the routing table. Forwarding is all about extracting destination address from an incoming packet, look into routing table to see what is the ideal next neighbour for that packet and then send it over the line where that neighbour is connected.

However simple it looks like, forwarding is an extremely complex process as it is to happen in real time. That means the packets are to be processed as fast as they arrive. Consider router having five incoming lines each of which having a capacity of 10Gb. In the worst case, when each of the lines is blasting at the full speed, a router has to process packets 50 Gb/sec which sounds phenomenal but common across routers. Consider the capacity of CISCO CRS -3 type of router's high-end version can crunch 322 Terabits per second.

Forwarding, like many other things in networks, can be done in two different ways. Connection-oriented and connectionless. In the connection-oriented fashion forwarding, the sender network layer establishes a connection with receiver's network layer before transmission and tears off once it is done. Every packet belonging to that connection travels over that path decided and does not roam around anywhere else. Connectionless forwarding just sends the packets across.

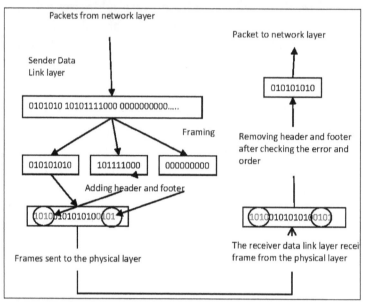

How data link layer works, at sender as well as receiver.

## The Transport Layer

The transport layer is working as per instructions by the application layer. Suppose we type www. oup.com in our browser. The browser, which is technically a client process running HTTP (Hypertext Transfer Protocol) client, then communicates with the web server located at Oxford University Press website. How does it do it? It instructs the TCP (Transmission Control Protocol) running on your machine to establish the connection with the server at www.oup.com and once the connection is established, sends this URL to that server. The server sends back the home page of the website and the browser displays it in return.

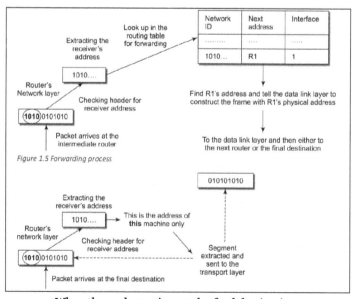

When the packet arrives at the final destination.

The underlying networks which carry our traffic remain as unreliable as they were in past. The communication lines have improved but there are many wireless links added which drops packets quite frequently and thus the application (like our browser, and OUP's server), needs a reliable connection which delivers the content reliable at the other end despite communication line being unreliable. The transport layer promises reliability and fulfills it by a simple trick.

That trick is known as timeout and retransmits with acknowledgment. Every data unit that is being sent, is acked by the receiver. When the data unit (called segment in TCP/IP parlance), is corrupted, the receiver won't send the ack back. Thus either if the data unit itself is lost (in that case the receiver won't receive that segment) or it is corrupted, the sender won't get the ack back. In the case ack is not received in time which is known as Time Out in TCP parlance, the transport layer is designed to send it again. That is known as retransmission. Thus TCP recovers from a lost segment or a corrupted segment without informing the application layer. Whenever we send the URL and receives the page, we do not find anything missing because of this mechanism.

The event Time Out and the process of retransmission are managed using a timer. Whenever a segment is sent, TCP remembers the time and also calculates an expected time of ack coming back.

Take an example of sending a video to the other end. Suppose in a cartoon movie, Mickey Mouse is shown moving from left to right. There is a creature sitting in the middle of the screen. Frame by frame, Mickey is coming closer to that creature. In one of the frames, Mickey kicks that creature, the next frame shows the creature in the sky, and the next sequence shows the creature falling on top of Mickey. Now assume the frames are sent one by one and the kicking frame is lost. Then the viewers will automatically assume that the creature must have been kicked. It is absolutely fine till now. If the kicking frame is retransmitted, then we have a sequencing problem. If Mickey is shown kicking that creature after the creature falls down, then it will create a confusion in the minds of the viewers as to how Mickey came out from beneath the crashed creature and kicked it.

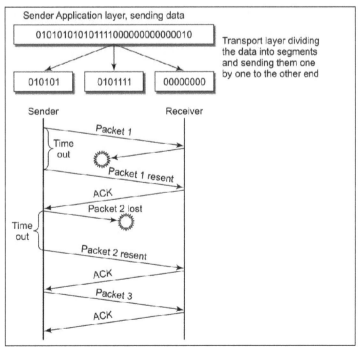

Timeout and Retransmission.

So it is better not to transmit the lost frame and keep it lost. Another example in order. Suppose we are sending a message to the server as follows. "Allow Virendra, Jayant Ashwin Disallow Root Bairstow Cook". What is Disallow is little delayed and played after Bairstow? The receiver incorrectly concludes and allow Root and Bairstow. Now the question arises—if we do not need retransmission of lost data, then what is the necessity to have timers and count the number of transmitted frames? If nothing is required, TCP becomes an overhead. Same is the case with sending audio. A word is lost and retransmitted would create a lot of confusion in listener's mind. In fact, the best option is to skip the lost or delayed frame. Human listeners will learn about it intuitively. Retransmitting them later is the last thing that one should do. If ever need, human listener may ask the sender to repeat everything (and not the lost segment!) to clarify any doubt.

When there is no need for retransmission, what is the need to keep timers, check for each segments time and do all that accounting? Thus TCP is not used for such cases, UDP (User Datagram Protocol) is a better choice where there is no such formality is maintained. It is a transport protocol with the only option for sending the segment across and forget afterward. In fact, there is one more alternative called SCTP (Stream Control Transfer Protocol) which is more suited for such cases but most of the installations do not provide SCTP. The great thing about TCP/IP model is that it provides all these options while older OSI model did not have any such options.

## Application Layer

All applications, when run, talk to the application layer for all their communication requirements. Consider FTP. When we run an FTP client on our machine and download or upload a file, our client communicates the FTP server at the other end and download and upload files, we execute commands like cd, get, put, mput, mget etc. The commands are processed at the application layer. The client program and the server program both runs at the application layer. When the user types command, the application layer realizes that the communication is to be made and ask TCP to send that command (get) across. TCP uses all its ability to send that command on the server's side. When the FTP server receives that command from its TCP, it processes that command, decide to send that specific file (if exists) and ask the TCP to send that file across.

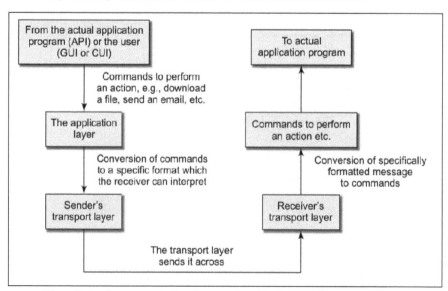

The relation between application, application layer and transport layer.

Thus application layer, the topmost layer, is the one which takes help of transport layer to send and receive messages related to applications they are part of. The transport layer takes the help of the network layer to route that message to the other end, the network layer takes the help of data link layer to make it error free. The data link layer takes the help of physical layer to convert that message into signals to send them across.

# Types of Computer Network

A computer network can be categorized by their size. A computer network is mainly of four types:

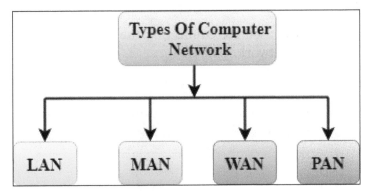

- LAN(Local Area Network).

- PAN(Personal Area Network).

- MAN(Metropolitan Area Network).

- WAN(Wide Area Network).

## LAN (Local Area Network)

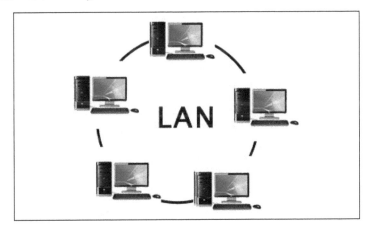

- Local Area Network is a group of computers connected to each other in a small area such as building, office.

- LAN is used for connecting two or more personal computers through a communication medium such as twisted pair, coaxial cable, etc.

- It is less costly as it is built with inexpensive hardware such as hubs, network adapters, and Ethernet cables.

- The data is transferred at an extremely faster rate in Local Area Network.

- Local Area Network provides higher security.

## PAN (Personal Area Network)

- Personal Area Network is a network arranged within an individual person, typically within a range of 10 meters.

- Personal Area Network is used for connecting the computer devices of personal use is known as Personal Area Network.

- Personal Area Network covers an area of 30 feet.

- Personal computer devices that are used to develop the personal area network are the laptop, mobile phones, media player and play stations.

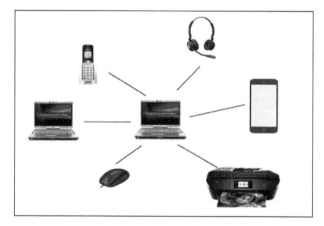

There are Two Types of Personal Area Network:

- Wireless Personal Area Network: Wireless Personal Area Network is developed by simply using wireless technologies such as WiFi, Bluetooth. It is a low range network.

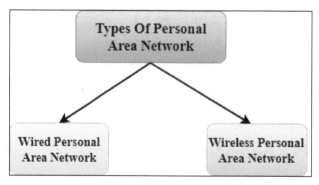

- Wired Personal Area Network: Wired Personal Area Network is created by using the USB.

## Examples of Personal Area Network

- Body Area Network: Body Area Network is a network that moves with a person. For example, a mobile network moves with a person. Suppose a person establishes a network connection and then creates a connection with another device to share the information.

- Offline Network: An offline network can be created inside the home, so it is also known as a home network. A home network is designed to integrate the devices such as printers, computer, television but they are not connected to the internet.

- Small Home Office: It is used to connect a variety of devices to the internet and to a corporate network using a VPN.

## MAN (Metropolitan Area Network)

- A metropolitan area network is a network that covers a larger geographic area by interconnecting a different LAN to form a larger network.

- Government agencies use MAN to connect to the citizens and private industries.

- In MAN, various LANs are connected to each other through a telephone exchange line.

- The most widely used protocols in MAN are RS-232, Frame Relay, ATM, ISDN, OC-3, ADSL, etc.

- It has a higher range than Local Area Network(LAN).

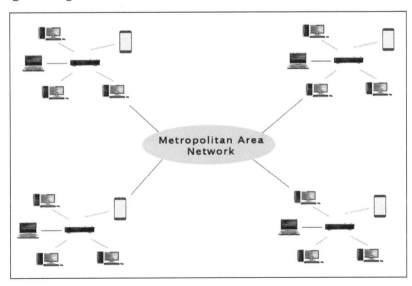

## Uses of Metropolitan Area Network

- MAN is used in communication between the banks in a city.

- It can be used in an Airline Reservation.

- It can be used in a college within a city.

- It can also be used for communication in the military.

## WAN (Wide Area Network)

- A Wide Area Network is a network that extends over a large geographical area such as states or countries.

- A Wide Area Network is quite bigger network than the LAN.

- A Wide Area Network is not limited to a single location, but it spans over a large geographical area through a telephone line, fibre optic cable or satellite links.

- The internet is one of the biggest WAN in the world.

- A Wide Area Network is widely used in the field of Business, government, and education.

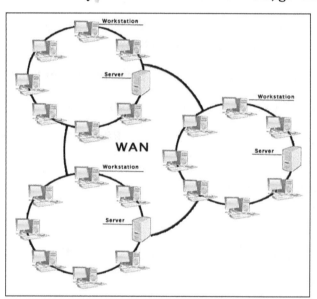

## Examples of Wide Area Network

- Mobile Broadband: A 4G network is widely used across a region or country.

- Last mile: A telecom company is used to provide the internet services to the customers in hundreds of cities by connecting their home with fiber.

- Private network: A bank provides a private network that connects the 44 offices. This network is made by using the telephone leased line provided by the telecom company.

## Advantages of Wide Area Network

- Geographical area: A Wide Area Network provides a large geographical area. Suppose if the branch of our office is in a different city then we can connect with them through WAN. The internet provides a leased line through which we can connect with another branch.

- Centralized data: In case of WAN network, data is centralized. Therefore, we do not need to buy the emails, files or back up servers.

- Get updated files: Software companies work on the live server. Therefore, the programmers get the updated files within seconds.

- Exchange messages: In a WAN network, messages are transmitted fast. The web application like Facebook, Whatsapp, and Skype allows you to communicate with friends.

- Sharing of software and resources: In WAN network, we can share the software and other resources like a hard drive, RAM.

- Global business: We can do the business over the internet globally.

- High bandwidth: If we use the leased lines for our company then this gives the high bandwidth. The high bandwidth increases the data transfer rate which in turn increases the productivity of our company.

## Disadvantages of Wide Area Network

- Security issue: A WAN network has more security issues as compared to LAN and MAN network as all the technologies are combined together that creates the security problem.

- Needs Firewall & antivirus software: The data is transferred on the internet which can be changed or hacked by the hackers, so the firewall needs to be used. Some people can inject the virus in our system so antivirus is needed to protect from such a virus.

- High Setup cost: An installation cost of the WAN network is high as it involves the purchasing of routers, switches.

- Troubleshooting problems: It covers a large area so fixing the problem is difficult.

## Internetwork

- An internetwork is defined as two or more computer network LANs or WAN or computer network segments are connected using devices, and they are configured by a local addressing scheme. This process is known as internetworking.

- An interconnection between public, private, commercial, industrial, or government computer networks can also be defined as internetworking.

- An internetworking uses the internet protocol.

- The reference model used for internetworking is Open System Interconnection(OSI).

## Types of Internetwork

- Extranet: An extranet is a communication network based on the internet protocol such as Transmission Control protocol and internet protocol. It is used for information sharing.

The access to the extranet is restricted to only those users who have login credentials. An extranet is the lowest level of internetworking. It can be categorized as MAN, WAN or other computer networks. An extranet cannot have a single LAN, atleast it must have one connection to the external network.

- Intranet: An intranet is a private network based on the internet protocol such as Transmission Control protocol and internet protocol. An intranet belongs to an organization which is only accessible by the organization's employee or members. The main aim of the intranet is to share the information and resources among the organization employees. An intranet provides the facility to work in groups and for teleconferences.

## Intranet Advantages

- Communication: It provides a cheap and easy communication. An employee of the organization can communicate with another employee through email, chat.

- Time-saving: Information on the intranet is shared in real time, so it is time-saving.

- Collaboration: Collaboration is one of the most important advantages of the intranet. The information is distributed among the employees of the organization and can only be accessed by the authorized user.

- Platform independency: It is a neutral architecture as the computer can be connected to another device with different architecture.

- Cost effective: People can see the data and documents by using the browser and distributes the duplicate copies over the intranet. This leads to a reduction in the cost.

# 3

# Communications in Computer Networks

Communication in computer networks can take place through wired or wireless channels. Some of the important topics associated with this domain are bandwidth and data rates, network topology, EM spectrum, Wi-Fi standards, Network layer services, etc. All these diverse principles of communications in computer networks have been carefully analyzed in this chapter.

## Bandwidth and Data Rates

There are two types of channels through which data transfer takes place, wired and wireless. The quality of the communication is highly influenced by the characteristics of the medium it passes through. Bandwidth and data rate are two important parameters of us to consider. Bandwidth is the inherent property of the media which is analogous to the width of the road. The data rate is the amount of data passing through, which is analogous to a number of people passing through the highway (which depends on a number of vehicles passes through which in turn depends on the width of the road). Thus, they are not independent to each other. The data rate has some dependency on the bandwidth.

The bandwidth of a media is the range of frequencies that can pass through that medium. The bandwidth of the signal is the range of frequencies that signal carries. The media bandwidth is analogous to the width of the road, wider the road more vehicles can pass per unit time (usually per second) and thus larger the range, more the bandwidth. The maximum data rate also depends on the width and length of the wire.

A copper cable of category 6A can provide 500 Mbps for 100-meter distance. The same wire can provide speeds in excess of 10 Gb if the distance is reduced to 1 meter. If we increase the distance to say 500 meters, the capacity may reduce to 100 Mb or less. Category 5 cable was able to provide 100 Mbps for the same range of 100 meters. The ability of Category 6A cable to provide higher bandwidth for the same range depends on many things including better width. Data rate depends on the amount of data that the user is sending and thus, is a variable thing. It can increase, decrease and may become zero if the user is not sending. On the contrary, the bandwidth depends on the natural property of the media and thus, a fixed value. The maximum data rate is the maximum amount of data that one can send over that communication channel, the value, that depends on the bandwidth, and thus a fixed value.

The data rate, a number of people traveling over the highway, is varying and can be zero if nobody is traveling on the highway right now. On the other hand, the capacity of the road is a fixed amount. Similarly, a maximum number of people traveling over the road, is also a fixed amount, depending on the capacity of the road.

Drivers cherish the widest possible road; similarly, the network users prefer large bandwidth. Drivers expect no obstacles and network users prefer no delay while accessing data. This demands very wide roads and fast media pipes. However, the administrators, who are concerned about the cost, would like the roads and the network cables to be utilized optimally so striking some balance is essential. One would like to have enough bandwidth that every user can work satisfactorily. However, one would also like to squeeze the maximum amount of data rate given the bandwidth.

A signal is an EM wave of some type. The data is encoded in the signal; i.e. the typical type of signal represents typical data. For example, one may represent 1 as a wave with frequency 10 Hz and 0 as a wave with frequency 20 Hz. Thus there are two different things, signals, and data. The data is 1 or 0 and signals are EM signals.

Let us first of all list some factors on which the data rate depends:

- Data can be sent using either analog or digital signaling. Analog signals are continuous curved signals produced by people like us when we speak. Digital signals are discrete in nature and are square in shape. Analog signals require less bandwidth to travel and digital signal requires more bandwidth. The data rate depends on different factors based on which type of signaling is used.

- Apart from signaling, the data rate depends on how signals code the data. Continuing with our analogy of highway traffic, vehicles are signals and people are data. The road capacity determines the maximum amount of vehicles that can pass at any given point of time. Thus the bandwidth of the media determines the number of signals that can pass through. However, the number of people passing through depends on both, the number of vehicles that can pass through and the number of people carried by a single vehicle. Thus if a single signal can carry multiple bits (which is usually done), the maximum data rate also depends on how many bits a signal can carry, apart from the bandwidth itself.

- If analog signals are used, the data rate depends on how the data is modulated. There are few methods of modulation used in practice. For example, in the case of cable TV, transmission from the server to the TV, it is possible to use the type of modulation known as QAM (Quadrature Amplitude Modulation) 256 which allows 8 bits per signal. The same cable TV, while uploading data from TV to server, uses a type of modulation called QPSK (Quadrature Phase Shift Keying) which only carries 2 bits per signal. Number of bits a signal carries depends on constellation point value, which in above QAM256 case is 256. In case of QPSK, it is 4.

- If Digital signal is used, the data rate depends on how many numbers of digital levels are used.

- In either case, the data rate is proportional to $\log_2(L)$ where L is a number of constellation points a signal can carry in the case of analog and L is the number of signal levels used in case of digital signaling. This is a normal way while you deal with binary numbers. If we have n bit to store a binary value, we can have $2^n$ total such values. On the other hand, for L are total such values, we need a $\log_2(L)$ bits long value.

- The data rate also depends on how sensitive the receiver is. The communication media, for natural and environmental reasons, introduce noise. The noise distorts the signals to some extent. When the signal travels longer, it is more likely to encounter some noise. Due to natural characteristics, even without a noise, the signal tends to distort based on the distance covered. In the case of digital signaling, noise is possible to be removed to some extent, but it is impossible in analog signals. The problem with digital signaling is that the distortion also increases with the data rate. Thus, the receiver, in no case, receives the signal intact. One of the critical components is determining the data rate is the ability of the receiver to sustain distortion. The high-data-rate signal is more distorted than low rate signal and thus there is always some data rate, beyond which the signal is distorted to a point that receiver cannot decide what is the original signal is. One cannot send beyond that point, which is decided by the sensitivity of the receiver. In short, if the receiver is more sensitive and can recover from the higher level of distortion, it is capable of managing higher data rate.

- Media like copper cables which are used in practice offer some resistance to the passing EM waves. The amount of resistance offered depends on a number of stray electrons in the copper cable. A number of stray electrons depend on the temperature of the cable. Like the sensitivity of the receiver, the amount of noise introduced by these stray electrons impacts the flow of waves depends on the data rate, higher the temperature, more the resistance. Thus temperature determines the resistance and thus influences the data rate. Over a typical data rate limit, it is impossible to increase the data rate for any given media. This discussion is not applicable to fiber optic cables as they carry photons and not electrons.

- The data is also affected by external noise. The devices which work in vicinity, interferes with the communicating devices if they happen to work on the same frequency. When a scooter or a mixer starts in vicinity and our TV starts showing snowy images, or radio starts reflecting that noise, it is due to this phenomenon. The data rate can be improved by reducing the external noise. That is done by properly shielding and structuring the wires. When properly shielded, the external signals have reduced effect on the signal being propagated.

## The Frequency and Frequency Band

The bandwidth of the signal is represented by the range of frequencies of a given signal. The difference between highest and lowest frequencies of the signal, in other words, is a bandwidth of that signal. Sometimes the range is also referred to as a frequency band.

The bandwidth of the signal is the bandwidth of the caravan of few vehicles that we would like to pass on the highway together. If a number of vehicles in a caravan is more than the capacity of the highway, they cannot travel together. Same way, if the signal frequency is more than the media frequency, only those frequencies which can pass through the media, goes through, rest are filtered out. Unlike the highway case, we cannot carry that part of the signal in the second cycle. For two reasons, first, there is no way of cutting and pasting signals which can be practically used here, and second, the second cycle is not empty, the next signal is scheduled in next cycle. Another analogy we can provide is a swimming pool. If we have 8 lanes in a swimming pool (the capacity of the pool), and the competition has 9 registrations, only 8 swimmers can swim at a time, the 9th swimmer is not included (cut off).

Carrying on with our swimming pool analogy, we can also see that it is not possible for two swimmers to swim just next to each other, they need some space between them. Similarly, two frequency bands cannot stay just next to each other, they need guard bands in between. The reason is, the transmission on a specific frequency band cannot be confined to that band, some part of it 'spills over' the adjacent frequencies. For example, if you try listening radio on 98.4 instead or 98.3, you will be able to listen to a few bits of the transmission. It is because the transmission on 98.3 also affects adjacent frequencies. Running another radio station at 98.4 will result in a lot of disturbance in the transmission of 98.3. We will have to run it much further apart. Another analogy is to have two different groups communicating in adjacent rooms, both will feel disturbance if their voice goes out of the room. The question is, can we make sure that even with disturbance, they can still communicate? One clever trick of using orthogonal frequencies for adjacent channels. It is possible for the receiver to listen only on the frequency intended to and omit the frequencies orthogonal to it, thus enabling to pack the frequencies much tighter. That trick is popularly known as Orthogonal Frequency Division Multiplexing and is used by a few versions of Wi-Fi.

A number of frequencies available in band determine the number of users who can send and receive at a given point of time. For example, Wi-Fi uses an ISM band between 2.4 GHz and 2.48GHz. As each Wi-Fi channel need 22 MHz, it is possible accommodate 14 channels (out of which 13 are available in India and 11 in the US, as two of them are used for low powered device communications) out of which 3 are non-overlapping and can be used together. That means between two channels, we need to keep 3 to 4 channels to avoid interference. Another version, 802.11g uses OFDM and thus can use number of channels compared to 802.11b, which result into better bandwidth from the same frequency band.

## The Media Affects the Signal

When a signal passes through media and signal has higher frequencies than the media can pass, those frequencies are cut off and the signal is said to be distorted. In simple terms, The resultant signal = original signal − frequency components which are cut off by media.

However strange it looks like, another problem with media is, it favors some frequencies than others. Let us extend our swimming pool analogy to understand. Assume all 8 swimmers indicate the signal. Also, assume all 8 swimmers have the same speed. What if all of them starts swimming at the same point in time? Middle lanes offer less resistance and thus provide better movement for swimmers while the lanes at the outmost edge are comparatively harder. That means swimmers on the edge will lag behind others and middle lane swimmers forge ahead. The original shape (a straight line) now distorts into a shape like a > sign. Same thing happens with different frequency components of a signal. Some of them travel faster than others and thus when they reach at the receiver, the shape is not the same as they start with. If we represent the starting position of the swimmers as the original shape of the signal and the final position of the swimmers as the shape what the receiver receives, the difference represents the distortion.

## The Composite Signal and Harmonics

All signals used in data communication contains multiple frequencies, and thus a combination of multiple signals. Such a signal, which is a collection of other signals of different frequencies, is known as a composite signal. Jean Fourier, a French scientist, proved that a square signal is a composite signal and made up of an infinite number of components, each of which being an analog periodic sine wave. The first components of a given square signal are of the same frequency and amplitude of the square wave itself. The second component is of three times the frequency of the first component and has $1/3^{rd}$ of the amplitude of the first component. The third component has 5 times the frequency of the first component and has the $1/5^{th}$ amplitude of the first component, and so on. This means that the second component completes three cycles and the third component completes five cycles while the first component completes one. These components are also known as harmonics.

The frequency of the first component is known as the fundamental frequency, let us call it f, the amplitude of that first component is highest, let us call it A. In a mathematical form, a frequency of $n^{th}$ component is $(2n + 1) * f$ while the amplitude is $\dfrac{1}{2n+1} * A$.

First three rows describe the components combined to generate the signal are depicted. The fourth signal is the addition of first three components. If such infinite components are collected, we have a square signal. What can we learn from this figure? Here are some observations.

- In a square signal, which is basically a composite signal, the frequency of the components increases and the amplitude decreases, in the linear fashion?

- Only first few components contribute to the shape of the signal in a significant way. The rest add very little. In our figure, when we only add three components, the signal looks quite near to square.

- These components are called harmonics or Fourier components. Signal, its shape and components are critical to understanding the relation between the bandwidth of a given medium and maximum data rate.

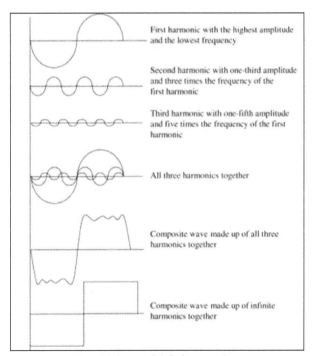

Combining multiple harmonics.

- When the signal has n components and the media can only pass m components, the resultant signal is a signal with n-m components and thus is a distorted signal. For example, in the case of 7.1, if only three harmonics pass through, we will have a signal which is the combination of first three harmonics and looks like last but one signal. However, with a human eye, it is not difficult to judge their original value. If the receiver is sensitive enough, it can only reconstruct the signal from the first three components in this case and do not mind if other components are cut off. The reason is that the higher frequency parts also have smaller amplitude and contribute little to the final shape of the signal.

## Properties of a Channel

Two rules of thumb for communication:

- More the bandwidth of the media, more components pass through the media.

- Higher the data rate, lesser components pass through the media.

When we have higher data rate, the first or the fundamental frequency is higher and thus each subsequent component has higher frequency value than the previous one. That means given a cap, the media will be able to pass less number of components when data rate increases. As a consequence, when we increase the data rate continuously, lesser and lesser harmonics pass through and eventually no harmonic passes through once a limit is reached. Based on the sensitivity of the receiver, some number of harmonics must pass through and that puts a cap on the data rate.

In a way, this cap is on a number of signals and not bits. That means we are fixing a number of vehicles passes through the highway and not the number of people. Interestingly, our aim is not to increase the signal rate but the bit rate, (number of people passes through and not the number of vehicles that carry them). If we increase the number of people per vehicle, we can still increase the number of people passing through highway in unit time. The same approach is used here.

Suppose the signal has the binary state; thus have two different types of signals passing through the channel. Consider two types are +5V and -5V signals. Also assume that +5V indicates 0 and -5V indicate 1. Thus each of the signal carries one bit each.

Thus for sending 101101000110, We will be sending,

+5V, -5V, +5V, +5V, -5V, +5V, -5V, +5V, -5V, -5V, -5V, +5V, +5V, -5V

Now assume the signal to contain four different states (or consider four different signals). Each signal contains 2 bits now. How? Assume we have a square signal represented by +5V, -5V, +10V, -10V; thus four different states (you can also call them four different signals with these values). Each signal, now, can represent two bits. One of the possible mappings is as follows.

+5V <-> 00, -5V <-> 01, +10V <-> 10, and -10V <-> 11

So, while we are sending 101101000110, We will be sending,

+10V, -10V, -5V, +5V, -5V, +10V

Now let us assume the signal has eight states, +5, -5, +10, -10, +15, -15, +20, -20. How many bits can each of the states contain? 3 bits. Here is one typical mapping.

+5V <-> 000, -5V <-> 001, +10V <-> 010, and -10V <-> 011

+15V <-> 100, -15V <-> 101, +20V <-> 110, and -20V <-> 111

now, while we are sending 101101000110, We will be sending,

-15V, -15V, +5V, +20V

In a way, we need less number of vehicles if we accommodate more people in the single vehicle, to carry the same number of people. On the other hand, if we are sending the same number of symbols (when each signal can carry multiple bits), we can send more and more bits, without really increasing the number of signals. Thus, having more bits per symbol helps us achieve arbitrary bit rates, irrespective of a number of symbols possible to be sent based on the bandwidth of the media If we extend the analogy, we can send as many people as we want across, if we can accommodate arbitrary number of people in the vehicle. However, there is a limit that we can accommodate people for a vehicle. Similarly, we cannot accommodate an arbitrary number of bits in a symbol because of noise in the channel. Above discussion holds true only when the channel is noiseless.

Nyquist realized what we have discussed here and gave a simple equation for calculating Maximum Data Rate (MDR) of a noiseless channel.

MDR = 2 * Bandwidth * $Log_2 L$ where L is levels or states of signals.

When we have only two signals, $Log_2 2 = 1$ and thus MDR is calculated as,

MDR = 2 * Bandwidth

Claude Shannon, a well-known scientist, furthered this work for noisy channels and proved that when a signal to noise ratio is S/N, the Maximum Data Rate (MDR) of a noisy channel, is

MDR = 2 * Bandwidth * $log_2(1 + S/N)$

Signal to noise ratio of any channel is fixed for a given temperature. For example, conventional telephone lines use cat-3 and cat-5 copper wires, at room temperature, has 30 dB S/N value. (Signal to Noise ratio is measured in dB, decibel). Given that, we cannot have arbitrary levels. If the Shannon equation gives us the MDR to be 50 Mb, we can increase signal levels to the extent it reaches 50 Mb. Increasing signal levels after that do not yield higher data rate.

The S/N ratio represented in dB, which is 10 log (Ps/Pn) where Ps is the signal strength and Pn is noise strength. An interesting observation can be made when both these quantities are equal. The Ps/Pn ratio is 1. In that case, the MDR is calculated as,

MDR = 2 * Bandwidth $log_2 (1 + 10 * log_2 1)$

= Bandwidth * $log_2 (1 + 0)$ (as $log_2 1 = 0$)

= Bandwidth * $log_2 1$

= 0

The meaning is, when the noise is as strong as the signal itself, nothing will pass through, irrespective of everything else. Quite logical.

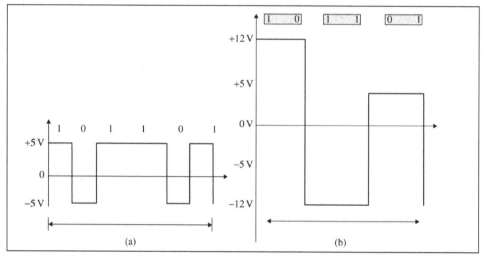

Using multiple signal levels.

The (a) use two levels while (b) use four levels. Thus it is possible in (b) to accommodate two bits for a symbol. Thus we only need to send three symbols for the same data as compared to (a). Looking at the Shannon limit, we can continue increasing the signal levels and increase the bit rate only till we reach the Shannon limit.

# Network Topology

Network Topology is the schematic description of a network arrangement, connecting various nodes (sender and receiver) through lines of connection.

## Bus Topology

Bus topology is a network type in which every computer and network device is connected to single cable. When it has exactly two endpoints, then it is called Linear Bus topology.

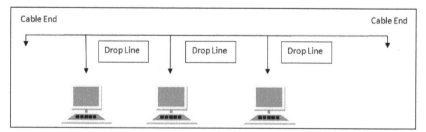

## Features of Bus Topology

- It transmits data only in one direction.

- Every device is connected to a single cable.

## Advantages of Bus Topology

- It is cost effective.
- Cable required is least compared to other network topology.
- Used in small networks.
- It is easy to understand.
- Easy to expand joining two cables together.

## Disadvantages of Bus Topology

- Cables fails then whole network fails.
- If network traffic is heavy or nodes are more the performance of the network decreases.
- Cable has a limited length.
- It is slower than the ring topology.

## Ring Topology

It is called ring topology because it forms a ring as each computer is connected to another computer, with the last one connected to the first. Exactly two neighbours for each device.

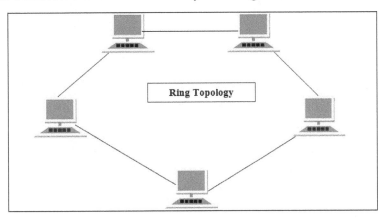

## Features of Ring Topology

- A number of repeaters are used for Ring topology with large number of nodes, because if someone wants to send some data to the last node in the ring topology with 100 nodes, then the data will have to pass through 99 nodes to reach the 100th node. Hence to prevent data loss repeaters are used in the network.

- The transmission is unidirectional, but it can be made bidirectional by having 2 connections between each Network Node, it is called Dual Ring Topology.

- In Dual Ring Topology, two ring networks are formed, and data flow is in opposite direction in them. Also, if one ring fails, the second ring can act as a backup, to keep the network up.

- Data is transferred in a sequential manner that is bit by bit. Data transmitted, has to pass through each node of the network, till the destination node.

## Advantages of Ring Topology

- Transmitting network is not affected by high traffic or by adding more nodes, as only the nodes having tokens can transmit data.

- Cheap to install and expand.

## Disadvantages of Ring Topology

- Troubleshooting is difficult in ring topology.

- Adding or deleting the computers disturbs the network activity.

- Failure of one computer disturbs the whole network.

## Star Topology

In this type of topology all the computers are connected to a single hub through a cable. This hub is the central node and all others nodes are connected to the central node.

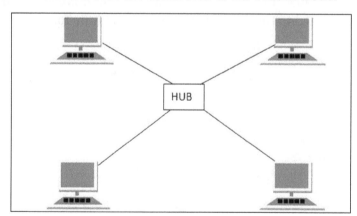

## Features of Star Topology

- Every node has its own dedicated connection to the hub.

- Hub acts as a repeater for data flow.

- Can be used with twisted pair, Optical Fibre or coaxial cable.

## Advantages of Star Topology

- Fast performance with few nodes and low network traffic.

- Hub can be upgraded easily.

- Easy to troubleshoot.

- Easy to setup and modify.

- Only that node is affected which has failed, rest of the nodes can work smoothly.

## Disadvantages of Star Topology

- Cost of installation is high.

- Expensive to use.

- If the hub fails then the whole network is stopped because all the nodes depend on the hub.

- Performance is based on the hub that is it depends on its capacity.

## Mesh Topology

It is a point-to-point connection to other nodes or devices. All the network nodes are connected to each other. Mesh has n(n-1)/2 physical channels to link n devices. There are two techniques to transmit data over the Mesh topology, they are:

- Routing.

- Flooding.

## Mesh Topology: Routing

In routing, the nodes have a routing logic, as per the network requirements. Like routing logic to direct the data to reach the destination using the shortest distance. Or, routing logic which has information about the broken links, and it avoids those node etc. We can even have routing logic, to re-configure the failed nodes.

## Mesh Topology: Flooding

In flooding, the same data is transmitted to all the network nodes, hence no routing logic is required. The network is robust, and the its very unlikely to lose the data. But it leads to unwanted load over the network.

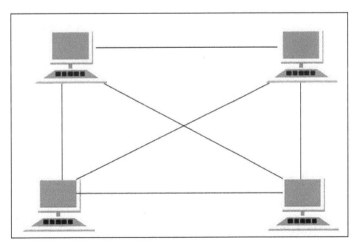

## Types of Mesh Topology

- Partial Mesh Topology : In this topology some of the systems are connected in the same fashion as mesh topology but some devices are only connected to two or three devices.

- Full Mesh Topology : Each and every nodes or devices are connected to each other.

## Features of Mesh Topology

- Fully connected.

- Robust.

- Not flexible.

## Advantages of Mesh Topology

- Each connection can carry its own data load.

- It is robust.

- Fault is diagnosed easily.

- Provides security and privacy.

## Disadvantages of Mesh Topology

- Installation and configuration is difficult.

- Cabling cost is more.

- Bulk wiring is required.

## Tree Topology

It has a root node and all other nodes are connected to it forming a hierarchy. It is also called hierarchical topology. It should at least have three levels to the hierarchy.

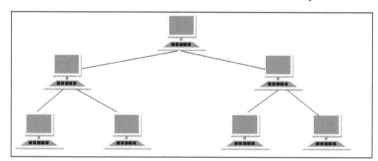

## Features of Tree Topology

- Ideal if workstations are located in groups.

- Used in Wide Area Network.

## Advantages of Tree Topology

- Extension of bus and star topologies.

- Expansion of nodes is possible and easy.

- Easily managed and maintained.

- Error detection is easily done.

## Disadvantages of Tree Topology

- Heavily cabled.

- Costly.

- If more nodes are added maintenance is difficult.

- Central hub fails, network fails.

## Hybrid Topology

It is two different types of topologies which is a mixture of two or more topologies. For example if in an office in one department ring topology is used and in another star topology is used, connecting these topologies will result in Hybrid Topology (ring topology and star topology).

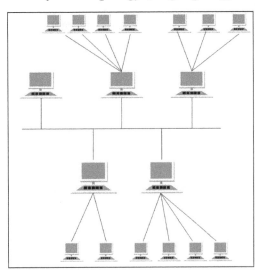

## Features of Hybrid Topology

- It is a combination of two or topologies.

- Inherits the advantages and disadvantages of the topologies included.

## Advantages of Hybrid Topology

- Reliable as Error detecting and trouble shooting is easy.

- Effective.

- Scalable as size can be increased easily.

- Flexible.

## Disadvantages of Hybrid Topology

- Complex in design.

- Costly.

# EM Spectrum

### Radio Waves

The radio waves are at the lowest part of the spectrum. The frequency range of the radio wave is $10^4$ to $10^7$ Hz. The frequency, thus, is less and the corresponding wavelength is more, i.e. the waves are long. Following famous equation describes a well-known principle of physics.

$$\lambda f = c$$

The f is the frequency of the wave, c is the velocity of the wave in the vacuum (which is same as the speed of light) and $\lambda$ is the wavelength of the wave in the vacuum. This equation clearly indicates that the multiplication of both wavelength and frequency being a constant, increasing value of one will decrease the value of the other.

Such waves are easy to produce and transmitted across comparatively long distance. They are able to pass through obstacles and are omnidirectional so sender and receiver do not need to be aligned carefully. Thus the old fashioned radio can be placed anywhere which suits the listener. Even when we use a radio in a moving car, the orientation of the car does not matter in the quality of the transmission. Unlike that, the higher range transmission used in TV sets, the antenna (a dish antenna or a typical TV antenna with multiple pipes of varying length) must exactly point to the TV tower or satellite in the right direction, otherwise, the transmission cannot be achieved. Another desirable property of the radio wave is that they can pass through obstacles. Thus the old fashioned radio was able to work even indoors. The TV antenna cannot work indoors, on the contrary, as it works on microwaves and not radio waves.

Radio waves have quite a few subcategories and each has different physical properties. One common property is that a radio wave travels a long distance. Most radio stations are heard at long distances due to this reason. The downside of this characteristic is that it is possible for multiple radio waves to merge into each other and thus garble. When radio signals travel longer than expected, a radio set sometimes produces mixed output due to this reason. This is the reason FCC in US and DoT in India are established for regulating the use of radio spectrum. All radio stations can only use frequency slot dedicated to them and no other.

Our interest is to use the radio frequency for data communication. Unfortunately, there are a few reasons which make radio spectrum not very suitable for data communication. First, a law of physics. At lower frequencies, data encoding per frequency is much lesser than higher frequencies. At 1 MHz, a radio wave is capable of carrying 1 Mb of data. Higher frequency microwaves, for example, can carry 4 Mb to 5Mb on the contrary. Second reason is that radio spectrum is quite crowded.

The properties that we generally attached to radio waves are actually frequency dependent. Lower range radio waves pass through thicker obstacles and travel in all directions but they have very high attenuation. When a signal is traveling in any direction, the signal tends to spread in all directions surrounding that signal, and drastically lose power. The power loss is in proportion to the square of the distance traveled. That means if the wave travels double the distance, lose power 4 times the original. This power loss is also known as path loss. As the signals travel in all directions, the path loss is huge. At higher frequencies, the radio waves move from omnidirectional travel to single directional travel and at higher and higher frequencies, they tend to travel in straight line. Higher the frequency, more they stop passing through obstacles and bounce off them. Path loss still occurs but to the lesser extent as the wave does not travel in all directions and lose power in all directions.

There are many devices which work in that range and that is why the radio waves always face interference. Moreover, there are other devices like electric motors, and scooters which produce (as a side effect of their work), some radio waves. When somebody starts the electric motor in the vicinity and if your radio voice is distorted.

Attenuation in the air is quite analogous to attenuation in media. The power of the signal drops with respect to distance it travels. The attenuation, also, is a property of a typical frequency of the radio waves. The radio spectrum is divided into multiple sub-bands. It begins with VLF (very low frequency), LF (Low Frequency), MF (medium frequency), HF (High Frequency), VHF (Very high frequency), UHF (ultra-high frequency), SHF (super high frequency), EHS (extremely high frequency), THF (tremendously high frequency).

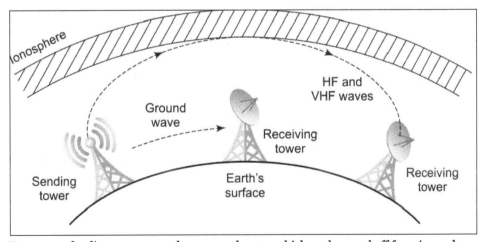

Two types of radio waves, ground waves, and waves which are bounced off from ionosphere.

Last few names may surprise you. This is a problem of premature naming. After naming HF as high frequency (which actually is quite low), when higher level frequencies started being used, naming them in the as funny manner as above was devised. Also, the ranges UHF to THF are considered under microwave by most others.

The LF, MF and VF waves travel along the earth surface. They follow the curvature of the earth and thus can go a long way without needing any towers (which are needed for higher frequency waves). The downside is that their power drastically drops with distance as mentioned before. The advantage is that such waves can move anywhere without reflection. Navigation signals, AM radio stations, submarine communication etc. use this range.

HF and VHF, on the contrary, travel in straight lines and curvature of the earth comes in between any transmission. We need tall towers to overcome that problem and make sure the signals travel as long as they can. Again, to double the distance we need to increase the size of the towers (on both sides, a sender's as well as receiver's) four-fold.

HF and VHF waves have one more advantage. There is an atmospheric layer consisting of charged particles around the earth, known as ionosphere at about 100 km above the earth surface. The HF and VHF waves tend to bounce off from the ionosphere and thus can travel a much longer distance. Most of the long range radio stations (for example, BBC) use this range to transmit their signals, so are heard very far, even other continents at times. There are ham radio enthusiasts who use radio transmission to communicate to other like-minded people over the world. These people built their own radio sets and use them over these frequency bands. In a case of some calamities in past, these ham radio operators have helped to signal messages for relief and directions for saving people. The other operator who uses this range is military. Aircraft to aircraft communication also use this range. Maritime mobile communication also is benefited by this range. The figure showcases both ground waves and waves which bounce off from the ionosphere.

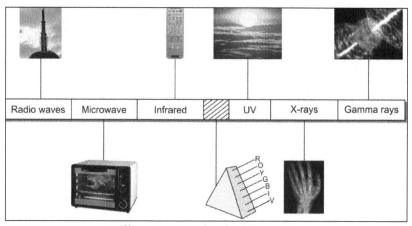

Different ranges of each of the waves.

Figure shows the position of each of the types of waves. The radio waves are at the lowest frequency range. The next in that range is the microwave.

## Microwave Transmission

The microwave range is about 100 MHz to $10^{11}$ Hz. In the beginning, the higher end of the microwave was not used but now some part of it, most notably, one range at around 10GHz and another at around 50GHz is started being used. The higher range of frequencies of the microwave are highly directional; i.e. they travel in very straight line so much so that even if a sender and receiver move a millimetre sideways they lose the sync. Both sender and receiver need to be aligned precisely for communication. This requirement is called line of sight (LOS) requirement. Sometimes special mechanism for defocusing the beam is needed to make sure the communication is not disturbed even when sender and receiver are little misaligned. Unlike radio waves, they only travel in the single direction and thus experience much lesser path loss. That means microwaves can travel much longer distance than radio waves.

The difference between the radio and microwave range does not come abruptly. The waves gradually become more focused as they go shorter in length. In the lower range, if the communicating parties are little misaligned, they can still communicate with a lower data rate but at the higher frequencies, special defocusing is needed. On the other hand, such a focused transmission allows the sender to use a technology called MIMO (Multiple Input Multiple Output). MIMO is a method to increase the capacity of the carrier to be multiplied by pairs of antennas used for transmission. In MIMO, there are multiple antennas sending and receiving (like multiple wires are used together for sending and receiving), and thus multiply the effective bandwidth by a number of such pairs of antennas used. Multiple transmitters are lined up in a single row to multiple receivers without having any interference from each other. Thus if one such pair of antenna gives a 10 Mb and we have 10 such pairs of antennas lined up, we get an effective bandwidth of 100Mb without using additional frequency band. Latest Wi-Fi solutions have increased the capacity of the transmission using many techniques, one of them is MIMO.

The antennas used by the microwave is the parabolic antenna. It helps focus the beam precisely at the center of the antenna and travel much longer. These parabolic antennas must be aligned precisely for clear communication. Unlike HF and VHF, microwaves do not bounce off the ionosphere and we need towers at sender and receiver for communication. However, the microwave is an attractive solution when no wiring is possible between sender and receiver. Microwave is the only solution when the terrain in between the sender and the receiver requires right-of-way to dig trench for wired communication (for example, between two high-rise building in the city where the connecting line passes through resident colony), or impossible to lay cables (for example, between islands, or peaks of hills etc.). The sheer dimension of the obstacle prevents a wired solution. The Microwave can bypass these obstacles and thus can be really handy. It is relatively inexpensive as one just need to raise sender and receiver towers. The mobile phone companies save a lot when whey use high-rise building rooftops to raise their towers for communications. They avoid wiring the passage containing the busy government owned roads and other buildings. They use repeaters atop rooftops of tall buildings at the distance of 50 to 60 km to further their coverage. The microwave communication is not affected by natural disasters like flood or earthquake, as long as the sender, receiver, and repeaters are intact and aligned, the transmission remains unaffected.

The microwaves do not pass through the obstacles like radio waves and bounce off the obstacles. Even when traveling in straight lines, some divergence is introduced by atmospheric conditions. Due to typical atmospheric conditions, a typical range of microwaves refracted from atmospheric layers and thus reach to the receiver little later than the direct wave. This little delay is good enough to make them out of phase with the direct wave. If they reach the receiver in an out of phase with the original wave, they will cancel out the original wave and the receiver does not get any signal. This is known as multipath fading and happen quite often. Different atmospheric conditions affect different frequency bands and generally, there is no alternative for the sender to use some other frequency to transmit. It is a natural phenomenon and there is no way to prevent it. As a practical solution, sender usually keeps a spare frequency. When one of the transmitting range experience multipath fading, they use the spare frequency band instead and transfer the communicating going on that frequency to the reserved band.

Another problem with the high-end microwave is that they are so short that they are absorbed by rain and vegetation. The reason for dish television programs stops working while there is a heavy rain is due to this reason. The waves coming from the satellite are absorbed by rain drops. This is also true for cases where the trees come in between.

However, microwaves are quite useful for many applications like mobile phone communication, long range communication by other mobile devices like satellite phones, long range point to point communication and communication satellite to dish antenna communication and also between ground stations of TV channels to satellites. Due to all these usages (especially use of this spectrum by mobile companies), they are highly in demand and invite arbitration from the government. The government, from time to time, auction these bands. International bodies like ITU (International Telecommunication Union) are working in the direction. The advantage of such international agreement is huge. It is always a good idea to have consistent frequency allocation across countries as devices working in one country (for example mobile phones and TV sets) also work in other countries as they use the same frequency spectrum. One can mass produce the device in a country where such manufacturing is cheaper. Government bodies like DoT (Department of Telecommunication) in India and FCC (Federal Communications Commission) in the US are controlling the auction process. Instead of technological reasons, decisions of such bodies are controlled by strong lobbies who has acquired or would like to acquire specific frequency band and do not want to release. That means, there is a little consensus across countries to adopt the suggestions by bodies like ITU for a typical spectrum. The politically influenced parties do not allow any such agreement between countries. One such example is of 3G. It took almost 10 years to arrive and lose the advantage it would have otherwise. ITU recommended it but nobody except China reserved the specified bandwidth on the specified spectrum. Originally designed to be 2 Mb, it has to be reduced to 384 kb and even that is not actually possible to be delivered in most cases. The next range that is used is called infrared which has the size of wave reduced to millimeters in size and thus are also known as millimeter waves.

## Infrared Transmission

The infrared is used for short range transmission, for example, the remote controls of our TV sets and other electronic devices use infrared transmission. The devices which one need to generate such rays can be built easily so quite cheap, it is not hazardous to human health (microwaves are) so one can use them in household operations and remote controlled toys etc., and contains a huge bandwidth so can carry a lot of data. It is highly directional so one needs to align sender with the receiver and it cannot pass obstacles. Both of these properties anyone would have realized if ever stood between a TV set and a remote.

The infrared waves are very focused so much so that if the sender and receiver are not properly aligned, the communication cannot happen. Older mobile phones used to have infrared ports. When one uses such ports, both devices must be kept exactly opposite to each other. The infrared cannot work outdoors as well. A portion of the sunlight contains infrared waves apart from visible light and many other waves. We cannot 'see' anything other than the visible light as our eyes are equipped to see only a small part of the spectrum. If we use an infrared device outdoors, the signals will collide with the infrared signals present in the sunlight and result in garbage. Governments do not impose any licensing on the usage of infrared waves.

The confinement to indoors and the inability of pass through obstacles can actually be boon for devices which demand security. For example, one cannot remotely operate our TV from outside our house and play a prank. A communication will not be 'heard' in the adjacent rooms. However, infrared use is limited to connecting wireless devices like mice and printers in past. That job is taken over by the Bluetooth in recent years.

## The Unlicensed Bands (ISM Bands)

Looking at the issues of licensing and politics associated with, one may wonder if we can forgo licensing and start using the spectrum in some collaborative fashion. There are indeed some ranges known as "Industrial, Scientific and Medical" bands which are free for anybody to use primarily set aside to be used in industrial equipment, apparatus used for the scientific purpose and medical devices. However, they have used for non-ISM purposes also. Out of a few ISM ranges, there are three different ranges used worldwide for non-ISM usage. The exact ranges available are different from place to place and there is no worldwide consensus except for 2.4 GHz range. Looking at the use of such bands, many prefer to call these range as "unlicensed" and not ISM bands. Calling them ISM may be considered misnomer in future. Let us concentrate on three ranges that are primarily used for such non-ISM purpose.

The first range is about 915 MHz which is used by 802.15.4 networks and ZigBee networks. That range is also used by cordless telephones. The second range is 2.4 GHz to 2.48 GHz, popularly known as middle ISM range. Unlike the first range, this range is available worldwide in most countries. The Wi-Fi network's two version 802.11b and 802.11g works in this range. Bluetooth also works in this range. Some of the 802.15.4 and ZigBee devices also use this band. Many remote controlled devices, toys, garage door openers, microwave ovens, etc. also use this band. The third range which exists at 5 GHz, is basically a collection of three different ranges. One is between 5.25 GHz to 5.35 GHz (a 100 MHz band), another is between 5.47 to 5.7 GHz which is 255 MHz wide, and last is 5.725 GHz to 5.825 GHz which is also 100 MHz wide. These ranges are known as Unlicensed National Information Infrastructure (U-NIII). The range is also known as Broadband Radio Access Network (BARN). One typical version of Wi-Fi, the 802.11a, uses this range. HyperLAN which is a wireless LAN used in Europe also uses this range.

Out of three bands available, the lower bands have less bandwidth compared to higher end bands. However, they better for some reasons cited as follows:

- They consume less power as compared to higher end band to cover the same distance. That means the devices used in this range need less power and battery runs longer.

- For the same power, the range they cover is more than double the range covered by high-frequency bands.

- High-frequency bands suffer from absorption by rain and vegetation, these bands do not have any such problem.

The downside is that there are many devices which use this range. The range is highly occupied by many radio devices and other long range communicating devices. There is every chance that the transmission experiences some interference.

## Optical Light, FSO and Li-Fi

The final band that is used for transmission is the visible light that we are used to. Light is also a wave with frequency and well suited for transmission except for the case that there is a lot of interference due to the existence of our normal light. The term Optical Wireless Communication is used to describe unguided visible, infrared and UV light for carrying the data signal. FSO or free space optics is a way of transmitting the optical light in free space. FSO is generally used to provide a terrestrial point to point link. The very light pulses which work in FO cable can work without the confinement of cable. The idea about data transmission using optical light has emerged from that idea. Thus we will be using the very light that we use for our day to day life for data communication purpose without using any physical media. It is quite similar to use the torch to signal a message.

FSO can be used wherever laying an FO cable is inappropriate, or impossible, for example, when we want two aircraft to communicate. FSO is demonstrated to work even with distances of 40,000 of kilometers between spacecrafts. In other experiments, it was demonstrated to work at 1Gbps speed for about 2 kilometers. Though the FSO is the quite attractive proposition from that ground, has a few limitations as well. The atmosphere is the biggest issue. Everything including sunlight, fog, vegetation, rain, lightning, dust can hinder the propagation of light, and thus, data communication.

In recent years, an interesting indoor application has emerged called Li-Fi, which is basically a Wi-Fi for home. The difference is, instead of using the 2.4GHz spectrum, it uses visible light, infrared and near UV spectrum for data communication. The sender uses LED and receiver uses a photodiode, like an FO cable.

The LED switches off and on while transmitting the light pulses, too fast for the human eye to notice. The light is dimmed below human visibility to make sure humans do not get disturbed by the transmission. Li-Fi is a boon for cases like aircraft cabins, nuclear plants, hospitals where any form of radiation is unwelcome. Li-Fi is capable of achieving much better data speeds than Wi-Fi. Researchers are able to generate speeds of 224 Gb in a closed space. Even when the senders and receivers are not aligned, the light bouncing off the walls can provide about 70 Gb of speed. The light cannot pass through walls which make this network much more secure than Wi-Fi.

## Using the Spectrum

In most cases, the devices which use the spectrum focus on a very small part of it. For example, a radio station generally picks up a very small band a few kb wide. A GSM mobile phone uses a 200 MHz band. Such bands are known as the narrow band and most transmission works in that fashion. The benefit for such narrow band transmission is clear. It uses very less bandwidth and thus many such transmissions can be packed in the available range.

Some transmissions favor a wide band transmission, i.e. use a much wider range than needed. This method seems wasteful but it is not in true sense. One typical method, known as DSSS or direct sequence spread spectrum was used in Wi-Fi transmission. Another method, known as CDMA or Code Division Multiple Access, is one popular method of mobile communication. Yet another version, known as FHSS (Frequency Hopping Spread Spectrum) is also used in Bluetooth and other cases. All these methods use more bandwidth than they actually need.

The FHSS utilizes the large bandwidth in a typical way. The transmission which uses FHSS moves from one frequency to another from time to time. The sender and receiver both have the clear idea about the sequence in which the frequency changes and the time it spends in a given frequency band. An intruder fails to jam signals from such transmission for a long period as he might use trial and error to capture a transmission but cannot hold on to it for a longer period.

The DSSS uses a larger band to avoid errors related to big signals (higher frequency harmonics will cut off if the transmission uses a big signal. It uses multiple smaller signals. This mechanism can use the spectrum more efficiently and is more immune to other transmission related errors.

CDMA allows multiple users to use the same frequency and thus can entertain a much larger number of users in a given band than a narrow band transmission might allow. So CDMA was a popular choice in 3G mobile phones.

Another mechanism which uses a wider band is called UWB or Ultra-Wide Band. It spreads the radio energy over a very wide frequency band, with very low power spectral density. Usually, the range is many GHz and the data rate is also around some GHz speed. However, it is spread over a much larger band. That means for any narrow frequency part chosen out of this wide band, the power used is very less and a number of bits it covers are also less. The high bandwidth allows very high data rate for a short distance or reasonably good data rate for a longer distance. The advantage of UWB is its capacity to withstand interference, pass through obstacles and even share the bandwidth with another narrow band transmission. For a narrow band transmission, the low powered UWB transmission going on in that very range seems like little noise and nothing else. The UWB signal is said to underlay the narrow band signal in that case.

UWB actually is designed to transmit using such a wide range that it also covers many bands which are commercially licensed to transmit narrow band. The proponents of it claim that the interference the UWB devices generate is less than the normal noise that the narrow band transmission is expected to encounter during normal transmission. Thus UWB does not cause significant interference with other licensed users.

There are a few advantages of this wide band. The multipath fading problem does not affect UWB and low power utilization improves the battery life of the devices. UWB is well suited for sensor devices with constrained power. Normally UWB operates in 3 GHz to the 10GHz range. Vehicular networks use UWB in the range of 22Gb to 29Gb frequency range. PANs also use UWB and get about 1Gbps speed.

## Wi-Fi Standards

The term Wi-Fi is synonymous with wireless access in general, despite the fact that it is a specific trademark owned by the Wi-Fi Alliance, a group dedicated to certifying that Wi-Fi products meet the IEEE's set of 802.11 wireless standards.

These standards, with names such as 802.11b (pronounced "Eight-O-Two-Eleven-Bee", ignore the "dot") and 802.11ac, comprise a family of specifications that started in the 1990s and continues to grow today. The 802.11 standards codify improvements that boost wireless throughput and range as well as the use of new frequencies as they become available. They also address new technologies that reduce power consumption.

## What is Wi-Fi 6, Wi-Fi 5 and Wi-Fi 4?

The IEEE naming scheme for the standard is a little tough to get used to, and in an effort to make it easier to understand, the Wi-Fi Alliance has come up with some simpler names.

Under its naming convention, the alliance calls 802.11ax Wi-Fi 6. 802.11ac is now Wi-Fi 5, and 802.11n is Wi-Fi 4. The idea, according to the Wi-Fi Alliance, is to make matching endpoint and router capabilities a simpler matter for the rank-and-file user of Wi-Fi technology.

There is a subcategory of Wi-Fi 6 called Wi-Fi 6E, which was written into the 802.11ax specification to accommodate additional spectrum that might be added down the road.

Meanwhile it's important to know that the Wi-Fi Alliance has not made up simpler names for all the 802.11 standars, so it's important to be familiar with the traditional designations. Also, the IEEE, which continues to work on newer versions of 802.11, has not adopted these new names, so trying to track down details about them using the new names will make the task more complicated.

The traditional names of these standards create quite an alphabet soup, made all-the-more confusing because they are not arranged alphabetically. To help clarify the situation, here's an update on these physical-layer standards within 802.11, listed in reverse chronological order, with the newest standards at the top, and the oldest toward the bottom.

## 802.11ah

Also known as Wi-Fi HaLow, 802.11ah defines operation of license-exempt networks in frequency bands below 1GHz (typically the 900 MHz band), excluding the TV White Space bands. In the U.S., this includes 908-928MHz, with varying frequencies in other countries. The purpose of 802.11ah is to create extended-range Wi-Fi networks that go beyond typical networks in the 2.4GHz and 5GHz space (remember, lower frequency means longer range), with data speeds up to 347Mbps. In addition, the standard aims to have lower energy consumption, useful for Internet of Things devices to communicate across long ranges without using a lot of energy. But it also could compete with Bluetooth technologies in the home due to its lower energy needs. The protocol was approved in September 2016 and published in May 2017.

## 802.11ad

Approved in December 2012, 802.11ad is very fast - it can provide up to 6.7Gbps of data rate across the 60 GHz frequency, but that comes at a cost of distance – you achieve this only if your client device is situated within 3.3 meters (only 11 feet) of the access point.

## 802.11ac (Wi-Fi 5)

Current home wireless routers are likely  802.1ac-compliant, and operate in the 5 GHz frequency space. With Multiple Input, Multiple Output (MIMO) – multiple antennas on sending and receiving devices to reduce error and boost speed – this standard supports data rates up to 3.46Gbps. Some router vendors include technologies that support the 2.4GHz frequency via 802.11n, providing support for older client devices that may have 802.11b/g/n radios, but also providing additional bandwidth for improved data rates.

## 802.11n (Wi-Fi 4)

The first standard to specify MIMO, 802.11n was approved in October 2009 and allows for usage in two frequencies - 2.4GHz and 5GHz, with speeds up to 600Mbps. When you hear wireless LAN vendors use the term "dual-band", it refers to being able to deliver data across these two frequencies.

## 802.11g

Approved in June 2003, 802.11g was the successor to 802.11b, able to achieve up to 54Mbps rates in the 2.4GHz band, matching 802.11a speed but within the lower frequency range.

## 802.11a

The first "letter" following the June 1997 approval of the 802.11 standard, this one provided for operation in the 5GHz frequency, with data rates up to 54Mbps. Counterintuitively, 802.11a came out later than 802.11b, causing some confusion in the marketplace because eople expected that the standard with the "b" at the end would be backward compatible with the one with the "a" at the end.

## 802.11b

Released in September 1999, it's most likely that your first home router was 802.11b, which operates in the 2.4GHz frequency and provides a data rate up to 11 Mbps. Interestingly, 802.11a products hit the market before 802.11a, which was approved at the same time but didn't hit the market until later.

## 802.11-1997

The first standard, providing a data rate up to 2 Mbps in the 2.4GHz frequency. It provided a range of a whopping 66 feet of indoors (330 feet outdoors), so if you owned one of these routers, you probably only used it in a single room.

## Pending Wi-Fi Standards

### 802.11aj

Also known as China Millimeter Wave, this defines modifications to the 802.11ad physical layer and MAC layer to enable operation in the China 59-64GHz frequency band. The goal is to maintain backward compatibility with 802.11ad (60GHz) when it operates in that 59-64GHz range and to operate in the China 45GHz band, while maintaining the 802.11 user experience.

## 802.11ak

There are some products in the home-entertainment and industrial-control spaces that have 802.11 wireless capability and 802.3 Ethernet function. The goal of this standard is to help 802.11 media provide internal connections as transit links within 802.1q bridged networks, especially in the areas of data rates, standardized security and quality-of-service improvements.

## 802.11ax (Wi-Fi 6)

Known as High Efficiency WLAN, 802.11ax aims to improve the performance in WLAN deployments in dense scenarios, such as sports stadiums and airports, while still operating in the 2.4GHz and 5GHz spectrum. The group is targeting at least a 4X improvement in throughput compared to 802.11n and 802.11ac., through more efficient spectrum utilization.

## 802.11ay$\frac{1}{8}$

Also known as Next Generation 60GHz, the goal of this standard is to support a maximum throughput of at least 20Gbps within the 60GHz frequency (802.11ad currently achieves up to 7Gbps), as well as increase the range and reliability.

## 802.11az

Called Next Generation Positioning (NGP), a study group was formed in January 2015 to address the needs of a "Station to identify its absolute and relative position to another station or stations it's either associated or are not $\frac{1}{8}$associated with." The goals of the group would be to define modifications to the MAC and PHY layers that enable "determination of absolute and relative position with better accuracy with respect to the Fine Timing Measurement (MTM) protocol executing on the same PHY-type, while reducing existing wireless medium use and power consumption, and is scalable to dense deployments."

## 802.11ba

Otherwise known as "Wake-Up Radio" (WUR), this isn't a crazy morning zoo-crew thing, but rather a new technology aimed at extending the battery life of devices and sensors within an Internet of Things network. The goal of the WUR is to "greatly reduce the need for frequent recharging and replacement of batteries while still maintaining optimum device performance.

# Network Layer Services

Apart from routing and forwarding, a few other duties that a network layer should provide is listed below:

- Identify each machine uniquely. This is the prerequisite for all services including routing and forwarding. Addressing mechanism should be able to handle an increase in a number of machines and should help faster routing.

- Account the usage of network layer services by every user, for reporting and billing. The volume of data and duration for which the services used are two common parameters considered.

- Implement forwarding process in fastest possible manner. Considering the amount of data modern routers are used to process, this is the most critical function of most routers.

- Multiplex TCP and UDP data (sometimes even SCTP data) and also manage multiple cards (which contain data link and physical layers).

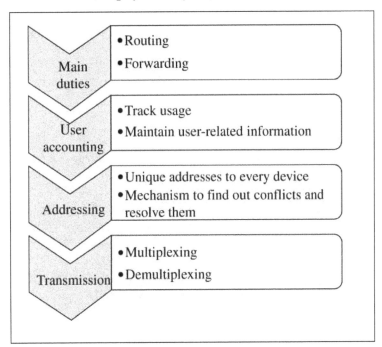

Network Layer Services.

## Routing

An autonomous system or AS is a collection of networks owned by a single party. When a packet needs to be routed between two divisions of the same company or between two departments of the University, the communicating networks, and the interconnecting infrastructure belongs to the single party, i.e. the routing is to be performed within the AS. In that case, the routing is called intra-AS or interior routing. All company networks together and all university departmental networks together are examples of AS. Sometimes, the packet starts from one AS needs to be delivered to another AS. For example, a packet from network-1 of company 1 to be delivered to network -7 of company-2. In that case, in addition to intra-AS routing, the packet also needs to find a path from AS of company-1 to AS of company-2. This is another type of routing, called exterior routing or inter-AS routing. The internal and external traffic need different types of routing because they need different treatment. Routing algorithms are quite close to the type of network we are using, therefore, wired and wireless networks need different types of routing. Smaller IoT devices need their own process of routing. Figure depicts a case where four Autonomous Systems are communicating with each other. You can see internal communication, as well as Inter-AS communication, is carried out by those connecting lines.

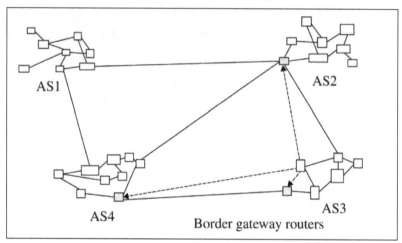

Inter and Intra-Autonomous Routing.

## Accounting

Accounting is a critical function of the network layer when the user is charged for the volume of the traffic. Two reasons demand an accounting by network layer.

- How many packets users have sent and received, counting the amount of data he has consumed for billing him or checking if he has exceeded the limit imposed by the package he has paid for.

- Checking if the packet volume shows some sign of abnormal activity, to check if there is a security breach of some sort or policy imposed is violated.

## Receive Services from the Data Link Layer

Once the network layer decides the destination address, it must pass that information to data link layer to construct the frame with that destination address and place the content (the packet), it has generated in that frame. The data link layer provides the service of delivering the frame to the next immediate recipient. The process is not as simple as it seems, the network layer has an IP address while the frame must contain a MAC address. There has to be a process for finding the MAC address for an IP address. This is performed by a process called Address Resolution.

## Provide Service to the Transport Layer

On one hand the network layer takes services of data link layer to send data across to the next immediate recipient, it also provides services to the transport layer by taking a segment from it, decide the next immediate recipient from the routing table as well as the destination address, and ask data link layer to deliver that to the next immediate recipient.

An IP address identifies a machine and a port number identifies an application running within. For example, a pair of values 128.66.203.37, 80 indicates a machine with given IP address and a process (a web server) running within. This pair is called an end point. When we talk about a network connection, it is between two such endpoints, for example, 128.66.203.37, 80 and 128.66.203.7, 1234 indicate two endpoints, one server and another is a client, communicating with each other, and forming a connection. That means, two endpoints identify a connection. IP provides machine-to-machine and not process to process communication. We that is why need a pair of IP address and port number to identify a process running on a machine.

## Global Machine Level Addressing

Unless every machine is uniquely identified, it is impossible for the network layer to do the routing process correctly. The Internet has begun with classful addressing mechanism, now getting obsolete and another mechanism based on classless addressing is increasingly used.

## Classful Addressing

The classful addressing mechanism identifies each network as either class A, B or C. Class A are small in number but contain very large number of hosts (nodes), Class B are moderately large networks and their quantity also belongs to that range. Class C network is much smaller (in a number of nodes) but very large in number.

The network address is 32 bits in IPv4 and classful addresses are designed according to dividing that 32-bit number into four divisions and manipulating them as per the type of address. The numbers are represented in dotted decimal notation; a typical scheme of representing each byte as its decimal equivalent, separated by a dot (.). For example, 10000000 00010100 00000000 00000000 is represented as 128.20.0.0. In fact, this is an address of a network of type B. A type B network has first two bytes reserved for a network address. Every address in a classful mechanism is denoted as Network Address + Node Address. For example, a node 128.20.5.6 is a node belongs to a network 128.20 with node id as 5.6. Another node belongs to the same network may be 128.20 6.7. Here the first two bytes are same, which is not a coincidence. All nodes of the same network share the same prefix. i.e. all nodes of network 128.20.0.0 have first two bytes as 128.20 only.

## Classless Addressing

Classful addresses are not in vogue today. A mechanism which provides a more optimized way of assignment of the network addresses is used here. In classful addresses, the network and node addresses are byte level addresses, thus a network address is one byte and node address can be of 3 bytes (class A) or network address of two bytes and node address of two bytes (class B), and network address of 3 bytes and node address of one byte (class C) are the only three varieties possible. That resulted in huge waste of addresses. The classless mechanism allows the users to choose the network as well as the host address size. For example, if a user wants to get a network address for two computers, he can get an address of the network with 30 bit size with node address of two bits. If the classful addressing mechanism is used, the user must get a minimum class C address which has 254 host addresses and thus would waste 252 addresses. The uniqueness of every address is a must, even in classless addressing case. When we allow arbitrarily long network addresses, a slash notation is used to indicate a number of bits used for network id. For example, 128.20.0.0/24 indicates that this address has first 24 bits as the network address and last 8 bits are host address.

When a host is connected to multiple networks, it will have multiple network addresses, as every address contains both networks as well as host ids. The figure indicates the addressing issue. A router R1 and a node which is connected to two networks (called a multihomed host) have two addresses.

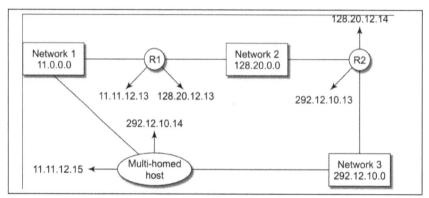

Network layer addressing.

The routers, interestingly, do not store complete addresses in the routing table but try to provide aggregated entries. Figure depicts a typical setup and 20.5 showcases a typical routing table one may think a router should have. 20.6 showcases an aggregated table a router will normally provide. The ISPs usually have limited addresses so they deploy a method known as Network Address Translation (NAT), which allows them to share addresses among multiple subscribers at the same point in time.

Both of above solutions are useful for IPv4 addresses. The Internet is moving towards using IPv6 everywhere and provide a (seemingly) final solution to addressing issues. An IPv6 has total $2^{128}$ addresses which are sufficient for almost all atoms on earth. The world is going towards billions of interconnected very small devices networks (IoT), IPv6 is most suitable option for addressing nodes of such networks. IPv6 provides a much more hierarchical way of addressing. Both geographical and ISP based hierarchy is possible to be provided in IPv6.

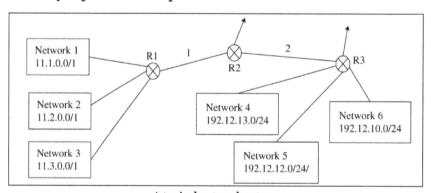

A typical network setup.

Table: A routing table with all entries.

| Network ID | Next hop address | Interface | (other fields) |
|---|---|---|---|
| 11.1.0.0/16 | R1 | 1 | |
| 11.2.0.0/16 | R1 | 1 | |
| 11.3.0.0/16 | R1 | 1 | |
| 192.12.10.0/12 | R3 | 2 | |

| 192.12.12.0/24 | R3 | 2 | |
|---|---|---|---|
| 192.12.13.0/24 | R3 | 2 | |

Table: Aggregated entries.

| Network ID | Next hop address | Interface | (other fields) |
|---|---|---|---|
| 11./16 | R1 | 1 | |
| 192.12./24 | R3 | 2 | |

## Multiplexing and Managing Multiple Transport Layer and Data Link Layer Connections

TCP and UDP data is both runs multiple connections together and the single network layer provides their multiplexing and demultiplexing. Multiple data link layers are to be managed under a single network layer.

## Forwarding Approaches at Network Layer

Network layer, before communicating to the next immediate network layer, might establish a connection or otherwise. When a connection is established between two network layers before sending it is called virtual circuit while when a connection is not established, the approach is called datagram based. The TCP/IP model which is prevalent on the Internet uses a datagram based approach. A method normally chosen by high-level ISPs is called MPLS (Multiprotocol Label Switching) MPLS uses a connection-oriented approach. In fact, the current mantra is forwarding based on service.

## Connectionless Forwarding

The IP uses connectionless forwarding. This process works like this. The sender just sends the packet and forget about it. Whether that packet reaches the receiver or not, it is not IP's concern. The connectionless forwarding acts like sending postcards or SMS, sent and forgotten. The receiver usually gets one, but might not get in sequence, might get is after a variable delay and might just be lost and not delivered. The sender won't even get the feedback.

A better mechanism may be based on connection-oriented delivery where the receiver gets the feedback about delivery and the receiver gets the data in right sequence. This seemingly inferior approach is chosen to provide autonomy of routers. The connectionless delivery mechanism just pumps the packets into the network, without establishing the connection. That means the packet can take any path the intermediary routers deem fit. The routers get the power to send the packet in any direction they prefer. That helps routers to avoid paths which are closed, dynamically, for each packet that they forward.

If a connection-oriented approach for packet delivery was chosen instead, a router or a line failure would cost all connections passing through it. In a case of this connectionless forwarding process, the previous router can decide to avoid a dead router or line. The most important thing, the process of forwarding continues despite line or router start malfunctioning or stop working.

Closely observe the figure. Sender and Receiver are nodes which want to communicate. The network layer has multiple options possible out of which it chooses a typical path. Case number-1 shows the normal path including lines from A to B and B to Receiver. If a router B runs into a snag and A learns about it, the router A learns about that and chooses an alternate path via D for subsequent packets. Even when the communication line B-Receiver goes down, B can choose another path via D to reach to the receiver for remaining packets. Thus, such a scheme, based on connectionless delivery is quite tolerant to line and node failures and thus chosen for network layer delivery at Internet.

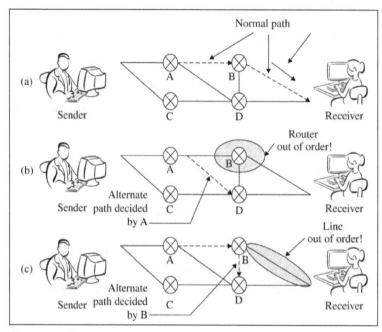

The power of autonomy given to routers, a connection sustaining failures.

Another question may arise; how many packets are lost if a snag is suddenly introduced in the network? In above case, for example, if A realizes that B has run into a snag, and diverts the remaining traffic through D, the packets that it sent and not forwarded by B may be lost. However, if B has not acked those packets, we know that the sender (A here) keeps a copy of such packets and thus those packets are still with A. In that case, when A decides to change path, it will also send those packets along the new path and thus they are also not lost. Only those packets which acked by B and not forwarded are lost.

Here A and B are said to autonomous routers, they can choose the paths of incoming packets on their own, in the best interest of the network. This is a great freedom, enabling them to choose lightly loaded or faster paths etc. SDN extends this functionality to administrator's policy based forwarding. That means the routers (called forwarding devices in the context of SDN), choose paths which best suits the policies designed by administrators. One can choose different paths for 2G and 3G subscriber's packets, for example, or even a VOIP packet or a data download packet between the same pair of nodes can be routed differently.

Even during congestion (traffic jam), where a typical line or router has more packets than it can handle, previous routers can choose alternate paths to relieve that ailing router and thus help in controlling the congestion process.

The networks, in the modern era, are getting more and more reliable as interconnections by FO cables and technical conditions of routers are getting better and better. There are many solutions not allowing such autonomy are used, one of the most common methods is to use MPLS.

## The Process of Connectionless Forwarding

When a sender wants to send, it won't decide the path beforehand but rely on intermediate routers to eventually find the receiver. Each intermediary routers find the best path on their own, based on their local circumstances. Thus there is no connection establishment process preceding the data transmission.

When the sends the first packet, the path has no snag and the packet passes through A and B to the receiver. How do they find the path to the receiver? All routers of the network, including A and B, periodically review their surrounding and exchange information so they are aware of the best paths to all other nodes of the network. When A gets the packet from Sender, it looks into his routing table and finds that B is the best next router for destination Receiver. So it sends it across to B. Once B receive that packet, it also finds the direct entry in the routing table indicating that the Receiver is on the direct path. B sends the packet over that path and the packet reached its final destination! It is also important to note that the routing tables are not fixed. Periodically, routing algorithms run, take the stock of the nodes of the network, decide the current best neighbour for every other network as a destination in a given AS, and update the routing table accordingly.

For the second packet, though, the problem is there at B, so when it reaches at A, and A looks for paths to Receiver, it finds the B is not reachable and found another path through D. So A forwards the second packet to D. Before the third packet arrives, the B is up and running and informs all neighbours including A that it is available now. So A forwards the third packet to B. Now when B updates itself, it finds that the response from Receiver arrives from D and not the direct link. Thus it learns that the direct link is down and forwards the third packet to D.

What if the line between B and D starts working now? Both B and D periodically poke at all their outgoing lines and if they get a response back, they conclude that the line is working. So if the line is working, they will soon learn about it and the fourth packet again travels through the original path. There are a few things we have overlooked in the entire process. First, we have assumed that the routing tables are already there and we will be using them straight away. That may not be the case, when the router is newly added or gone down and come up again, it loses everything it has learned including the routing table.

Second, the periodic updates are what they are, periodic. When a routing table is updated they remain as it is for a while and again updated. Between two updates, they continue with the same details they have updated in the previous cycle. That means, what they use is not exactly current status of the network but a snapshot taken a few moments back. It is quite possible that some late changes are not reflected in the routing table entries and a packet may be misdirected. The packet may also be misdirected if the information is updated but not reached to the router which is taking a decision. The point is, the routing table may not direct the packet to optimum path always.

Third, each router decides its own path based on the local information. In example, we are fortunate to have the complete topology of the network at our disposal and thus we can confirm that the decisions taken by A and B are correct. The network administrators cannot see the topology like our academic image enables us and thus it is not easy for them to determine the decisions being right or otherwise. When the router's decision is wrong, the packet sometimes roams around in the network. Special mechanisms need to be devised for informing the sender about problems associated with incorrect routing. A protocol called ICMP (Internet Control and Message Protocol) is used to report routing related errors back. An IP packet contains a field 'time to live'. When the packet roams around long enough, this field helps the router to drop the packet rather than forwarding it.

## Pros and Cons of Connectionless Approach

Connectionless approach forgoes connection establishment and close. Thus the sender can start sending anytime it wants and without really knowing if the path to the receiver is intact or receiver is up and running. There are two disadvantages of this approach. First, the exercise may be fruitless if the path is broken or the receiver is out of order. Second, if one needs to have guaranteed delivery process, for example, a video transmission demands minimum delay for every packet. The connectionless approach has no way of providing it. If some connection oriented mechanism would have been used instead, it would have been possible to ask for and get those service from intermediary routers. As the path does not change during the complete connection, once the quality is guaranteed, it is likely to be provided throughout the connection.

The routing process invites every router to make a decision. The routers have local information and different than the global view. A better solution demands a global view. The conventional routing process slowed down due to two things, first, every router deliberates on the packet and second, routing table size is dauntingly huge in most cases. Many techniques are devised to reduce routing table entries as well as faster decision making.

The connectionless design is really good in dealing with congestion as the routers can redirect traffic away from congested area. However, some type of traffic also demands process of admission control. Let us try to understand. In a connectionless architecture, any sender can send the packet whenever he wishes to. He won't check network condition or readiness of the receiver. When other users are downloading files, they experience additional delay and that is fine with most of us. Unfortunately, if others are video conferencing or audio conferencing, they experience jitter and none of us likes it. What we need is a solution of connection-oriented type, known as admission control. When a new user wants to have a connection to send data, it is allowed only if the network can handle it and not otherwise.

Figure shows how a congested area of the network is possible to be avoided in connectionless forwarding mechanism. The network topology is redrawn assuming the congested part does not exist. For example, C wants to send something to S. A normal path is through Q-G-M but the encircled path is congested right now. The routing tables are updated in a way that the nodes of the congested part are omitted from the entries. That means C can only find one way to send anything to S, via U-V-W path and thus only forwards to U. When all others follow this mechanism, the congestion resolves much faster. This is one of the biggest advantages of connectionless forwarding.

Connectionless forwarding demands complete receiver address in the packet. This is so because whenever a router needs to forward a packet, it looks at the complete address and then decides.

When we do not have any special purpose routers along the path (in a case of MANets or IoT networks), processing longer addresses may take inordinate time. MPLS-like mechanisms use much shorter tags and thus are more useful.

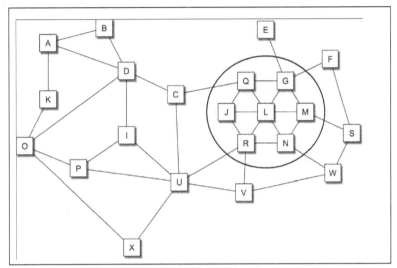

Avoiding congested path.

## Connecting Networks at Network Layer

The network layer is a better candidate for interconnection. When a packet moves from an Ethernet network to a wireless network, for example, we won't find any problems, if connected at the network layer. An entirely new frame, based in the recipient network is just created. The IP packet remains the same.

Sometimes one more problem needs to be addressed. Not all networks support the same maximum size of packets. A packet entering a network may be larger than the maximum size the network can handle. Unlike Ethernet or 802.11 type of networks, IP has an elaborate mechanism to fragment incoming packets to the required size when they enter such network. The fragments travel to the recipient as they are and the receiver defragments them. IP also provides that facility.

Another problem is of different types of network layers along the path. For example, we may find a sender sending IPv6 packet which travels through a network consisting only IPv4 routers. In that case, the network layer provides another solution. An IP packet can embed another IP packet inside. Thus when an IPv6 packet enters an IPv4 network, a new IPv4 packet header is generated and IPv6 packet is embedded within as data. When it crosses IPv4 network, the outer IPv4 packet header is removed and IPv6 packet starts traveling like before.

A final problem that a network layer may encounter is, the incoming packet may be of IPv4 or IPv6. The network layer must be able to handle such case. The solution to this problem is called dual stack. The network layer runs both IPv4 and IPv6 processes together. The Ethernet TYPE field will tell the packet belongs to which process and the required network layer is roped in for handling that packet.

That means, the process of interconnection can be easily managed at the network layer, unlike MAC layer. That is why most of the interconnecting solutions work at the network layer. The Internet is also designed as a network layer transit system. The sender machine and the routers communicate at the network layer and the routers communicate to each other using the network layer. Routing processes concentrate on network layer packet exchanges and also information each router share at the network layer.

# Transport Layer Services

TCP/IP model offers two choices to applications, for application demanding reliable, stream like (what is sent is delivered in the same order, as is) service, TCP is used. For applications demanding real time, no-retransmission type service, UDP is used. There is no service for multimedia traffic. UDP provides no-frills service which is augmented by some application layer protocols to provide services to multimedia traffic. SCTP is actually designed to bridge that gap but most of the operating systems do not yet provide support for SCTP so it is not in real use yet.

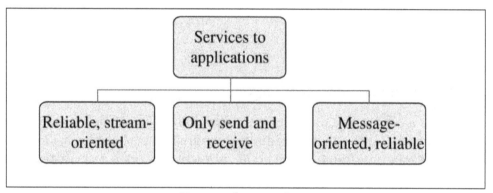

Transport layer services.

The transport layer services are divided into four categories for our convenience. Figure describes those four categories.

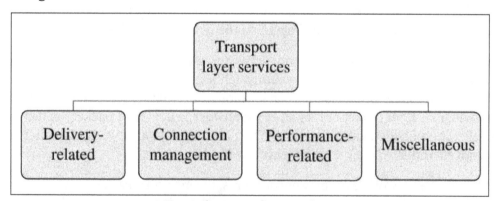

Types of transport layer services.

Delivery based services are designed to provide better delivery to the recipient. TCP connection needs to adjust as per the connecting line, sender and receiver conditions and network load, next type of services manage them. The performance of the TCP process and connection management result into better application services and thus user satisfaction.

## Delivery Related Services

Many applications, including a file transfer or web access, demands the data to reach the recipient as it was sent by the sender. Even if the content is altered in transit, the transport layer should make sure that the content is not delivered in invalid form. TCP handles that problem by using a method called checksum. The receiver TCP does not respond back with proper ack when checksum do not match and the sender TCP is forced to resend that segment. This service is called reliable delivery. The reliable delivery is provided using another service called retransmission.

The TCP also makes sure that the line is completely utilized. That means, when the line is free, it sends as much data it can and when the line is constrained, it reduces its speed. When the line is free, the ack comes back fast while the line is congested, the ack takes some time to arrive. The TCP is good enough to adjust its retransmission timer as per speed of arriving of ack.

TCP also provides a guarantee to deliver the segments in the order that was sent. We know that receiver window is designed to provide this service. All out of order frames are kept on hold until proper segment in order arrives. The application running above TCP always receives segments in the order sent by the sender, independents of actual order in which they arrive.

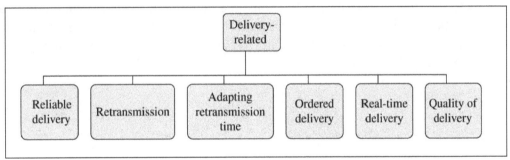

Delivery related services provided by transport layer.

UDP provides provisioning for real-time delivery as it does not offer retransmission and no holding back to reduce its speed. TCP, as soon as retransmission occurs, assumes segment loss and reduce its speed. Such a behavior does not suit the real-time sender who prefers a segment lost as compared to slowing down the transmission. In the case of congestion, if a few frames are lost, the human receiver can still gather the meaning of transmission. He would be unhappy if the video slows down and look jittery.

In some cases, quality of delivery is equally important. Consider a remote medical assistance problem. An image of an X-ray is sent over to a doctor to decide whether the patient is to be operated or requires an urgent medical assistance. The X-ray image must not be degraded when sent over. The doctor won't appreciate a blurred image or an image with less resolution.

## Connection Related Services

Managing connections at the transport layer is one of the most complicated tasks. The transport layer might have no connection at one point in time and have hundreds of connections at another moment. Not only that, different types of connections demand different services. For example, a file download connection demands high bandwidth solution and can accept the little additional delay. On the other hand, a remote login connection demands minimum delay and can sustain low bandwidth. TCP tries to provide a few services related to connection related problems. Let us try to look at some of the most crucial services. Figure lists those services.

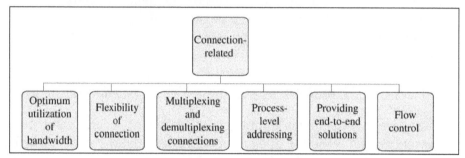

TCP's connection related services.

The first such service is called optimum utilization of bandwidth. TCP increases and reduces its sender's window based on the traffic. TCP also makes sure that enough number of data is accumulated before sending it over. Every segment sent has at least 20 byte TCP and a 20 byte IP header apart from MAC layer headers, making it unacceptable if of a very small size of data within. Thus TCP normally buffers incoming data and sends only when the buffer is full. Unfortunately, such a behavior tends to disfavor interactive applications like Telnet which sends small data like 'ls' and 'ps' etc. and expects an almost immediate response. TCP is smart enough to even handle that case. For interactive applications, it smartly sends data so the user does not feel starved of attention and does not feel that system is slowed down.

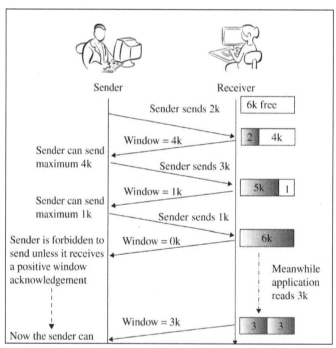

Flow control using Window Advertisement in TCP.

Interestingly, a programmer can choose either TCP or UDP depending on his requirements. Such a flexibility is indeed a very clever move by the designers of the Internet. One size does not fit all and a single solution does not work for all, TCP and UDP provides a choice to the programmer. So if you want "a service which sends my data at the other end, maintains the order of the items that I sent, manage if there is an error in the middle, retransmit if need be but make sure to check whatever I sent is received intact" you can use TCP and if you ask for "give me a service without any fuss, send data if you can with minimum overhead, I will manage the rest myself" you can use UDP.

TCP is the first end-to-end layer. Anything which is sent at the transport layer is only opened and looked at by the final recipient only. Checking if the segment is received intact at the other end, TCP deploys the checksum method. The receiver can check if the segment is erroneous and invite sender TCP to retransmit. This is an example of end to end service. Flow control, which we have listed as a separate service, also is one type of end to end service. TCP provides flow control using window advertisement. Figure indicates how TCP does so.

The sender sends 2k while the receiver has only 6k free. After receiving 2k, receiver TCP can accept only 4k now, so he advertises so. When the sender sends 3k in the next cycle, he is informed that only 1k is available at the receiver. When the sender sends 1k in the next cycle, the receiver is in no position of receiving any data from the sender on this connection and he sends back a zero window advertisement. Only when the application reads 3k, receiver allows the sender to send 3k of data by sending a nonzero ack. You can easily see how the receiver controls the process not to get swamped by the sender blasting at the full speed. Once we have looked at connection related services, it is time for performance related services.

## Performance Related Services

Performance related services are critical for the processing of TCP process. The process must make sure three things, as mentioned as different services in the figure.

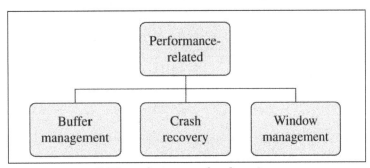

TCP's performance related services.

Buffer management is the first such service. TCP has multiple connections open at any given point of time. The number of connections varies every moment as well as the memory and processing requirements of those connections. Buffer management deals with those dynamic requirements. It is also possible that connections go down once in a while and leaves the communicating TCP processes in a limbo. One of the jobs of TCP is to make sure to recover from such connection crashes. Window management also is a critical point in maintaining required performance.

## Miscellaneous Services

We have classified three services together under this head. The first such service is related to handling multiple connections together. TCP, might have varieties of connections and a dynamic number of them at any given point of time. The connection management part manages connections, their status and related information in a separate database. The other service provided by TCP is related to timers.

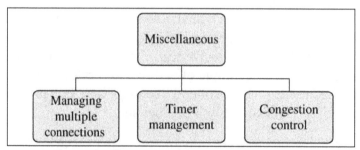

Three miscellaneous services provided by the TCP.

Along with retransmission, there are other timers used by TCP as well. Another critical job of TCP to manage congestion.

## Services not Provided by TCP

TCP was designed in the late 70s. It is still running but in a radically different environment than for which it was designed. Today's transport layer demands a few additional services which TCP does not supply.

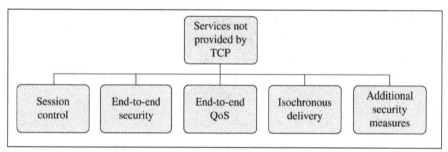

Services not provided by TCP.

Session control enables us to resume that session. For example, while downloading a file, if the connection is closed and we need to restart, if session control is enabled we can restart from the place it stopped. TCP does not provide session control as it demands to store a lot of other information about the connection. Storing and processing such information is a huge overhead which outweighs the advantages of the session control.

The other such service is to provide encryption and authentication from sender's TCP process to receiver's TCP process. Current users demand such services and an extension to TCP called TLS (Transport Layer Security, the older version is known as SSL or secure socket layer) is used in combination with TCP. There are few other services like a user conversing over a video conferencing demand a sustained bandwidth for a specific period, or the time difference between two consecutive packets should not increase beyond 500 ns, are expected by some applications. TCP cannot provide such service. Some protocols like RTP (Real Time Protocol) and few other protocols are designed to provide some subset of these services.

When a landline or mobile phone is used for voice communication, a word spoken and a pause between are maintained as it is. When we use Skype or WhatsApp calling, such strict ordering is not maintained. This is because TCP does not provide isochronous delivery service. Unlike other services, one cannot even provide an additional protocol to solve this problem.

Communicating parties today demands many other security-related services, for example, some of them demand authentication, making sure both parties check the identity of each other before revealing any secret information. Some others demand non-repudiation, so once a party has committed something, for example, placing an order for 100 computers, he cannot deny later of doing so.

Providing non-repudiation is also impossible for a conventional transport layer like TCP. Some additional protocols are provided to handle this case. Authentication is provided by TLS.

After looking at services provided and not provided by TCP, there is a time to look at a typical service in little more detail; how TCP calculates a retransmission timeout value for a given connection.

## Timeout Calculation

Whenever a segment is sent, it starts a timer known as retransmission timer. It also sets the value called time out. When the ack of the segment does not reach TCP before the timeout (time elapsed is more than timeout value), the segment is retransmitted. The TCP will have to have an estimate of the time by which such ack comes back and set the timeout value accordingly. Shorter than required value inflicts unnecessary retransmission and larger than required value adds unnecessary delay to the proceedings. Such unnecessary delay, if goes beyond a limit, frustrates the user and thus is unwanted for. For example, if we type a URL which is lost and TCP waits longer than required time to resend, the page takes that much longer time to download and the user will have to wait that much longer.

The solution to this problem is to estimate the round trip time (RTT) as tight as we can. Having some default or a priori value is out of the question as two communicating parties may be part of the same LAN where the RTT is almost zero. They may also be continents apart in which case the RTT value is quite significant, in terms of a few milliseconds.

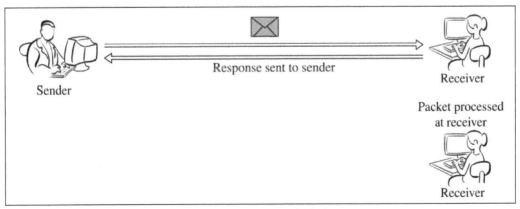

The round trip time calculation.

Figure describes the process of calculating the RTT value. The sender sends the segment and record that time, receiver processes that segment and sends back the ACK of that segment. The sender records the time to receive the ACK and finds the time difference between these values and calculate the RTT. Unfortunately, this simple scheme is not perfect as the RTT for each segment does not remain constant. It changes with the current network load and the current path taken by the specific packet. The same pair of sender & receiver using the same path also experiences different delays between consecutive packets due to many reasons, including the load on intermediary routers and their queue lengths and how much data others are sending etc. So RTT is not taken as it is. The next best choice is to take a few sample RTT values and calculate an average. This is a good solution and better than the previous but with another problem. Usually, next RTT is more like recent RTT values rather than an RTT value observed 10 minutes before. So we need to take a weighted average where the recent readings have more weight than the older ones. Moreover, the connection conditions change every second and thus demands continuous tuning of the RTT values. The solution is to continue calculating this weighted average and estimate the timeout value based on latest estimated RTT value.

For each ongoing connection, TCP subtracts the ACK receipt time from the time it sent the segment to get the RTT for that segment. Before sending the segment TCP estimated the RTT value of that segment. For estimating the RTT for any segment TCP calculates estimated RTT as follows:

$$\text{Estimated RTT} = [(1 - \alpha) \times \text{previous estimated RTT}] + [(\alpha \times \text{current RTT value})]$$

The value $\alpha$ is chosen as $1/8 = 1/2^3 = 0.125$. Choosing a multiple of 2 has a distinct advantage. The multiplication or division can be carried out by either left shifting or right shifting the number. For example, in above case, dividing by multiple of 2 is a right shift that many times so multiplying with $\alpha$ is right shifting 3 times. This is a very fast operation and thus preferred. Eventually, the calculation comes out to be as follows:

$$\text{Estimated RTT} = [(0.875 \times \text{previous estimated RTT})] + [(0.125 \times \text{current RTT value})]$$

When a new segment is sent, estimated RTT is calculated like above and when the ACK comes back, the actual RTT value is also found out. Armed with these two values, the TCP can calculate the estimated RTT for the next segment and the process goes on. The weighted average, as you can see, stresses more on recent values of RTT. Not only the current value which we multiply with $\alpha$ but previous estimate also has a larger share of latest RTT value then and so on. Thus recent values have a larger share in the calculation of estimated RTT.

Once we have learned to decide how to calculate RTT values, the next thing we need to do is to decide when to timeout. Timeout, when the RTT is over, is overkill. The estimated RTT is what it is named estimated; i.e. not exact. The segment's RTT values do vary over a period of time and eagerly resending the segment when an ACK is marginally delayed wastes precious network bandwidth. A wiser solution is to wait a little more to avoid a retransmission when an ack is delayed by some value. The next question is to find out that additional value for which we continue waiting for the ACK after the estimated RTT is over.

To manage that part, TCP plays one more trick. With the RTT, the TCP also calculates another quantity, the variance. A variance is a difference between the actual value and an estimate. Thus,

TCP estimate two things, the RTT value and the variance as well. Like RTT, the variance also is a variable quantity and continuously changing. That is why TCP also continuously manages a weighted average to calculate the variance in following way:

Estimated deviation = [(1 − β ) × previous estimate of deviation] + [(β × current deviation)]

The previous deviation is the difference between the previous estimate and current RTT value. So it is calculated as follows:

Previous deviation = (previous estimation of RTT − current actual value of RTT)

In other words, if we estimated RTT to be 0.7 ms and ACK comes back in 0.5 ms, the deviation is calculated as 0.7 - 0.5 = 0.2ms. Thus the estimated deviation is calculated as follows:

Estimated deviation = [(1 − β) × previous estimate of deviation] + [β × (previous estimation of RTT − current actual value of RTT)

The value β is taken as ¼ = $1/2^2$ is chosen as it only requires two right shifts. That means the estimated deviation is calculated as follows:

Estimated deviation = (0.75 × old deviation) + (0.25 × current deviation)

Once both the RTT and deviation is estimated, calculating timeout is a trivial job. The timeout is calculated as round trip time estimate plus four times the estimated deviation. That means:

Timeout value = Estimated RTT + (4 × Estimated deviation)

where the multiplier is sometimes denoted as η and thus the equation is written as follows:

Timeout value = Estimated RTT + (η × Estimated deviation)

The value of η is chosen as 4 as multiplying with η is right to shift twice.

Thus the complete process of timeout calculation is summarized as follows:

- When the ack comes back, RTT is calculated.

- Deviation is calculated as estimate vs actual value.

- Weighted averages are recalculated based on above equations.

The same process is repeated when every packet is sent and when every ack arrives. You can now see why utmost care is taken to do this calculation swiftly.

## Karn's Algorithm

The RTT calculation process runs into a problem in two different cases. Whenever there is a need to retransmit, the ack that comes back is called ambiguous as it can be attached to either of the transmission.

Attaching the RTT value to the earlier transmission when it is actually associated with the second unnecessarily stretches the timeout value too much larger than actual. This is especially true if it is expected that every transmission is lost at least once and demand such calculation, in which case RTT increases to exponentially large value and the user feels like no communication taking place. Another problem occurs when we associate the RTT with the later transmission when it actually belongs to the earlier. In this case, it inflicts unnecessary retransmission. Research has shown that in such a case, every packet is transmitted at least twice.

Solution to this problem is provided by Karn, which is ridiculously simple. It says "Do not recalculate RTT in such case, double timeout values for each of the segments in sender's window at this point of time". When it does not recalculate the RTT, it saves us from the first problem and when the timeout value is doubled, the second problem is attended. Simple solutions like make a lot of sense in high-speed networks of today.

# Hyper Text Transfer Protocol

HTTP is a protocol which allows the fetching of resources, such as HTML documents. It is the foundation of any data exchange on the Web and it is a client-server protocol, which means requests are initiated by the recipient, usually the Web browser. A complete document is reconstructed from the different sub-documents fetched, for instance text, layout description, images, videos, scripts, and more.

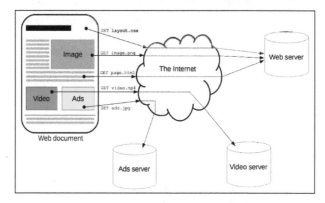

Clients and servers communicate by exchanging individual messages (as opposed to a stream of data). The messages sent by the client, usually a Web browser, are called requests and the messages sent by the server as an answer are called responses.

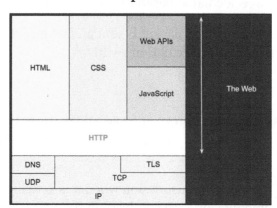

Designed in the early 1990s, HTTP is an extensible protocol which has evolved over time. It is an application layer protocol that is sent over TCP, or over a TLS-encrypted TCP connection, though any reliable transport protocol could theoretically be used. Due to its extensibility, it is used to not only fetch hypertext documents, but also images and videos or to post content to servers, like with HTML form results. HTTP can also be used to fetch parts of documents to update Web pages on demand.

## Components of HTTP-based systems

HTTP is a client-server protocol: requests are sent by one entity, the user-agent (or a proxy on behalf of it). Most of the time the user-agent is a Web browser, but it can be anything, for example a robot that crawls the Web to populate and maintain a search engine index. Each individual request is sent to a server, which handles it and provides an answer, called the response. Between the client and the server there are numerous entities, collectively called proxies, which perform different operations and act as gateways or caches, for example:

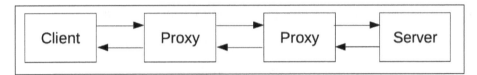

In reality, there are more computers between a browser and the server handling the request: there are routers, modems, and more. Thanks to the layered design of the Web, these are hidden in the network and transport layers. HTTP is on top, at the application layer. Although important to diagnose network problems, the underlying layers are mostly irrelevant to the description of HTTP.

## Client: The User-agent

The user-agent is any tool that acts on the behalf of the user. This role is primarily performed by the Web browser; other possibilities are programs used by engineers and Web developers to debug their applications. The browser is always the entity initiating the request. It is never the server.

To present a Web page, the browser sends an original request to fetch the HTML document that represents the page. It then parses this file, making additional requests corresponding to execution scripts, layout information (CSS) to display, and sub-resources contained within the page (usually images and videos). The Web browser then mixes these resources to present to the user a complete document, the Web page. Scripts executed by the browser can fetch more resources in later phases and the browser updates the Web page accordingly.

A Web page is a hypertext document. This means some parts of displayed text are links which can be activated to fetch a new Web page, allowing the user to direct their user-agent and navigate through the Web. The browser translates these directions in HTTP requests, and further interprets the HTTP responses to present the user with a clear response.

## The Web Server

On the opposite side of the communication channel, is the server, which serves the document as requested by the client. A server appears as only a single machine virtually: this is because it may actually be a collection of servers, sharing the load (load balancing) or a complex piece of software interrogating other computers (like cache, a DB server, or e-commerce servers), totally or partially generating the document on demand.

A server is not necessarily a single machine, but several server software instances can be hosted on the same machine. With HTTP/1.1 and the Host header, they may even share the same IP address.

## Proxies

Between the Web browser and the server, numerous computers and machines relay the HTTP messages. Due to the layered structure of the Web stack, most of these operate at the transport, network or physical levels, becoming transparent at the HTTP layer and potentially making a significant impact on performance. Those operating at the application layers are generally called proxies. These can be transparent, forwarding on the requests they receive without altering them in any way, or non-transparent, in which case they will change the request in some way before passing it along to the server. Proxies may perform numerous functions:

- Caching (the cache can be public or private, like the browser cache).

- Filtering (like an antivirus scan or parental controls).

- Load balancing (to allow multiple servers to serve the different requests).

- Authentication (to control access to different resources).

- Logging (allowing the storage of historical information).

## Basic Aspects of HTTP

- HTTP is simple: HTTP is generally designed to be simple and human readable, even with the added complexity introduced in HTTP/2 by encapsulating HTTP messages into frames. HTTP messages can be read and understood by humans, providing easier testing for developers, and reduced complexity for newcomers.

- HTTP is extensible: Introduced in HTTP/1.0, HTTP headers make this protocol easy to extend and experiment with. New functionality can even be introduced by a simple agreement between a client and a server about a new header's semantics.

- HTTP is stateless, but not session less: HTTP is stateless: there is no link between two requests being successively carried out on the same connection. This immediately has the prospect of being problematic for users attempting to interact with certain pages coherently, for example, using e-commerce shopping baskets. But while the core of HTTP itself is stateless, HTTP cookies allow the use of stateful sessions. Using header extensibility, HTTP Cookies are added to the workflow, allowing session creation on each HTTP request to share the same context, or the same state.

## HTTP and Connections

A connection is controlled at the transport layer, and therefore fundamentally out of scope for

HTTP. Though HTTP doesn't require the underlying transport protocol to be connection-based; only requiring it to be reliable, or not lose messages (so at minimum presenting an error). Among the two most common transport protocols on the Internet, TCP is reliable and UDP isn't. HTTP therefore relies on the TCP standard, which is connection-based.

Before a client and server can exchange an HTTP request/response pair, they must establish a TCP connection, a process which requires several round-trips. The default behavior of HTTP/1.0 is to open a separate TCP connection for each HTTP request/response pair. This is less efficient than sharing a single TCP connection when multiple requests are sent in close succession.

In order to mitigate this flaw, HTTP/1.1 introduced pipelining (which proved difficult to implement) and persistent connections: the underlying TCP connection can be partially controlled using the Connection header. HTTP/2 went a step further by multiplexing messages over a single connection, helping keep the connection warm and more efficient. Experiments are in progress to design a better transport protocol more suited to HTTP.

## What can be Controlled by HTTP?

This extensible nature of HTTP has, over time, allowed for more control and functionality of the Web. Cache or authentication methods were functions handled early in HTTP history. The ability to relax the origin constraint, by contrast, has only been added in the 2010s. Here is a list of common features controllable with HTTP:

- Caching: How documents are cached can be controlled by HTTP. The server can instruct proxies and clients, about what to cache and for how long. The client can instruct intermediate cache proxies to ignore the stored document.

- Relaxing the origin constraint: To prevent snooping and other privacy invasions, Web browsers enforce strict separation between Web sites. Only pages from the same origin can access all the information of a Web page. Though such constraint is a burden to the server, HTTP headers can relax this strict separation on the server side, allowing a document to become a patchwork of information sourced from different domains; there could even be security-related reasons to do so.

- Authentication: Some pages may be protected so that only specific users can access them. Basic authentication may be provided by HTTP, either using the WWW-Authenticate and similar headers, or by setting a specific session using HTTP cookies.

- Proxy and tunnelling: Servers or clients are often located on intranets and hide their true IP address from other computers. HTTP requests then go through proxies to cross this network barrier. Not all proxies are HTTP proxies. The SOCKS protocol, for example, operates at a lower level. Other protocols, like ftp, can be handled by these proxies.

- Sessions: Using HTTP cookies allows you to link requests with the state of the server. This creates sessions, despite basic HTTP being a state-less protocol. This is useful not only for e-commerce shopping baskets, but also for any site allowing user configuration of the output.

## HTTP Flow

When a client wants to communicate with a server, either the final server or an intermediate proxy, it performs the following steps:

- Open a TCP connection: The TCP connection is used to send a request, or several, and receive an answer. The client may open a new connection, reuse an existing connection, or open several TCP connections to the servers.

- Send an HTTP message: HTTP messages (before HTTP/2) are human-readable. With HTTP/2, these simple messages are encapsulated in frames, making them impossible to read directly, but the principle remains the same. For example:

```
GET / HTTP/1.1

Host: developer.mozilla.org

Accept-Language: fr
```

- Read the response sent by the server, such as:

```
HTTP/1.1 200 OK

Date: Sat, 09 Oct 2010 14:28:02 GMT

Server: Apache

Last-Modified: Tue, 01 Dec 2009 20:18:22 GMT

ETag: "51142bc1-7449-479b075b2891b"

Accept-Ranges: bytes

Content-Length: 29769

Content-Type: text/html


<!DOCTYPE html... (here comes the 29769 bytes of the requested web page)
```

- Close or reuse the connection for further requests:

  If HTTP pipelining is activated, several requests can be sent without waiting for the first response to be fully received. HTTP pipelining has proven difficult to implement in existing networks, where old pieces of software coexist with modern versions. HTTP pipelining has been superseded in HTTP/2 with more robust multiplexing requests within a frame.

## HTTP Messages

HTTP messages, as defined in HTTP/1.1 and earlier, are human-readable. In HTTP/2, these messages are embedded into a binary structure, a frame, allowing optimizations like compression of headers and multiplexing. Even if only part of the original HTTP message is sent in this version of HTTP, the semantics of each message is unchanged and the client reconstitutes (virtually) the original HTTP/1.1 request. It is therefore useful to comprehend HTTP/2 messages in the HTTP/1.1 format.

There are two types of HTTP messages, requests and responses, each with its own format.

## Requests

An example HTTP request:

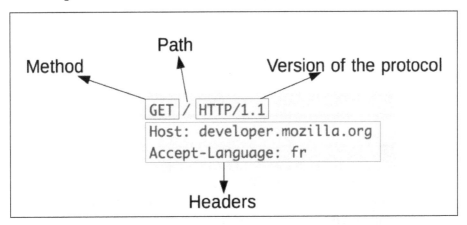

Requests consists of the following elements:

- An HTTP method, usually a verb like GET, POST or a noun like OPTIONS or HEAD that defines the operation the client wants to perform. Typically, a client wants to fetch a resource
  (using GET) or post the value of an HTML form (using POST), though more operations may
  be needed in other cases.

- The path of the resource to fetch; the URL of the resource stripped from elements that are
  obvious from the context, for example without the protocol (http://), the domain (here,
  developer.mozilla.org), or the TCP port.

- The version of the HTTP protocol.

- Optional headers that convey additional information for the servers.

- Or a body, for some methods like POST, similar to those in responses, which contain the
  resource sent.

## Responses

Responses consist of the following elements:

- The version of the HTTP protocol they follow.

- A status code, indicating if the request was successful, or not, and why.

- A status message, a non-authoritative short description of the status code.

- HTTP headers, like those for requests.

- Optionally, a body containing the fetched resource.

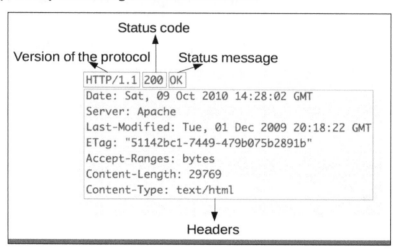

## APIs based on HTTP

The most commonly used API based on HTTP is the XMLHttpRequest API, which can be used to exchange data between a user agent and a server. The modern Fetch API provides the same features with a more powerful and flexible feature set.

Another API, server-sent events, is a one-way service that allows a server to send events to the client, using HTTP as a transport mechanism. Using the EventSource interface, the client opens a connection and establishes event handlers. The client browser automatically converts the messages that arrive on the HTTP stream into appropriate Event objects, delivering them to the event handlers that have been registered for the events' type if known, or to the onmessage event handler if no type-specific event handler was established.

# Mail Transfer Protocols

E-mail Protocols are set of rules that help the client to properly transmit the information to or from the mail server.

## SMTP

SMTP stands for Simple Mail Transfer Protocol. It was first proposed in 1982. It is a standard protocol used for sending e-mail efficiently and reliably over the internet.

### Key Points of SMTP

- SMTP is application level protocol.

- SMTP is connection oriented protocol.

- SMTP is text based protocol.

- It handles exchange of messages between e-mail servers over TCP/IP network.

- Apart from transferring e-mail, SMPT also provides notification regarding incoming mail.

- When you send e-mail, your e-mail client sends it to your e-mail server which further contacts the recipient mail server using SMTP client.

- These SMTP commands specify the sender's and receiver's e-mail address, along with the message to be send.

- The exchange of commands between servers is carried out without intervention of any user.

- In case, message cannot be delivered, an error report is sent to the sender which makes SMTP a reliable protocol.

## SMTP Commands

The following table describes some of the SMTP commands:

| S.N. | Command Description |
|------|---------------------|
| 1 | HELLO: This command initiates the SMTP conversation. |
| 2 | EHELLO: This is an alternative command to initiate the conversation. ESMTP indicates that the sender server wants to use extended SMTP protocol. |
| 3 | MAIL FROM: This indicates the sender's address. |
| 4 | RCPT TO: It identifies the recipient of the mail. In order to deliver similar message to multiple users this command can be repeated multiple times. |
| 5 | SIZE: This command let the server know the size of attached message in bytes. |
| 6 | DATA: The DATA command signifies that a stream of data will follow. Here stream of data refers to the body of the message. |
| 7 | QUIT: This commands is used to terminate the SMTP connection. |
| 8 | VRFY: This command is used by the receiving server in order to verify whether the given username is valid or not. |
| 9 | EXPN: It is same as VRFY, except it will list all the users name when it used with a distribution list. |

## IMAP

IMAP stands for Internet Message Access Protocol. It was first proposed in 1986. There exist five versions of IMAP as follows:

- Original IMAP

- IMAP2

- IMAP3

- IMAP2bis

- IMAP4

## Key Points of IMAP

- IMAP allows the client program to manipulate the e-mail message on the server without downloading them on the local computer.

- The e-mail is hold and maintained by the remote server.

- It enables us to take any action such as downloading, delete the mail without reading the mail.It enables us to create, manipulate and delete remote message folders called mail boxes.

- IMAP enables the users to search the e-mails.

- It allows concurrent access to multiple mailboxes on multiple mail servers.

## IMAP Commands

The following table describes some of the IMAP commands:

| S.N. | Command Description |
|------|---------------------|
| 1 | IMAP_LOGIN: This command opens the connection. |
| 2 | CAPABILITY: This command requests for listing the capabilities that the server supports. |
| 3 | NOOP: This command is used as a periodic poll for new messages or message status updates during a period of inactivity. |
| 4 | SELECT: This command helps to select a mailbox to access the messages. |
| 5 | EXAMINE: It is same as SELECT command except no change to the mailbox is permitted. |
| 6 | CREATE: It is used to create mailbox with a specified name. |
| 7 | DELETE: It is used to permanently delete a mailbox with a given name. |
| 8 | RENAME: It is used to change the name of a mailbox. |
| 9 | LOGOUT: This command informs the server that client is done with the session. The server must send BYE untagged response before the OK response and then close the network connection. |

## POP

POP stands for Post Office Protocol. It is generally used to support a single client. There are several versions of POP but the POP 3 is the current standard.

## Key Points of POP

- POP is an application layer internet standard protocol.

- Since POP supports offline access to the messages, thus requires less internet usage time.

- POP does not allow search facility.

- In order to access the messaged, it is necessary to download them.

- It allows only one mailbox to be created on server.

- It is not suitable for accessing non mail data.

- POP commands are generally abbreviated into codes of three or four letters. Eg. STAT.

## POP Commands

The following table describes some of the POP commands:

| S.N. | Command Description |
|------|---------------------|
| 1 | LOGIN: This command opens the connection. |
| 2 | STAT: It is used to display number of messages currently in the mailbox. |
| 3 | LIST: It is used to get the summary of messages where each message summary is shown. |
| 4 | RETR: This command helps to select a mailbox to access the messages. |
| 5 | DELE: It is used to delete a message. |
| 6 | RSET: It is used to reset the session to its initial state. |
| 7 | QUIT: It is used to log off the session. |

## Comparison between POP and IMAP

| S.N. | POP | IMAP |
|------|-----|------|
| 1 | Generally used to support single client. | Designed to handle multiple clients. |
| 2 | Messages are accessed offline. | Messages are accessed online although it also supports offline mode. |
| 3 | POP does not allow search facility. | It offers ability to search emails. |
| 4 | All the messages have to be downloaded. | It allows selective transfer of messages to the client. |
| 5 | Only one mailbox can be created on the server. | Multiple mailboxes can be created on the server. |
| 6 | Not suitable for accessing non-mail data. | Suitable for accessing non-mail data i.e. attachment. |
| 7 | POP commands are generally abbreviated into codes of three or four letters. Eg. STAT. | IMAP commands are not abbreviated, they are full. Eg. STATUS. |
| 8 | It requires minimum use of server resources. | Clients are totally dependent on server. |
| 9 | Mails once downloaded cannot be accessed from some other location. | Allows mails to be accessed from multiple locations. |
| 10 | The e-mails are not downloaded automatically. | Users can view the headings and sender of e-mails and then decide to download. |
| 10 | POP requires less internet usage time. | IMAP requires more internet usage time. |

## Simple Mail Transfer Protocols

## Components of SMTP

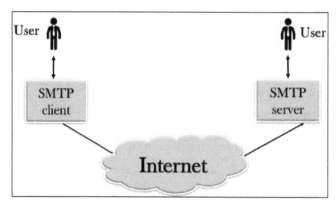

- First, we will break the SMTP client and SMTP server into two components such as user agent (UA) and mail transfer agent (MTA). The user agent (UA) prepares the message, creates the envelope and then puts the message in the envelope. The mail transfer agent (MTA) transfers this mail across the internet.

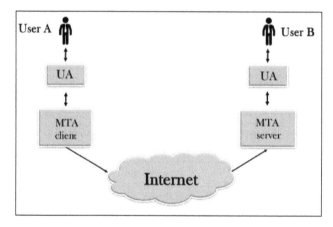

- SMTP allows a more complex system by adding a relaying system. Instead of just having one MTA at sending side and one at receiving side, more MTAs can be added, acting either as a client or server to relay the email.

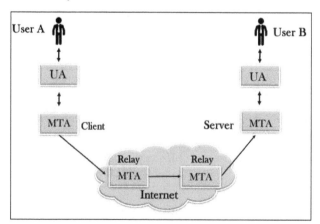

- The relaying system without TCP/IP protocol can also be used to send the emails to users, and this is achieved by the use of the mail gateway. The mail gateway is a relay MTA that can be used to receive an email.

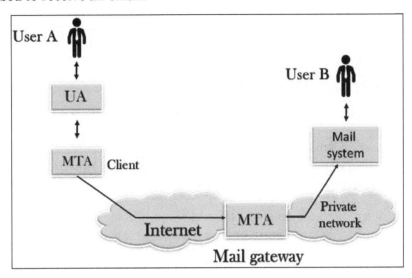

Mail gateway

## Working of SMTP

- Composition of Mail: A user sends an e-mail by composing an electronic mail message using a Mail User Agent (MUA). Mail User Agent is a program which is used to send and receive mail. The message contains two parts: body and header. The body is the main part of the message while the header includes information such as the sender and recipient address. The header also includes descriptive information such as the subject of the message. In this case, the message body is like a letter and header is like an envelope that contains the recipient's address.

- Submission of Mail: After composing an email, the mail client then submits the completed e-mail to the SMTP server by using SMTP on TCP port 25.

- Delivery of Mail: E-mail addresses contain two parts: username of the recipient and domain name. For example, vivek@gmail.com, where "vivek" is the username of the recipient and "gmail.com" is the domain name. If the domain name of the recipient's email address is different from the sender's domain name, then MSA will send the mail to the Mail Transfer Agent (MTA). To relay the email, the MTA will find the target domain. It checks the MX record from Domain Name System to obtain the target domain. The MX record contains the domain name and IP address of the recipient's domain. Once the record is located, MTA connects to the exchange server to relay the message.

- Receipt and Processing of Mail: Once the incoming message is received, the exchange server delivers it to the incoming server (Mail Delivery Agent) which stores the e-mail where it waits for the user to retrieve it.

- Access and Retrieval of Mail: The stored email in MDA can be retrieved by using MUA (Mail User Agent). MUA can be accessed by using login and password.

# Software-Defined Networks

Software-Defined Networking (SDN) is an emerging architecture that is dynamic, manageable, cost-effective, and adaptable, making it ideal for the high-bandwidth, dynamic nature of today's applications. This architecture decouples the network control and forwarding functions enabling the network control to become directly programmable and the underlying infrastructure to be abstracted for applications and network services.

Here are common requirements of the modern day admin:

- Packet classification is to be used but must have hardware implementation so that process happens faster and more complex and multiple forwarding rules, based on administrator's wish and convenience, can be executed in real time.

- Forwarding logic, for speed, may be embedded in hardware. The current routers cannot do so directly because they have to do both, routing and forwarding.

- The solution is able to provide traffic engineering, thus network operators or administrators can choose the rules to route traffic based on their policies and not merely on the destination address.

- The solution should also be reliable; thus the operators can check if there is any problem with routing. Conventional routers and switches, when misconfigured, can lead to serious problems. Such problems are avoided in SDN. In fact, the reason is the lack of global view from individual routers. SDN is designed with that global view.

- Thus they should have much finer control over routing; choosing every route for every packet, based on any item of the packet header or content they wish.

- The solution should be scalable, that means, when the networks grow or shrink, the solution should be able to adjust accordingly.

- The network control should be programmable. That means the administrators' policies should be implemented as programs. There has to be an interface which can accept such programs and automate the implementation part of the policies. The programming is done in higher level languages instead of low-level vendor specific commands.

- The control should be agile enough to dynamically adjust. That means network-wide policies can be implemented and changed with very few unambiguous steps.

- The control is to be managed centrally. Network intelligence (how to route traffic, how to find a malicious process or a node, how to balance traffic etc.) is located in central part where the control is located. The idea is to use network intelligence to control network in a global and thus optimal way. When optimal routes based on specific quality is designed, for example, a common requirement is; there should not be any cycles in the route. The SDN solution will have data about all switches together located centrally and can see if there are cycles, immediately.

- The network managers or administrators should be able to configure, manage, secure and optimize network resources in a programmable manner. Thus, once the policy is set and configured, it automatically decides what to do in a given situation. More importantly, it does not depend on the propitiatory solutions which differ with different vendors for those devices. The administrators can allocate and deallocate switches or firewalls or IDS (Intrusion Detection System which can help find intrusions or attacks in the system, while the system is running) as the need be.

- The standards provided should be open and vendor neutral. That means the standards allow multiple devices to be controlled using a single, consistent interface. Being open, it is possible for anybody to manage.

The very idea of SDN begins with dividing the network device and eventually the network into different planes.

## Shortcomings of Traditional Networking Solution and Need for SDN

The networks are managed by routers and switches forwarding packets across the network. These traditional networks are hard to be customized for higher level management policies. The higher level policies, for example, 2G traffic should be given lesser priority than 3G demand routers to have two queues, one of 2G and one for 3G packets and allow 3G packets to be processed in higher proportion with respect to 2G packets. One will have to configure each individual network device separately for deploying a typical policy. Thus each router and switch which may be from different vendors need to be configured accordingly. This configuration requires vendor specific and many times low-level commands to execute. For example, the way CISCO router needs to be programmed for this job may be very different than Linksys router. Traditional networks are less fault tolerant and lead to problems when the devices start malfunctioning. For example, when one port of a switch stops working, administrators will receive problems like a typical connection to a typical node not working and they will have to manually figure out what is wrong. After some investigation, when they find that a typical port is not working, they may have to route the traffic over another port manually. Administrators also have to load balance manually. For example, if there are multiple ports possible to be used to reach a given destination, administrators love to divide traffic over them in an even manner but that is hard to be automated in general case.

Using one of the multiple ports to load balance and fail over when a port is not working demands re-configuring the switch. There is no mechanism to re-configure the network switch automatically in conventional networks. Achieving all of above goals need a better (and breakthrough) design. The idea is to identify the root cause of the problems and then eliminate that cause.

Network devices are designed to provide three primary functions. First, forwarding network traffic (the forwarding process) and how to treat different traffic differently (the logic for making the decisions about forwarding, usually done by routing and packet classification). The second function is implemented by protocols (routing protocols), which outputs the routing tables. These two functions are usually so tightly integrated that it is hard to separate them. One of the reasons for the transition from IPv4 to IPv6 took so long is due to the fact that these two different things are not separately modeled. Sometimes this tight coupling between these two components is called vertical integration. The third function is to participate in the network-wide management process.

For example, when the administrator wants to configure switches to provide higher priority to one type of traffic in the entire network, he needs to provide that by (usually) configuring each switch manually in accordance with the need.

The component of the router which forwards the packets is known as a data plane while the component which decides the forwarding policy is known as a control plane. Devices working at the data plane are known as forwarding devices (The devices working at the control plane are known as the controllers. The interface to the controller is the management plane, which is important and is usually vendor-dependent and also adds to the problem. Many authors claim to have two planes, data, and control and describe management plane as the interface to control. Whatever architecture one chooses to describe the SDN, it is clear that data and control function needs to be separated. To implement network-wide functions (by instructing the control plane accordingly), one needs an open interface which networking applications should use. For example, if the administrator needs to provide all VOIP traffic of the network to be given highest precedence over all other traffic, the forwarding devices are to be instructed to do so by all controllers. How does the admin instruct the controller to do so? Using an open interface such an open interface is the management plane. It is OPEN because any type of controller will be able to be addressed using this plane.

In conventional network devices, both control and data planes are tightly integrated into the device and thus routing and forwarding process happens quickly, remain in sync and provide reasonably good performance. The router acts as a single unit for both operations. Not only that, the output of one unit is used by another unit. Such a design is better for managing issues related to faulty devices and faulty configurations of devices, as the fault is limited to the device. For example, if a router is not routing as per policy the problem is confined to that router and administrators can identify that router as a culprit and set it right easily. The routers only communicate their prescribed routing packets with other routers and if they are malfunctioning, their routing tables will be able to reveal their fault. This design worked well and thus in use so far. Also, when the network size, line speeds and density of devices increased, the designers need to increase the number of such devices. Each device has its own control and data plane and all devices have built-in intelligence for its work and thus self-contained, the networks grew without much of a trouble. However, this design is difficult to manage, especially when common management policies are to be implemented in heterogeneous devices, many times, from different vendors, which is now becoming a norm, across the entire network.

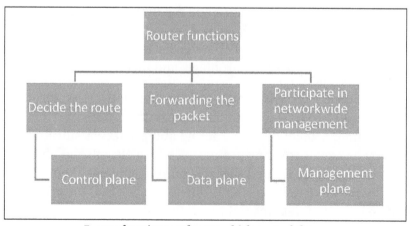

Router functions and parts which control them.

This tightly coupled architecture has one more problem. As network devices are to be manually and individually configured, and network administrators are heavily loaded, the "quick and dirty" ad hoc approach takes precedence over well planned, systematic approach. Such an approach resulted in many misconfigured devices in the networks. Forwarding loops (packets are roaming around in cycles in the network), sending data on wrong paths, violating SLAs unintentionally, and even packet loss were results of such misconfigurations.

## Virtualization and Overlay Networks

The idea of virtualization is to make sure the services provided to the upper layer in a transparent way, all underlying problems are handled by the layer which provides the service without passing the problems to the current layer. That means the problems faced while providing the service is not seen by the current layer which is taking that service. For example, TCP provides a reliable, circuit like, robust and fault tolerant service to the application. Virtual LANs are designed for the need of administrator to treat networks in a logical and not physical fashion. VPN solutions allow a customer to connect to a remote network as if he is physically part of that network and connecting locally to it. All problems are managed by the virtual network management system. Virtualization process began with storage and processor virtualization and has reached to providing virtual networks today.

The overlay network is an extension of the virtualization idea. The overlay network can have a remote member and provide a service to it as if it is a local member. A member may not always be a node, it can even be another network. That means an overlay network can provide service to the administrators of those networks and users of the underlying networks as if they are all connected to each other directly. The interconnection issues and other complexities are managed in a way that user does not realize that the network or the other node that he is communicating is not local.

Let us take an example to understand. Consider an education institute, having their central office situated in New York and having other sister institutes in few other cities like Texas, Los Angeles, San Fransisco, and Florida, four cities in the close vicinity. The academic institute also has three campuses in New York which run different courses. What are the needs of administrators and management of these institutes, located at the central office in New York? Quite a few, but we will take two which help us understand the need for an overlay network.

First, they may want secure connections between these centers, even from other cities and within New York. A question paper or mark sheet sent should not be seen by any third party. Examination orders and many other exams related information also should be kept and transmitted in a secret fashion. Also, accountants at these centers should communicate to the central office where chief accounts officer seats, in a way that others cannot poke into their communication, not even users of the network they belong to. In a way, these computers used by accountants should be separated from their own networks but required to be connected to this virtual network. There may be 100 other requirements but these two are enough for us to learn about the need to have an overlay network. The designers can solve this problem by providing an overlay network which we call Overlay-1. Routers at all four cities and three centers connect to each other using some tunneling protocol. In fact, not all lines are needed. All centres and cities, if only connects to the central office, above requirements can be met with. The tunnels may be designed as per required security criteria. Additionally, another overlay network, let us call it Overlay-2, is formed between all accountants across all these networks. These machines are part of the overlay network Overlay-2 but no other networks. Even though they communicate over tunnels passing through the Internet, they cannot communicate to other machines of Internet if the routers are configured accordingly. Thus both problems are possible to be solved by overlay networks Overlay-1 and Overlay-2.

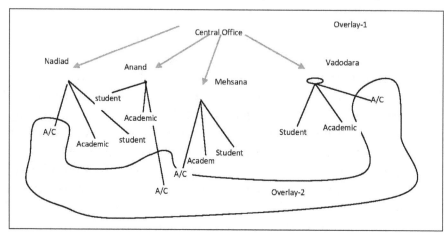

Two overlays out of multiple networks. A/C departments having their separate overlay while others having combined in the other overlay.

## Virtual Private Network

The virtual private network or VPN helps a remote machine to communicate to a network as if it is locally connected, in a secure fashion. The process is enabled by a technique which provides two things:

- The data is communicated from sending machine or sending network router to the router of the network where the machine would like to be part of.

- The data is tunneled. That means the sending router encapsulates the entire packet inside another packet where sender's address is his own and receiver as the destination network router. Before encapsulation, the data is also encrypted to make sure others do not get anything from snooping into the communication.

You can understand that the overlay networks extend this idea and allow even networks to be a member of a remote network. One more critical difference is, overlay networks are transparent; users does not realize that they are part of the overlay network and not a conventional network. They do not feel that difference. The VPN, on the contrary, has to be set and configured and the user is aware of the fact that he is using VPN and not a local network.

## Need for Routing Differently

The basic idea of SDN is derived from the need of routing differently. Conventionally, when the routing tables are set up, the packet for the same destination follows the same path irrespective of the content of the packet. The customers demand routing packets based on many quality-of-service parameters and they expect routing process to follow those policies. The routers, instead of routing based on destination address, route based on the tag value. Thus, two packets, destined to the same address, but belong to a different class of customers, can be given different routing treatment and thus, different service.

This QOS based routing process is known as traffic engineering as the traffic is manipulated, routed and given priorities based on the traffic parameters using specific demands. For example, routing VOIP traffic over a separate route as compared to data route is a common requirement. Giving higher priority to premium customers is another common requirement. Look at Figure. There are two paths between sender and receiver. The path using thicker line is short and used for VOIP while the path using dotted lines is used for normal traffic. When the traffic is designed to follow this requirement, it is an example of traffic engineering. Such traffic engineering is more important at higher level ISPs and data centers as they need to route packets based on who the sender ISP is and the MOU between themselves and the sending ISP.

The traffic to be routed is based on mutual agreements and their own policies which otherwise is impossible to manage. For examples, they might have volume based agreements (you pass my 1 Gb, I will pass your 2Gb in return) or speed based agreements (you pass my 1Gb data at 25 Mb/sec and I pass your 1Gb data at 10 Mb/Sec) etc. or the payment, for example, if you pay ₹10,000, I will allow 20 Tb traffic of yours or based on priority, for example, class-A customers are routed to path A while class B customers are routed on path B. Here we do not need to use conventional routing protocols which find the shortest paths or datagram may decide its path on its own. When traffic engineering is deployed, the vendor or the administrator should decide how each packet is routed, irrespective of the destination address or other things. MPLS-like solutions work very well for such demands. When they do so, these networks are known to be traffic engineered. Each such routing decision is known as flow. When a packet is routed as per a given flow, the administrators are said to provide routing per-flow. When traffic engineering is possible, administrators have per-flow control over routing.

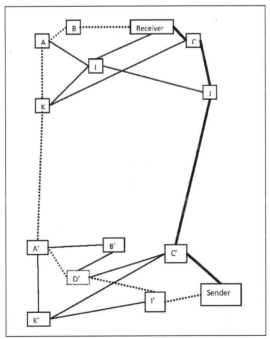

Two different paths from sender to receiver. Shorter path (Thick lines) for VOIP and dotted lines for normal traffic.

There are many other recent trends that drive the SDN movement. First, traffic patterns are changing. When data is located across the globe with distributed databases and servers needs very flexible traffic management. Let us take a few examples to understand. When a query is fired to a distributed database, the administrator would like to have some performance requirement, for example, all responses from all databases must come back by 2 msec. The queries are to be responded in real time irrespective of whether the database server is located in the US or in India.

When people bring their laptops and smartphones to the company, the "Bring your own device" mantra is being observed, treating those network devices with more flexible and stricter security is needed. The routing process and data movement should be tightly controlled. The network admins need much finer and stricter controls over packets moving across networks full of devices not completely under their control.

Cloud services are on the rise. If the organization prefers to provide services over a cloud, the first need is elasticity, i.e. service as per demand. Such flexibility is impossible to be achieved if the network traffic and servers are not under administrators' complete control and they are able to deploy them as and when the demand arises.

The era of "Big Data" is arrived; many applications use varieties of data coming from various sources like social networking sites and different types of databases and in a huge volume are on the rise. For example, a company getting feedbacks and comments about their products from all such methods. Collecting such direct and indirect feedbacks are complicated for many reasons. First, the amount of data is huge, second the data, especially which are coming in form of social media posts etc. are not structured and are of varieties of types and third, they change very fast. All in all, these type of solutions demand to manage the huge bandwidth networks with varieties of data with changing volume again demand flexible network management.

The conventional networks have some serious issues handling these problems. When there are complex policies, which are to be deployed network-wide, the conventional networks demand manual intervention. For example, deploying different services for 3G and 4G customers, each network device is to be locally and specifically configured using low-level commands of that specific device manually, and separately. Most administrators avoid such steps as system disruption is a major problem and users dislike disruption the most. Another problem with conventional network solution is that it is hard to scale them, especially when the demands are dynamic. For example, assume we have two servers. They are handling dedicated customers. It is quite possible that sometimes the load on one server is high and sometimes the load on the other server is high. The servers are quite good and can handle that load.

The problem is with the underlying network. The network should be designed in such a way that when the load on server-1 is high, the switches should distribute data going out from server-1 as much as possible and restrict the data going out from server 2 on a specific part of the network. Thus enabling flushing out data from both servers evenly. Similarly, when the server-2 is in high demand, the data going out from it should be distributed more. The network switches should be able to dynamically decide to either honor server-1 or server-2 as per the traffic volume. Such a solution is not possible to be provided automatically when the switches choose shortest paths. Ideally, the administrators should have a pool of switches (like other resources) and should be able to allocate them on demand. Another important point is, there is no standard for building network devices and their interfaces. A CISCO switch has a different interface than a Linksys switch. A Cyberoam Firewall has a different interface than a Fortinet firewall. Managing all switches or Firewalls of a network is always cumbersome with heterogeneous devices. It is always better to have a single consistent interface instead. SDN can provide traffic engineering, resource sharing, vendor neutral centralized control and the finer level of control for the administrators.

## Connection-oriented Networks and Routing Overlays

For flow-based routing, one method is to use a connection-oriented network and another is to use a routing overlay. In connection-oriented network approach allows the users to specify the exact path between sender and receiver (unlike IP-based connectionless delivery mechanism). An independent path for each flow is laid down by a connection-oriented connection. When the connection establishment process starts, it follows the path based on the policy suggested and thus the packets travel the exact route which the administrator wanted.

The process requires the switch to follow management policies implemented for all packets coming in. The path selection and forwarding are based on those policies. Thus the connection request indicates the policy to be obeyed and only those switches which accept that policy should be part of the path. Each switch along the path accepts the connection request only if they can accept the policy. For example, if the switch as the sender allows different paths for VOIP calls and other protocols like SMTP and HTTP, it can have two different routes already defined. One route contains the minimum of hops and switches along the path are designed to provide real-time service. On the other path, we can have switches which are used in the conventional network. Whenever the sender wants to establish a connection, the switch decides which type of connection is needed based on the request. If it is VOIP, it will choose the first route, and for others, it chooses the second route. The connections are established and executed accordingly and thus both types of traffic get the treatment they demand. Thus the connection-oriented connection is a great way to make sure such policies are enforced. Additionally, this connection orientation process can be embedded in hardware. When hardware is used to classify and label the packets, it happens at the real time and there is no performance degradation. Very high data rates can be sustained by this design.

A routing overlay is a network of virtual links (tunnels). Virtual links are established based on required policies. Thus a virtual link between network 1 and network 2 should be designed as per the policies of routing between them. It is also possible to have multiple virtual links between two networks for different policies. For example, if two networks need two different routes, one each for real-time and non-real-time traffic, then one can create two virtual links between them. A routing overlay is basically a set of tunnels between potential senders and receivers. Each tunnel acts like a direct link which the routers can choose to route. Each such channel offers a typical service set according to a specific policy. The administrator can design and deploy virtual links to set the policies that they deem fit. It is possible that the administrators design three different channels for 2G, 3G and 4G traffic between same pair or networks. Unlike connection oriented networks created by hardware, overlays are deployed entirely in software and thus have both advantages and disadvantages of software deployment. They are much more flexible and allows changes in the virtual link deployment on the fly. That means, a typical route for a user is by default 3G but when his quota is over, he can be easily shifted to another route which offers slower services. When he pays for the 3G network or 4G network, he is again shifted to a faster route. It is also possible that for these three services, the same route is used but each switch along the path has three priority queues. They always give the highest priority to 4G traffic and 2nd priority to 3G and the lowest priority to 2G traffic. Three different queues, one each for 4G, 3G and 2G traffic is deployed. Only when the 4G queue is empty or some specific time period is elapsed, a packet from the 3G queue is sent out. Only when both 4G and 3G queues are empty or a typical time period is elapsed, the packets belonging to the 2G queue is sent over the line.

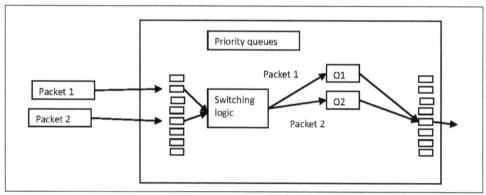

Implementing priority queues, for two different senders, going to the same port.

Thus, routing overlays provide an excellent opportunity for the administrators to dynamically control the networks. On the other hand, the routing overlays are much slower compared to connection oriented networks (as they are managed completely by software). The overlays can help existing network setup (which is working over the Internet) to act as per administrator's choice by just imposing the right type of overlay on top of it. Such an overlay can be easily changed if ISP's MOUs change and can be redesigned with changes if need be. Connection-oriented networks, as they are embedded in hardware, are hard to change. One can have multiple overlays implemented together for different types of services and different members. One overlay, for example, connects all accounts computers while another overlay might contain all who would like to connect to attendance server to insert everyday attendance.

Apart from being slow, overlays have other issues as well. They may result in routing which is not optimal. As the users are using virtual links to connect, they have no idea about associated actual links. The virtual link capacity (bandwidth) and delay (time to send the packet through) are set as per the underlying actual link in the beginning. However, we know that the actual link dimensions continuously vary and the bandwidth and delay assumed while establishing the virtual link may not remain true after some time. In that case, the routing over virtual link become incorrect or at least inefficient even if it remains correct. This is because the virtual link routing designed in overlays are independent of the actual links and both operate on their own.

The bottom line is, however useful, both connection-oriented networks and overlays look like, they do not solve the problem completely. We need a better solution, the SDN, which combines both of above approaches in a far more efficient way.

# Packet Switching

The practice of transferring data into small pieces to various networks is known as packet switching. Packet networks make use of circuit networks for the transmission of a formatted unit of data. The chapter closely examines the key concepts of packet switching to provide an extensive understanding of the subject.

Packet switching is a digital networking communications method that groups all transmitted data into suitably sized blocks, called *packets*, which are transmitted via a medium that may be shared by multiple simultaneous communication sessions. Packet switching increases network efficiency, robustness and enables technological convergence of many applications operating on the same network.

Packets are composed of a header and payload. Information in the header is used by networking hardware to direct the packet to its destination where the payload is extracted and used by application software.

Starting in the late 1950s, American computer scientist Paul Baran developed the concept *Distributed Adaptive Message Block Switching* with the goal to provide a fault-tolerant, efficient routing method for telecommunication messages as part of a research program at the RAND Corporation, funded by the US Department of Defense. This concept contrasted and contradicted then-established principles of pre-allocation of network bandwidth, largely fortified by the development of telecommunications in the Bell System. The new concept found little resonance among network implementers until the independent work of British computer scientist Donald Davies at the National Physical Laboratory (United Kingdom) in the late 1960s. Davies is credited with coining the modern name *packet switching* and inspiring numerous packet switching networks in Europe in the decade following, including the incorporation of the concept in the early ARPANET in the United States.

## Concept

A simple definition of packet switching is:

The routing and transferring of data by means of addressed packets so that a channel is occupied during the transmission of the packet only, and upon completion of the transmission the channel is made available for the transfer of other traffic.

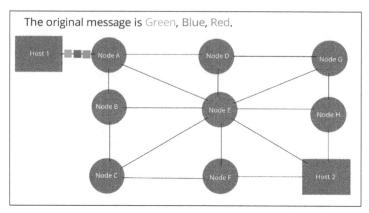

An animation demonstrating data packet switching across a network.

Packet switching features delivery of variable bit rate data streams, realized as sequences of packets, over a computer network which allocates transmission resources as needed using statistical multiplexing or dynamic bandwidth allocation techniques. As they traverse network nodes, such as switches and routers, packets are received, buffered, queued, and transmitted (stored and forwarded), resulting in variable latency and throughput depending on the link capacity and the traffic load on the network.

Packet switching contrasts with another principal networking paradigm, circuit switching, a method which pre-allocates dedicated network bandwidth specifically for each communication session, each having a constant bit rate and latency between nodes. In cases of billable services, such as cellular communication services, circuit switching is characterized by a fee per unit of connection time, even when no data is transferred, while packet switching may be characterized by a fee per unit of information transmitted, such as characters, packets, or messages.

Packet mode communication may be implemented with or without intermediate forwarding nodes (packet switches or routers). Packets are normally forwarded by intermediate network nodes asynchronously using first-in, first-out buffering, but may be forwarded according to some scheduling discipline for fair queuing, traffic shaping, or for differentiated or guaranteed quality of service, such as weighted fair queuing or leaky bucket. In case of a shared physical medium (such as radio or 10BASE5), the packets may be delivered according to a multiple access scheme.

## History

In the late 1950s, the US Air Force established a wide area network for the Semi-Automatic Ground Environment (SAGE) radar defense system. They sought a system that might survive a nuclear attack to enable a response, thus diminishing the attractiveness of the first strike advantage by enemies.

Leonard Kleinrock conducted early research in queueing theory which proved important in packet switching, and published a book in the related field of digital message switching (without the packets) in 1961; he also later played a leading role in building and management of the world's first packet-switched network, the ARPANET.

The concept of switching small blocks of data was first explored independently by Paul Baran at the RAND Corporation in the US and Donald Davies at the National Physical Laboratory (NPL) in the UK in the early to mid-1960s.

Baran developed the concept of *distributed adaptive message block switching* during his research at the RAND Corporation for the US Air Force into communications networks, that could survive nuclear wars, first presented to the Air Force in the summer of 1961 as briefing B-265, later published as RAND report P-2626 in 1962, and finally in report RM 3420 in 1964. Report P-2626 described a general architecture for a large-scale, distributed, survivable communications network. The work focuses on three key ideas: use of a decentralized network with multiple paths between any two points, dividing user messages into *message blocks*, later called packets, and delivery of these messages by store and forward switching.

Baran's work was known to Robert Taylor and J.C.R. Licklider at the Information Processing Technology Office, who advocated wide area networks, and it influenced Lawrence Roberts to adopt the technology in the development of the ARPANET.

Starting in 1965, Donald Davies at the National Physical Laboratory, UK, independently developed the same message routing methodology as developed by Baran. He called it *packet switching*, a more accessible name than Baran's, and proposed to build a nationwide network in the UK. He gave a talk on the proposal in 1966, after which a person from the Ministry of Defence (MoD) told him about Baran's work. A member of Davies' team (Roger Scantlebury) met Lawrence Roberts at the 1967 ACM Symposium on Operating System Principles and suggested it for use in the ARPANET.

Davies had chosen some of the same parameters for his original network design as did Baran, such as a packet size of 1024 bits. In 1966, Davies proposed that a network should be built at the laboratory to serve the needs of NPL and prove the feasibility of packet switching. The NPL Data Communications Network entered service in 1970.

The first computer network and packet switching network deployed for computer resource sharing was the Octopus Network at the Lawrence Livermore National Laboratory that began connecting four Control Data 6600 computers to several shared storage devices (including an IBM 2321 Data Cell in 1968 and an IBM Photostore in 1970) and to several hundred Teletype Model 33 ASR terminals for time sharing use starting in 1968.

In 1973, Vint Cerf and Bob Kahn wrote the specifications for Transmission Control Protocol (TCP), an internetworking protocol for sharing resources using packet-switching among the nodes.

## Connectionless and Connection-oriented Modes

Packet switching may be classified into connectionless packet switching, also known as datagram switching, and connection-oriented packet switching, also known as virtual circuit switching.

Examples of connectionless protocols are Ethernet, Internet Protocol (IP), and the User Datagram Protocol (UDP). Connection-oriented protocols include X.25, Frame Relay, Multiprotocol Label Switching (MPLS), and the Transmission Control Protocol (TCP).

In connectionless mode each packet includes complete addressing information. The packets are routed individually, sometimes resulting in different paths and out-of-order delivery. Each packet is labeled with a destination address, source address, and port numbers. It may also be labeled with the sequence number of the packet. This precludes the need for a dedicated path to help the packet find its way to its destination, but means that much more information is needed in the packet header, which is therefore larger, and this information needs to be looked up in power-hungry content-addressable memory. Each packet is dispatched and may go via different routes; potentially, the system has to do as much work for every packet as the connection-oriented system has to do in connection set-up, but with less information as to the application's requirements. At the destination, the original message/data is reassembled in the correct order, based on the packet sequence number. Thus a virtual connection, also known as a virtual circuit or byte stream is provided to the end-user by a transport layer protocol, although intermediate network nodes only provides a connectionless network layer service.

Connection-oriented transmission requires a setup phase in each involved node before any packet is transferred to establish the parameters of communication. The packets include a connection identifier rather than address information and are negotiated between endpoints so that they are delivered in order and with error checking. Address information is only transferred to each node during the connection set-up phase, when the route to the destination is discovered and an entry is added to the switching table in each network node through which the connection passes. The signaling protocols used allow the application to specify its requirements and discover link parameters. Acceptable values for service parameters may be negotiated. Routing a packet requires the node to look up the connection id in a table. The packet header can be small, as it only needs to contain this code and any information, such as length, timestamp, or sequence number, which is different for different packets.

## Packet Switching in Networks

Packet switching is used to optimize the use of the channel capacity available in digital telecommunication networks such as computer networks, to minimize the transmission latency (the time it takes for data to pass across the network), and to increase robustness of communication.

The best-known use of packet switching is the Internet and most local area networks. The Internet is implemented by the Internet Protocol Suite using a variety of Link Layer technologies. For example, Ethernet and Frame Relay are common. Newer mobile phone technologies (e.g., GPRS, i-mode) also use packet switching.

X.25 is a notable use of packet switching in that, despite being based on packet switching methods, it provided virtual circuits to the user. These virtual circuits carry variable-length packets. In 1978, X.25 provided the first international and commercial packet switching network, the International Packet Switched Service (IPSS). Asynchronous Transfer Mode (ATM) also is a virtual circuit technology, which uses fixed-length cell relay connection oriented packet switching.

Datagram packet switching is also called connectionless networking because no connections are established. Technologies such as Multiprotocol Label Switching (MPLS) and the Resource Reservation Protocol (RSVP) create virtual circuits on top of datagram networks. Virtual circuits are especially useful in building robust failover mechanisms and allocating bandwidth for delay-sensitive applications.

MPLS and its predecessors, as well as ATM, have been called "fast packet" technologies. MPLS, indeed, has been called "ATM without cells". Modern routers, however, do not require these technologies to be able to forward variable-length packets at multi-gigabit speeds across the network.

## X.25 vs. Frame Relay

Both X.25 and Frame Relay provide connection-oriented operations. X.25 provides it via the network layer of the OSI Model, whereas Frame Relay provides it via level two, the data link layer. Another major difference between X.25 and Frame Relay is that X.25 requires a handshake between the communicating parties before any user packets are transmitted. Frame Relay does not define any such handshakes. X.25 does not define any operations inside the packet network. It only operates at the user-network-interface (UNI). Thus, the network provider is free to use any procedure it wishes inside the network. X.25 does specify some limited re-transmission procedures at the UNI, and its link layer protocol (LAPB) provides conventional HDLC-type link management procedures. Frame Relay is a modified version of ISDN's layer two protocol, LAPD and LAPB. As such, its integrity operations pertain only between nodes on a link, not end-to-end. Any retransmissions must be carried out by higher layer protocols. The X.25 UNI protocol is part of the X.25 protocol suite, which consists of the lower three layers of the OSI Model. It was widely used at the UNI for packet switching networks during the 1980s and early 1990s, to provide a standardized interface into and out of packet networks. Some implementations used X.25 within the network as well, but its connection-oriented features made this setup cumbersome and inefficient. Frame relay operates principally at layer two of the OSI Model. However, its address field (the Data Link Connection ID, or DLCI) can be used at the OSI network layer, with a minimum set of procedures. Thus, it rids itself of many X.25 layer 3 encumbrances, but still has the DLCI as an ID beyond a node-to-node layer two link protocol. The simplicity of Frame Relay makes it faster and more efficient than X.25. Because Frame relay is a data link layer protocol, like X.25 it does not define internal network routing operations. For X.25 its packet IDs---the virtual circuit and virtual channel numbers have to be correlated to network addresses. The same is true for Frame Relays DLCI. How this is done is up to the network provider. Frame Relay, by virtue of having no network layer procedures is connection-oriented at layer two, by using the HDLC/LAPD/LAPB Set Asynchronous Balanced Mode (SABM). X.25 connections are typically established for each communication session, but it does have a feature allowing a limited amount of traffic to be passed across the UNI without the connection-oriented handshake. For a while, Frame Relay was used to interconnect LANs across wide area networks. However, X.25 and well as Frame Relay have been supplanted by the Internet Protocol (IP) at the network layer, and the Asynchronous Transfer Mode (ATM) and or versions of Multi-Protocol Label Switching (MPLS) at layer two. A typical configuration is to run IP over ATM or a version of MPLS. <Uyless Black, X.25 and Related Protocols, IEEE Computer Society, 1991> <Uyless Black, Frame Relay Networks, McGraw-Hill, 1998> <Uyless Black, MPLS and Label Switching Networks, Prentice Hall, 2001> < Uyless Black, ATM, Volume I, Prentice Hall, 1995>

## Packet-switched Networks

The history of packet-switched networks can be divided into three overlapping eras: early networks before the introduction of X.25 and the OSI model, the X.25 era when many postal, telephone, and telegraph companies introduced networks with X.25 interfaces, and the Internet era.

## Early Networks

ARPANET and SITA HLN became operational in 1969. Before the introduction of X.25 in 1973, about twenty different network technologies had been developed. Two fundamental differences involved the division of functions and tasks between the hosts at the edge of the network and the network core. In the datagram system, the hosts have the responsibility to ensure orderly delivery of packets. The User Datagram Protocol (UDP) is an example of a datagram protocol. In the virtual call system, the network guarantees sequenced delivery of data to the host. This results in a simpler host interface with less functionality than in the datagram model. The X.25 protocol suite uses this network type.

## Appletalk

AppleTalk was a proprietary suite of networking protocols developed by Apple Inc. in 1985 for Apple Macintosh computers. It was the primary protocol used by Apple devices through the 1980s and 90s. AppleTalk included features that allowed local area networks to be established *ad hoc* without the requirement for a centralized router or server. The AppleTalk system automatically assigned addresses, updated the distributed namespace, and configured any required inter-network routing. It was a plug-n-play system.

AppleTalk versions were also released for the IBM PC and compatibles, and the Apple IIGS. AppleTalk support was available in most networked printers, especially laser printers, some file servers and routers. AppleTalk support was terminated in 2009, replaced by TCP/IP protocols.

## ARPANET

The ARPANET was a progenitor network of the Internet and the first network to run the TCP/IP suite using packet switching technologies.

## BNRNET

BNRNET was a network which Bell Northern Research developed for internal use. It initially had only one host but was designed to support many hosts. BNR later made major contributions to the CCITT X.25 project.

## CYCLADES

The CYCLADES packet switching network was a French research network designed and directed by Louis Pouzin. First demonstrated in 1973, it was developed to explore alternatives to the early ARPANET design and to support network research generally. It was the first network to make the hosts responsible for reliable delivery of data, rather than the network itself, using unreliable datagrams and associated end-to-end protocol mechanisms. Concepts of this network influenced later ARPANET architecture.

## DECnet

DECnet is a suite of network protocols created by Digital Equipment Corporation, originally released in 1975 in order to connect two PDP-11 minicomputers. It evolved into one of the first peer-to-peer network architectures, thus transforming DEC into a networking powerhouse in the 1980s. Initially built with three layers, it later (1982) evolved into a seven-layer OSI-compliant networking protocol. The DECnet protocols were designed entirely by Digital Equipment Corporation. However, DECnet Phase II (and later) were open standards with published specifications, and several implementations were developed outside DEC, including one for Linux.

## DDX-1

This was an experimental network from Nippon PTT. It mixed circuit switching and packet switching. It was succeeded by DDX-2.

## EIN née COST II

European Informatics Network was a project to link several national networks. It became operational in 1976.

## EPSS

The Experimental Packet Switching System (EPSS) was an experiment of the UK Post Office. Ferranti supplied the hardware and software. The handling of link control messages (acknowledgements and flow control) was different from that of most other networks.

## GEIS

As General Electric Information Services (GEIS), General Electric was a major international provider of information services. The company originally designed a telephone network to serve as its internal (albeit continent-wide) voice telephone network.

In 1965, at the instigation of Warner Sinback, a data network based on this voice-phone network was designed to connect GE's four computer sales and service centers (Schenectady, New York, Chicago, and Phoenix) to facilitate a computer time-sharing service, apparently the world's first commercial online service. (In addition to selling GE computers, the centers were computer service bureaus, offering batch processing services. They lost money from the beginning, and Sinback, a high-level marketing manager, was given the job of turning the business around. He decided that a time-sharing system, based on Kemney's work at Dartmouth—which used a computer on loan from GE—could be profitable. Warner was right.)

After going international some years later, GEIS created a network data center near Cleveland, Ohio. Very little has been published about the internal details of their network. (Though it has been stated by some that Tymshare copied the GEIS system to create their network, Tymnet.) The design was hierarchical with redundant communication links.

## IPSANET

IPSANET was a semi-private network constructed by I. P. Sharp Associates to serve their time-sharing customers. It became operational in May 1976.

## IPX/SPX

The Internetwork Packet Exchange (IPX) and Sequenced Packet Exchange (SPX) are Novell networking protocols derived from Xerox Network Systems' IDP and SPP protocols, respectively. They were used primarily on networks using the Novell NetWare operating systems.

## Merit Network

Merit Network, Inc., an independent non-profit 501(c)(3) corporation governed by Michigan's public universities, was formed in 1966 as the Michigan Educational Research Information Triad to explore computer networking between three of Michigan's public universities as a means to help the state's educational and economic development. With initial support from the State of Michigan and the National Science Foundation (NSF), the packet-switched network was first demonstrated in December 1971 when an interactive host to host connection was made between the IBM mainframe computer systems at the University of Michigan in Ann Arbor and Wayne State University in Detroit. In October 1972 connections to the CDC mainframe at Michigan State University in East Lansing completed the triad. Over the next several years in addition to host to host interactive connections the network was enhanced to support terminal to host connections, host to host batch connections (remote job submission, remote printing, batch file transfer), interactive file transfer, gateways to the Tymnet and Telenet public data networks, X.25 host attachments, gateways to X.25 data networks, Ethernet attached hosts, and eventually TCP/IP and additional public universities in Michigan join the network. All of this set the stage for Merit's role in the NSFNET project starting in the mid-1980s.

## NPL

Donald Davies of the National Physical Laboratory, UK made many important contributions to the theory of packet switching. NPL built a single node network to connect sundry hosts at NPL.

## OCTOPUS

Octopus was a local network at Lawrence Livermore National Laboratory. It connected sundry hosts at the lab to interactive terminals and various computer peripherals including a bulk storage system.

## Philips Research

Philips Research Laboratories in Redhill, Surrey developed a packet switching network for internal use. It was a datagram network with a single switching node.

## PUP

PARC Universal Packet (PUP or Pup) was one of the two earliest internetwork protocol suites; it was created by researchers at Xerox PARC in the mid-1970s. The entire suite provided routing and packet delivery, as well as higher level functions such as a reliable byte stream, along with numerous applications. Further developments led to Xerox Network Systems (XNS).

## RCP

RCP was an experimental network created by the French PTT. It was used to gain experience with packet switching technology before the specification of Transpac was frozen. RCP was a virtual-circuit network in contrast to CYCLADES which was based on datagrams. RCP emphasised terminal to host and terminal to terminal connection; CYCLADES was concerned with host-to-host communication. TRANSPAC was introduced as an X.25 network. RCP influenced the specification of X.25.

## RETD

Red Especial de Transmisión de Datos was a network developed by Compañía Telefónica Nacional de España. It became operational in 1972 and thus was the first public network.

## SCANNET

"The experimental packet-switched Nordic telecommunication network SCANNET was implemented in Nordic technical libraries in 70's, and it included first Nordic electronic journal Extemplo. Libraries were also among first ones in universities to accommodate microcomputers for public use in early 80's."

## SITA HLN

SITA is a consortium of airlines. Their High Level Network became operational in 1969 at about the same time as ARPANET. It carried interactive traffic and message-switching traffic. As with many non-academic networks very little has been published about it.

## IBM Systems Network Architecture

IBM Systems Network Architecture (SNA) is IBM's proprietary networking architecture created in 1974. An IBM customer could acquire hardware and software from IBM and lease private lines from a common carrier to construct a private network.

## Telenet

Telenet was the first FCC-licensed public data network in the United States. It was founded by former ARPA IPTO director Larry Roberts as a means of making ARPANET technology public. He had tried to interest AT&T in buying the technology, but the monopoly's reaction was that this was incompatible with their future. Bolt, Beranack and Newman (BBN) provided the financing. It initially used ARPANET technology but changed the host interface to X.25 and the terminal interface to X.29. Telenet designed these protocols and helped standardize them in the CCITT. Telenet was incorporated in 1973 and started operations in 1975. It went public in 1979 and was then sold to GTE.

# Tymnet

Tymnet was an international data communications network headquartered in San Jose, CA that utilized virtual call packet switched technology and used X.25, SNA/SDLC, BSC and ASCII interfaces to connect host computers (servers)at thousands of large companies, educational institutions, and government agencies. Users typically connected via dial-up connections or dedicated async connections. The business consisted of a large public network that supported dial-up users and a private network business that allowed government agencies and large companies (mostly banks and airlines) to build their own dedicated networks. The private networks were often connected via gateways to the public network to reach locations not on the private network. Tymnet was also connected to dozens of other public networks in the U.S. and internationally via X.25/X.75 gateways. (Interesting note: Tymnet was not named after Mr. Tyme. Another employee suggested the name.)

# XNS

Xerox Network Systems (XNS) was a protocol suite promulgated by Xerox, which provided routing and packet delivery, as well as higher level functions such as a reliable stream, and remote procedure calls. It was developed from PARC Universal Packet (PUP).

# X.25 Era

There were two kinds of X.25 networks. Some such as DATAPAC and TRANSPAC were initially implemented with an X.25 external interface. Some older networks such as TELENET and TYMNET were modified to provide a X.25 host interface in addition to older host connection schemes. DATAPAC was developed by Bell Northern Research which was a joint venture of Bell Canada (a common carrier) and Northern Telecom (a telecommunications equipment supplier). Northern Telecom sold several DATAPAC clones to foreign PTTs including the Deutsche Bundespost. X.75 and X.121 allowed the interconnection of national X.25 networks. A user or host could call a host on a foreign network by including the DNIC of the remote network as part of the destination address.

# AUSTPAC

AUSTPAC was an Australian public X.25 network operated by Telstra. Started by Telecom Australia in the early 1980s, AUSTPAC was Australia's first public packet-switched data network, supporting applications such as on-line betting, financial applications — the Australian Tax Office made use of AUSTPAC — and remote terminal access to academic institutions, who maintained their connections to AUSTPAC up until the mid-late 1990s in some cases. Access can be via a dial-up terminal to a PAD, or, by linking a permanent X.25 node to the network.

## ConnNet

ConnNet was a packet-switched data network operated by the Southern New England Telephone Company serving the state of Connecticut.

## Datanet 1

Datanet 1 was the public switched data network operated by the Dutch PTT Telecom (now known as KPN). Strictly speaking Datanet 1 only referred to the network and the connected users via leased lines (using the X.121 DNIC 2041), the name also referred to the public PAD service *Telepad* (using the DNIC 2049). And because the main Videotex service used the network and modified PAD devices as infrastructure the name Datanet 1 was used for these services as well. Although this use of the name was incorrect all these services were managed by the same people within one department of KPN contributed to the confusion.

## Datapac

DATAPAC was the first operational X.25 network (1976). It covered major Canadian cities and was eventually extended to smaller centres.

## Datex-P

Deutsche Bundespost operated this national network in Germany. The technology was acquired from Northern Telecom.

## Eirpac

Eirpac is the Irish public switched data network supporting X.25 and X.28. It was launched in 1984, replacing Euronet. Eirpac is run by Eircom.

## HIPA-NET

Hitachi designed a private network system for sale as a turnkey package to multi-national organizations. In addition to providing X.25 packet switching, message switching software was also included. Messages were buffered at the nodes adjacent to the sending and receiving terminals. Switched virtual calls were not supported, but through the use of "logical ports" an originating terminal could have a menu of pre-defined destination terminals.

## Iberpac

Iberpac is the Spanish public packet-switched network, providing X.25 services. Iberpac is run by Telefonica.

## JANET

JANET was the UK academic and research network, linking all universities, higher education establishments, publicly funded research laboratories. The X.25 network was based mainly on GEC 4000 series switches, and run X.25 links at up to 8 Mbit/s in its final phase before being converted to an IP based network. The JANET network grew out of the 1970s SRCnet (later called SERCnet) network.

## PSS

Packet Switch Stream (PSS) was the UK Post Office (later to become British Telecom) national X.25 network with a DNIC of 2342. British Telecom renamed PSS under its GNS (Global Network Service) name, but the PSS name has remained better known. PSS also included public dial-up PAD access, and various InterStream gateways to other services such as Telex.

## Transpac

Transpac was the national X.25 network in France. It was developed locally at about the same time as DataPac in Canada. The development was done by the French PTT and influenced by the experimental RCP network. It began operation in 1978.

## VENUS-P

VENUS-P was an international X.25 network that operated from April 1982 through March 2006. At its subscription peak in 1999, VENUS-P connected 207 networks in 87 countries.

## Venepaq

Venepaq is the national X.25 public network in Venezuela. It is run by Cantv and allow direct connection and dial up connections. Provides nationalwide access at very low cost. It provides national and international access. Venepaq allow connection from 19.2 kbit/s to 64 kbit/s in direct connections, and 1200, 2400 and 9600 bit/s in dial up connections.

## Internet Era

When Internet connectivity was made available to anyone who could pay for an ISP subscription, the distinctions between national networks blurred. The user no longer saw network identifiers such as the DNIC. Some older technologies such as circuit switching have resurfaced with new names such as fast packet switching. Researchers have created some experimental networks to complement the existing Internet.

## CSNET

The Computer Science Network (CSNET) was a computer network funded by the U.S. National Science Foundation (NSF) that began operation in 1981. Its purpose was to extend networking benefits, for computer science departments at academic and research institutions that could not be directly connected to ARPANET, due to funding or authorization limitations. It played a significant role in spreading awareness of, and access to, national networking and was a major milestone on the path to development of the global Internet.

## Internet2

Internet2 is a not-for-profit United States computer networking consortium led by members from the research and education communities, industry, and government. The Internet2 community, in partnership with Qwest, built the first Internet2 Network, called Abilene, in 1998 and was a prime investor in the National LambdaRail (NLR) project. In 2006, Internet2 announced a partnership with Level 3 Communications to launch a brand new nationwide network, boosting its capacity from 10 Gbit/s to 100 Gbit/s. In October, 2007, Internet2 officially retired Abilene and now refers to its new, higher capacity network as the Internet2 Network.

## NSFNET

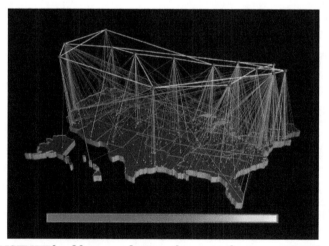

NSFNET Traffic 1991, NSFNET backbone nodes are shown at the top, regional networks below, traffic volume is depicted from purple (zero bytes) to white (100 billion bytes), visualization by NCSA using traffic data provided by the Merit Network.

The National Science Foundation Network (NSFNET) was a program of coordinated, evolving projects sponsored by the National Science Foundation (NSF) beginning in 1985 to promote advanced research and education networking in the United States. NSFNET was also the name given to several nationwide backbone networks operating at speeds of 56 kbit/s, 1.5 Mbit/s (T1), and 45 Mbit/s (T3) that were constructed to support NSF's networking initiatives from 1985-1995. Initially created to link researchers to the nation's

NSF-funded supercomputing centers, through further public funding and private industry partnerships it developed into a major part of the Internet backbone.

## NSFNET Regional Networks

In addition to the five NSF supercomputer centers, NSFNET provided connectivity to eleven regional networks and through these networks to many smaller regional and campus networks in the United States. The NSFNET regional networks were:

- BARRNet, the Bay Area Regional Research Network in Palo Alto, California;

- CERFNET, California Education and Research Federation Network in San Diego, California, serving California and Nevada;

- CICNet, the Committee on Institutional Cooperation Network via the Merit Network in Ann Arbor, Michigan and later as part of the T3 upgrade via Argonne National Laboratory outside of Chicago, serving the Big Ten Universities and the University of Chicago in Illinois, Indiana, Michigan, Minnesota, Ohio, and Wisconsin;

- Merit/MichNet in Ann Arbor, Michigan serving Michigan, formed in 1966, still in operation as of 2016;

- MIDnet in Lincoln, Nebraska serving Arkansas, Iowa, Kansas, Missouri, Nebraska, Oklahoma, and South Dakota;

- NEARNET, the New England Academic and Research Network in Cambridge, Massachusetts, added as part of the upgrade to T3, serving Connecticut, Maine, Massachusetts, New Hampshire, Rhode Island, and Vermont, established in late 1988, operated by BBN under contract to MIT, BBN assumed responsibility for NEARNET on 1 July 1993;

- NorthWestNet in Seattle, Washington, serving Alaska, Idaho, Montana, North Dakota, Oregon, and Washington, founded in 1987;

- NYSERNet, New York State Education and Research Network in Ithaca, New York;

- JVNCNet, the John von Neumann National Supercomputer Center Network in Princeton, New Jersey, serving Delaware and New Jersey;

- SESQUINET, the Sesquicentennial Network in Houston, Texas, founded during the 150th anniversary of the State of Texas;

- SURAnet, the Southeastern Universities Research Association network in College Park, Maryland and later as part of the T3 upgrade in Atlanta, Georgia serving Alabama, Florida, Georgia, Kentucky, Louisiana, Maryland, Mississippi, North Carolina, South Carolina, Tennessee, Virginia, and West Virginia, sold to BBN in 1994; and

- Westnet in Salt Lake City, Utah and Boulder, Colorado, serving Arizona, Colorado, New Mexico, Utah, and Wyoming.

## National LambdaRail

The National LambdaRail was launched in September 2003. It is a 12,000-mile high-speed national computer network owned and operated by the U.S. research and education community that runs over fiber-optic lines. It was the first transcontinental 10 Gigabit Ethernet network. It operates with high aggregate capacity of up to 1.6 Tbit/s and a high 40 Gbit/s bitrate, with plans for 100 Gbit/s.

## TransPAC, TransPAC2, and TransPAC3

TransPAC2 and TransPAC3, continuations of the TransPAC project, a high-speed international Internet service connecting research and education networks in the Asia-Pacific region to those in the US. TransPAC is part of the NSF's International Research Network Connections (IRNC) program.

## Very High-speed Backbone Network Service (vBNS)

The Very high-speed Backbone Network Service (vBNS) came on line in April 1995 as part of a National Science Foundation (NSF) sponsored project to provide high-speed interconnection between NSF-sponsored supercomputing centers and select access points in the United States. The network was engineered and operated by MCI Telecommunications under a cooperative agreement with the NSF. By 1998, the vBNS had grown to connect more than 100 universities and research and engineering institutions via 12 national points of presence with DS-3 (45 Mbit/s), OC-3c (155 Mbit/s), and OC-12c (622 Mbit/s) links on an all OC-12c backbone, a substantial engineering feat for that time. The vBNS installed one of the first ever production OC-48c (2.5 Gbit/s) IP links in February 1999 and went on to upgrade the entire backbone to OC-48c.

In June 1999 MCI WorldCom introduced vBNS+ which allowed attachments to the vBNS network by organizations that were not approved by or receiving support from NSF. After the expiration of the NSF agreement, the vBNS largely transitioned to providing service to the government. Most universities and research centers migrated to the Internet2 educational backbone. In January 2006, when MCI and Verizon merged, vBNS+ became a service of Verizon Business.

## Various Packet Switched Networks

### ARPANET

The Advanced Research Projects Agency Network (ARPANET) was an early packet switching network and the first network to implement the protocol suite TCP/IP. Both technologies became the technical foundation of the Internet. ARPANET was initially funded by the Advanced Research Projects Agency (ARPA) of the United States Department of Defense.

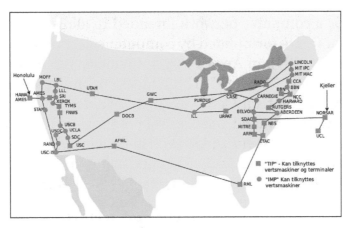

Arpanet 1974

The packet switching methodology employed in the ARPANET was based on concepts and designs by Americans Leonard Kleinrock and Paul Baran, British scientist Donald Davies, and Lawrence Roberts of the Lincoln Laboratory. The TCP/IP communications protocols were developed for ARPANET by computer scientists Robert Kahn and Vint Cerf, and incorporated concepts by Louis Pouzin for the French CYCLADES project.

As the project progressed, protocols for internetworking were developed by which multiple separate networks could be joined into a network of networks. Access to the ARPANET was expanded in 1981 when the National Science Foundation (NSF) funded the Computer Science Network (CSNET). In 1982, the Internet protocol suite (TCP/IP) was introduced as the standard networking protocol on the ARPANET. In the early 1980s the NSF funded the establishment for national supercomputing centers at several universities, and provided interconnectivity in 1986 with the NSFNET project, which also created network access to the supercomputer sites in the United States from research and education organizations. ARPANET was decommissioned in 1990.

## History

Packet switching—today the dominant basis for data communications worldwide—was a new concept at the time of the conception of the ARPANET. Prior to the advent of packet switching, both voice and data communications had been based on the idea of circuit switching, as in the traditional telephone circuit, wherein each telephone call is allocated a dedicated, end to end, electronic connection between the two communicating stations. Such stations might be telephones or computers. The (temporarily) dedicated line is typically composed of many intermediary lines which are assembled into a chain that stretches all the way from the originating station to the destination station. With packet switching, a data system could use a single communication link to communicate with more than one machine by collecting data into datagrams and transmitting these as packets onto the attached network link, as soon as the link becomes idle. Thus, not only can the link be shared, much as a single post box can be used to post letters to different destinations, but each packet can be routed independently of other packets.

The earliest ideas for a computer network intended to allow general communications among computer users were formulated by computer scientist J. C. R. Licklider of Bolt, Beranek and Newman (BBN), in April 1963, in memoranda discussing the concept of the "Intergalactic Computer Network". Those ideas encompassed many of the features of the contemporary Internet. In October 1963, Licklider was appointed head of the Behavioral Sciences and Command and Control programs at the Defense Department's Advanced Research Projects Agency (ARPA). He convinced Ivan Sutherland and Bob Taylor that this network concept was very important and merited development, although Licklider left ARPA before any contracts were assigned for development.

Sutherland and Taylor continued their interest in creating the network, in part, to allow ARPA-sponsored researchers at various corporate and academic locales to utilize computers provided by ARPA, and, in part, to quickly distribute new software and other computer science results. Taylor had three computer terminals in his office, each connected to separate computers, which ARPA was funding: one for the System Development Corporation (SDC) Q-32 in Santa Monica, one for Project Genie at the University of California, Berkeley, and another for Multics at the Massachusetts Institute of Technology. Taylor recalls the circumstance: "For each of these three terminals, I had three different sets of user commands. So, if I was talking online with someone at S.D.C., and I wanted to talk to someone I knew at Berkeley, or M.I.T., about this, I had to get up from the S.D.C. terminal, go over and log into the other terminal and get in touch with them. I said, "Oh Man!", it's obvious what to do: If you have these three terminals, there ought to be one terminal that goes anywhere you want to go. That idea is the ARPANET".

Meanwhile, since the early 1960s, Paul Baran at the RAND Corporation had been researching systems that could survive nuclear war and developed the idea of *distributed adaptive message block switching*. Donald Davies at the United Kingdom's National Physical Laboratory (NPL) independently invented the same concept in 1965. His work, presented by a colleague, initially caught the attention of ARPANET developers at a conference in Gatlinburg, Tennessee, in October 1967. He gave the first public demonstration, having coined the term *packet switching*, on 5 August 1968 and incorporated it into the NPL network in England. Larry Roberts at ARPA applied Davies' concepts of packet switching for the ARPANET. The NPL network followed by ARPANET were the first two networks in the world to use packet switching, and were themselves connected together in 1973. The NPL network was using line speeds of 768 kbit/s, and the proposed line speed for ARPANET was upgraded from 2.4 kbit/s to 50 kbit/s.

## Creation

By mid-1968, Taylor had prepared a complete plan for a computer network, and, after

ARPA's approval, a Request for Quotation (RFQ) was issued for 140 potential bidders. Most computer science companies regarded the ARPA–Taylor proposal as outlandish, and only twelve submitted bids to build a network; of the twelve, ARPA regarded only four as top-rank contractors. At year's end, ARPA considered only two contractors, and awarded the contract to build the network to BBN Technologies on 7 April 1969. The initial, seven-person BBN team were much aided by the technical specificity of their response to the ARPA RFQ, and thus quickly produced the first working system. This team was led by Frank Heart. The BBN-proposed network closely followed Taylor's ARPA plan: a network composed of small computers called Interface Message Processors (or IMPs), similar to the later concept of routers, that functioned as gateways interconnecting local resources. At each site, the IMPs performed store-and-forward packet switching functions, and were interconnected with leased lines via telecommunication data sets (modems), with initial data rates of 56kbit/s. The host computers were connected to the IMPs via custom serial communication interfaces. The system, including the hardware and the packet switching software, was designed and installed in nine months.

The first-generation IMPs were built by BBN Technologies using a rugged computer version of the Honeywell DDP-516 computer configured with 24KB of expandable magnetic-core memory, and a 16-channel Direct Multiplex Control (DMC) direct memory access unit. The DMC established custom interfaces with each of the host computers and modems. In addition to the front-panel lamps, the DDP-516 computer also features a special set of 24 indicator lamps showing the status of the IMP communication channels. Each IMP could support up to four local hosts, and could communicate with up to six remote IMPs via leased lines. The network connected one computer in Utah with three in California. Later, the Department of Defense allowed the universities to join the network for sharing hardware and software resources.

## Debate on Design Goals

In *A Brief History of the Internet*, the Internet Society denies that ARPANET was designed to survive a nuclear attack:

> It was from the RAND study that the false rumor started, claiming that the ARPANET was somehow related to building a network resistant to nuclear war. This was never true of the ARPANET; only the unrelated RAND study on secure voice considered nuclear war. However, the later work on Internetting did emphasize robustness and survivability, including the capability to withstand losses of large portions of the underlying networks.

The RAND study was conducted by Paul Baran and pioneered packet switching. In an interview he confirmed that while ARPANET did not exactly share his project's goal, his work had greatly contributed to the development of ARPANET. Minutes taken by Elmer Shapiro of Stanford Research Institute at the ARPANET design meeting of 9–10

Oct. 1967 indicate that a version of Baran's routing method and suggestion of using a fixed packet size was expected to be employed.

According to Stephen J. Lukasik, who as Deputy Director and Director of DARPA (1967–1974) was "the person who signed most of the checks for Arpanet's development":

> The goal was to exploit new computer technologies to meet the needs of military command and control against nuclear threats, achieve survivable control of US nuclear forces, and improve military tactical and management decision making.

The ARPANET incorporated distributed computation (and frequent re-computation) of routing tables. This was a major contribution to the survivability of the ARPANET in the face of significant destruction - even by a nuclear attack. Such auto-routing was technically quite challenging to construct at the time. The fact that it was incorporated into the early ARPANET made many believe that this had been a design goal.

The ARPANET was designed to survive subordinate-network losses, since the principal reason was that the switching nodes and network links were unreliable, even without any nuclear attacks. Resource scarcity supported the creation of the ARPANET, according to Charles Herzfeld, ARPA Director (1965–1967):

> The ARPANET was not started to create a Command and Control System that would survive a nuclear attack, as many now claim. To build such a system was, clearly, a major military need, but it was not ARPA's mission to do this; in fact, we would have been severely criticized had we tried. Rather, the ARPANET came out of our frustration that there were only a limited number of large, powerful research computers in the country, and that many research investigators, who should have access to them, were geographically separated from them.

The ARPANET was operated by the military during the two decades of its existence, until 1990.

## ARPANET Deployed

Historical document: First ARPANET IMP log: the first message ever sent via the ARPANET, 10:30 pm, 29 October 1969. This IMP Log excerpt, kept at UCLA, describes setting up a message transmission from the UCLA SDS Sigma 7 Host computer to the SRI SDS 940 Host computer.

The initial ARPANET consisted of four IMPs:

- University of California, Los Angeles (UCLA), where Leonard Kleinrock had established a Network Measurement Center, with an SDS Sigma 7 being the first computer attached to it;

- The Augmentation Research Center at Stanford Research Institute (now SRI International), where Douglas Engelbart had created the ground-breaking NLS system, a very important early hypertext system, and would run the Network Information Center (NIC), with the SDS 940 that ran NLS, named "Genie", being the first host attached;

- University of California, Santa Barbara (UCSB), with the Culler-Fried Interactive Mathematics Center's IBM 360/75, running OS/MVT being the machine attached;

- The University of Utah's Computer Science Department, where Ivan Sutherland had moved, running a DEC PDP-10 operating on TENEX.

The first successful message on the ARPANET was sent by UCLA student programmer Charley Kline, at 10:30 pm on 29 October 1969, from Boelter Hall 3420. Kline transmitted from the university's SDS Sigma 7 Host computer to the Stanford Research Institute's SDS 940 Host computer. The message text was the word *login*; on an earlier attempt the *l* and the *o* letters were transmitted, but the system then crashed. Hence, the literal first message over the ARPANET was *lo*. About an hour later, after the programmers repaired the code that caused the crash, the SDS Sigma 7 computer effected a full *login*. The first permanent ARPANET link was established on 21 November 1969, between the IMP at UCLA and the IMP at the Stanford Research Institute. By 5 December 1969, the entire four-node network was established.

## Growth and Evolution

In March 1970, the ARPANET reached the East Coast of the United States, when an IMP at BBN in Cambridge, Massachusetts was connected to the network. Thereafter, the ARPANET grew: 9 IMPs by June 1970 and 13 IMPs by December 1970, then 18 by September 1971 (when the network included 23 university and government hosts); 29 IMPs by August 1972, and 40 by September 1973. By June 1974, there were 46 IMPs, and in July 1975, the network numbered 57 IMPs. By 1981, the number was 213 host computers, with another host connecting approximately every twenty days.

In 1973 a transatlantic satellite link connected the Norwegian Seismic Array (NORSAR) to the ARPANET, making Norway the first country outside the US to be connected to the network. At about the same time a terrestrial circuit added a London IMP.

In 1975, the ARPANET was declared "operational". The Defense Communications Agency took control since ARPA was intended to fund advanced research.

In September 1984 work was completed on restructuring the ARPANET giving U.S. military sites their own Military Network (MILNET) for unclassified defense department communications. Controlled gateways connected the two networks. The combination was called the Defense Data Network (DDN). Separating the civil and military networks reduced the 113-node ARPANET by 68 nodes. The MILNET later became the NIPRNet.

## Rules and Etiquette

Because of its government funding, certain forms of traffic were discouraged or prohibited. A 1982 handbook on computing at MIT's AI Lab stated regarding network etiquette:

It is considered illegal to use the ARPANet for anything which is not in direct support of Government business ... personal messages to other ARPANet subscribers (for example, to arrange a get-together or check and say a friendly hello) are generally not considered harmful ... Sending electronic mail over the ARPANet for commercial profit or political purposes is both anti-social and illegal. By sending such messages, you can offend many people, and it is possible to get MIT in serious trouble with the Government agencies which manage the ARPANet.

## Technology

Support for inter-IMP circuits of up to 230.4 kbit/s was added in 1970, although considerations of cost and IMP processing power meant this capability was not actively used.

1971 saw the start of the use of the non-ruggedized (and therefore significantly lighter) Honeywell 316 as an IMP. It could also be configured as a Terminal Interface Processor (TIP), which provided terminal server support for up to 63 ASCII serial terminals through a multi-line controller in place of one of the hosts. The 316 featured a greater degree of integration than the 516, which made it less expensive and easier to maintain. The 316 was configured with 40 kB of core memory for a TIP. The size of core memory was later increased, to 32 kB for the IMPs, and 56 kB for TIPs, in 1973.

In 1975, BBN introduced IMP software running on the Pluribus multi-processor. These appeared in a few sites. In 1981, BBN introduced IMP software running on its own C/30 processor product.

In 1983, TCP/IP protocols replaced NCP as the ARPANET's principal protocol, and the ARPANET then became one subnet of the early Internet.

The original IMPs and TIPs were phased out as the ARPANET was shut down after the introduction of the NSFNet, but some IMPs remained in service as late as July 1990.

The *ARPANET Completion Report*, jointly published by BBN and ARPA, concludes that:

> ... it is somewhat fitting to end on the note that the ARPANET program has had a strong and direct feedback into the support and strength of computer science, from which the network, itself, sprang.

In the wake of ARPANET being formally decommissioned on 28 February 1990, Vinton Cerf wrote the following lamentation, entitled "Requiem of the ARPANET":

It was the first, and being first, was best, but now we lay it down to ever rest. Now pause with me a moment, shed some tears. For auld lang syne, for love, for years and years of faithful service, duty done, I weep. Lay down thy packet, now, O friend, and sleep.

-Vinton Cerf

Senator Albert Gore, Jr. began to craft the High Performance Computing and Communication Act of 1991 (commonly referred to as "The Gore Bill") after hearing the 1988 report toward a National Research Network submitted to Congress by a group chaired by Leonard Kleinrock, professor of computer science at UCLA. The bill was passed on 9 December 1991 and led to the National Information Infrastructure (NII) which Al Gore called the "information superhighway".

ARPANET was the subject of two IEEE Milestones, both dedicated in 2009.

## Software and Protocols

The starting point for host-to-host communication on the ARPANET in 1969 was the 1822 protocol, which defined the transmission of messages to an IMP. The message format was designed to work unambiguously with a broad range of computer architectures. An 1822 message essentially consisted of a message type, a numeric host address, and a data field. To send a data message to another host, the transmitting host formatted a data message containing the destination host's address and the data message being sent, and then transmitted the message through the 1822 hardware interface. The IMP then delivered the message to its destination address, either by delivering it to a locally connected host, or by delivering it to another IMP. When the message was ultimately delivered to the destination host, the receiving IMP would transmit a *Ready for Next Message* (RFNM) acknowledgement to the sending, host IMP.

Unlike modern Internet datagrams, the ARPANET was designed to reliably transmit 1822 messages, and to inform the host computer when it loses a message; the contemporary IP is unreliable, whereas the TCP is reliable. Nonetheless, the 1822 protocol proved inadequate for handling multiple connections among different applications residing in a host computer. This problem was addressed with the Network Control Program (NCP), which provided a standard method to establish reliable, flow-controlled, bidirectional communications links among different processes in different host computers. The NCP interface allowed application software to connect across the ARPANET by implementing higher-level communication protocols, an early example of the *protocol layering* concept incorporated to the OSI model.

In 1983, TCP/IP protocols replaced NCP as the ARPANET's principal protocol, and the ARPANET then became one component of the early Internet.

## Network Applications

NCP provided a standard set of network services that could be shared by several applications running on a single host computer. This led to the evolution of *application protocols* that operated, more or less, independently of the underlying network service, and permitted independent advances in the underlying protocols.

In 1971, Ray Tomlinson, of BBN sent the first network e-mail (RFC 524, RFC 561). By 1973, e-mail constituted 75 percent of ARPANET traffic.

By 1973, the File Transfer Protocol (FTP) specification had been defined (RFC 354) and implemented, enabling file transfers over the ARPANET.

The Network Voice Protocol (NVP) specifications were defined in 1977 (RFC 741), then implemented, but, because of technical shortcomings, conference calls over the ARPANET never worked well; the contemporary Voice over Internet Protocol (packet voice) was decades away.

## Password Protection

The Purdy Polynomial hash algorithm was developed for ARPANET to protect passwords in 1971 at the request of Larry Roberts, head of ARPA at that time. It computed a polynomial of degree $2^{24} + 17$ modulo the 64-bit prime $p = 2^{64} - 59$. The algorithm was later used by Digital Equipment Corporation (DEC) to hash passwords in the VMS Operating System, and is still being used for this purpose.

## ARPANET in Popular Culture

- *Computer Networks: The Heralds of Resource Sharing*, a 30-minute documentary film featuring Fernando J. Corbato, J.C.R. Licklider, Lawrence G. Roberts, Robert Kahn, Frank Heart, William R. Sutherland, Richard W. Watson, John R. Pasta, Donald W. Davies, and economist, George W. Mitchell.

- "Scenario", a February 1985 episode of the U.S. television sitcom *Benson* (season 6, episode 20), was the first incidence of a popular TV show directly referencing the Internet or its progenitors. The show includes a scene in which the ARPANET is accessed.

- There is an electronic music artist known as "Arpanet", Gerald Donald, one of the members of Drexciya. The artist's 2002 album *Wireless Internet* features commentary on the expansion of the internet via wireless communication, with songs such as *NTT DoCoMo*, dedicated to the mobile communications giant based in Japan.

- Thomas Pynchon mentions ARPANET in his 2009 novel *Inherent Vice*, which is set in Los Angeles in 1970, and in his 2013 novel *Bleeding Edge*.

- The 1993 television series *The X-Files* featured the ARPANET in a season 5 episode, titled "Unusual Suspects". John Fitzgerald Byers offers to help Susan Modeski (known as Holly . . . "just like the sugar") by hacking into the ARPANET to obtain sensitive information.

- In the spy-drama television series *The Americans*, a Russian scientist defector offers access to ARPANET to the Russians in a plea to not be repatriated (Season 2 Episode 5 "The Deal"). Episode 7 of Season 2 is named 'ARPANET' and features Russian infiltration to bug the network.

- In the television series *Person of Interest*, main character Harold Finch hacked ARPANET in 1980 using a homemade computer during his first efforts to built a prototype of the Machine. This corresponds with the real life virus that occurred in October of that year that temporarily halted ARPANET functions. The ARPANET hack was first discussed in the episode *2PiR* where a computer science teacher called it the most famous hack in history and one that was never solved. Finch later mentioned it to Person of Interest Caleb Phipps and his role was first indicated when he showed knowledge that it was done by "a kid with a homemade computer" which Phipps, who had researched the hack, had never heard before.

- In the third season of the television series *Halt and Catch Fire*, the character Joe MacMillan explores the potential commercialization of ARPANET.

## CYCLADES

The CYCLADES computer network was a French research network created in the early 1970s. It was one of the pioneering networks experimenting with the concept of packet switching, and was developed to explore alternatives to the ARPANET design. It supported general local network research.

The CYCLADES network was the first to make the hosts responsible for the reliable delivery of data, rather than this being a centralized service of the network itself. Datagrams were exchanged on the network using transport protocols that do not guarantee reliable delivery, but only attempt best-effort. To empower the network leaves, the hosts, to perform error-correction, the network ensured end-to-end protocol transparency, a concept later to be known as the end-to-end principle. This simplified network design, reduced network latency, and reduced the opportunities for single point failures. The experience with these concepts led to the design of key features of the Internet protocol in the ARPANET project.

The network was sponsored by the French government, through the *Institut de Recherche en Informatique et en Automatique* (IRIA), the national research laboratory for computer science in France, now known as INRIA, which served as the co-ordinating agency. Several French computer manufacturers, research institutes and universities contributed to the effort. CYCLADES was designed and directed by Louis Pouzin.

## Conception and Deployment

Design and staffing started in 1972, and November 1973 saw the first demonstration, using three hosts and one packet switch. Deployment continued in 1974, with three packet switches installed by February, although at that point the network was only operational for three hours each day. By June the network was up to seven switches, and was available throughout the day for experimental use.

A terminal concentrator was also developed that year, since time-sharing was still a prevalent mode of computer use. In 1975, the network shrank slightly due to budgetary constraints, but the setback was only temporary. At that point, the network provided remote login, remote batch and file transfer user application services.

By 1976 the network was in full deployment, eventually numbering 20 nodes with connections to NPL in London, ESA in Rome, and to the European Informatics Network (EIN).

## Technical Details

CYCLADES used a layered architecture, as did the Internet. The basic packet transmission like function, named CIGALE, was novel; however, it provided an unreliable *datagram* service (the word was coined by Louis Pouzin by combining *data* and *telegram*). Since the packet switches no longer had to ensure correct delivery of data, this greatly simplified their design.

"The inspiration for datagrams had two sources. One was Donald Davies' studies. He had done some simulation of datagram networks, although he had not built any, and it looked technically viable. The second inspiration was I like things simple. I didn't see any real technical motivation to overlay two levels of end-to-end protocols. I thought one was enough."

*— Louis Pouzin*

The CIGALE network featured a distance vector routing protocol, and allowed experimentation with various metrics. it also included a time synchronization protocol in all the packet switches. CIGALE included early attempts at performing congestion control by dropping excess packets.

The name CIGALE— which is French for *cicada*—originates from the fact that the developers installed a speaker at each computer, so that "it went 'chirp chirp chirp' like cicadas" when a packet passed a computer.

An end-to-end protocol built on top of that provided a reliable transport service, on top of which applications were built. It provided a reliable sequence of user-visible data units called *letters*, rather than the reliable byte stream of TCP. The transport protocol was able to deal with out-of-order and unreliable delivery of datagrams, using the now-standard mechanisms of end-end acknowledgments and timeouts; it also featured sliding windows and end-to-end flow control.

## Demise

By 1976, the French PTT was developing Transpac, a packet network based on the emerging X.25 standard. The academic debates between datagram and virtual circuit networks continued for some time, but were eventually cut short by bureaucratic decisions.

Data transmission was a state monopoly in France at the time, and IRIA needed a special dispensation to run the CYCLADES network. The PTT did not agree to funding by the government of a competitor to their Transpac network, and insisted that the permission and funding be rescinded. By 1981, Cyclades was forced to shut down.

## Legacy

The most important legacy of CYCLADES was in showing that moving the responsibility for reliability into the hosts was workable, and produced a well-functioning service network. It also showed that it greatly reduced the complexity of the packet switches. The concept became a cornerstone in the design of the Internet.

The network was also a fertile ground for experimentation, and allowed a generation of French computer scientists to experiment with networking concepts. Louis Pouzin and the CYCLADES alumni initiated a number of follow-on projects at IRIA to experiment with local area networks, satellite networks, the Unix operating system, and the message passing operating system Chorus.

Hubert Zimmermann used his experience in CYCLADES to influence the design of the OSI model, which is still a common pedagogical tool.

CYCLADES alumni and researchers at IRIA/INRIA were also influential in spreading adoption of the Internet in France, eventually witnessing the success of the datagram-based Internet, and the demise of the X.25 and ATM virtual circuit networks.

## IPSANET

IPSANET was a packet switching network written by I. P. Sharp Associates (IPSA). Operation began in May 1976. It initially used the IBM 3705 Communications Controller and Computer Automation LSI-2 computers as nodes. An Intel 80286 based-node was added in 1987. It was called the Beta node.

The original purpose was to connect low-speed dumb terminals to a central time sharing host in Toronto. It was soon modified to allow a terminal to connect to an alternate host running the SHARP APL software under license. Terminals were initially either 2741-type machines based on the 14.8 characters/s IBM Selectric typewriter or 30 character/s ASCII machines. Link speed was limited to 9600 bit/s until about 1984.

Other services including 2780/3780 Bisync support, remote printing, X.25 gateway and SDLC pipe lines were added in the 1978 to 1984 era. There was no general purpose data transport facility until the introduction of *Network Shared Variable Processor* (NSVP) in 1984. This allowed APL programs running on different hosts to communicate via Shared Variables.

The Beta node improved performance and provided new services not tied to APL. An X.25 interface was the most important of these. It allowed connection to a host which was not running SHARP APL.

IPSANET allowed for the development of an early yet advanced e-mail service, *666 BOX*, which also became a major product for some time, originally hosted on IPSA's system, and later sold to end users to run on their own machines. NSVP allowed these remote e-mail systems to exchange traffic.

The network reached its maximum size of about 300 nodes before it was shut down in 1993.

## Network Packet

A network packet is a formatted unit of data carried by a packet-switched network. Computer communications links that do not support packets, such as traditional point-to-point telecommunications links, simply transmit data as a bit stream. When data is formatted into packets, packet switching is possible and the bandwidth of the communication medium can be better shared among users than with circuit switching.

A packet consists of control information and user data, which is also known as the payload. Control information provides data for delivering the payload, for example: source and destination network addresses, error detection codes, and sequencing information. Typically, control information is found in packet headers and trailers.

## Terminology

In the seven-layer OSI model of computer networking, *packet* strictly refers to a data unit at layer 3, the Network Layer. The correct term for a data unit at Layer 2, the Data Link Layer, is a *frame*, and at Layer 4, the Transport Layer, the correct term is a *segment* or *datagram*. For the case of TCP/IP communication over Ethernet, a TCP segment is carried in one or more IP packets, which are each carried in one or more Ethernet frames.

## Packet Framing

Different communications protocols use different conventions for distinguishing between the elements and for formatting the data. For example, in Point-to-Point Protocol, the packet is formatted in 8-bit bytes, and special characters are used to delimit the different elements. Other protocols like Ethernet, establish the start of the header and data elements by their location relative to the start of the packet. Some protocols format the information at a bit level instead of a byte level.

A good analogy is to consider a packet to be like a letter: the header is like the envelope, and the data area is whatever the person puts inside the envelope.

A network design can achieve two major results by using packets: *error detection* and *multiple host addressing*. A packet has the following components.

## Addresses

The routing of network packets requires two network addresses, the source address of the sending host, and the destination address of the receiving host.

## Error Detection and Correction

Error detection and correction is performed at various layers in the protocol stack. Network packets may contain a checksum, parity bits or cyclic redundancy checks to detect errors that occur during transmission.

At the transmitter, the calculation is performed before the packet is sent. When received at the destination, the checksum is recalculated, and compared with the one in the packet. If discrepancies are found, the packet may be corrected or discarded. Any packet loss is dealt with by the network protocol.

In some cases modifications of the network packet may be necessary while routing, in which cases checksums are recalculated.

## Hop Counts

Under fault conditions packets can end up traversing a closed circuit. If nothing was done, eventually the number of packets circulating would build up until the network was congested to the point of failure. A time to live is a field that is decreased by one each time a packet goes through a network node. If the field reaches zero, routing has failed, and the packet is discarded.

Ethernet packets have no time-to-live field and so are subject to broadcast radiation in the presence of a switch loop.

## Length

There may be a field to identify the overall packet length. However, in some types of networks, the length is implied by the duration of transmission.

## Priority

Some networks implement quality of service which can prioritize some types of packets above others. This field indicates which packet queue should be used; a high priority queue is emptied more quickly than lower priority queues at points in the network where congestion is occurring.

## Payload

In general, payload is the data that is carried on behalf of an application. It is usually of variable length, up to a maximum that is set by the network protocol and sometimes the equipment on the route. Some networks can break a larger packet into smaller packets when necessary.

## Example: IP Packets

IP packets are composed of a header and payload. The IPv4 packet header consists of:

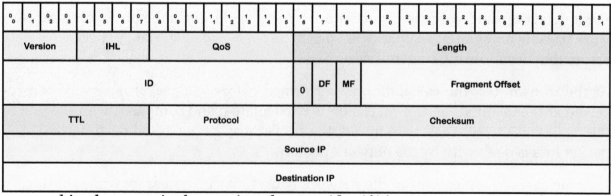

4 bits that contain the *version*, that specifies if it's an IPv4 or IPv6 packet,

1. 4 bits that contain the *Internet Header Length*, which is the length of the header in multiples of 4 bytes (e.g., 5 means 20 bytes).

2. 8 bits that contain the *Type of Service*, also referred to as Quality of Service (QoS), which describes what priority the packet should have.

3. 16 bits that contain the *length* of the packet in bytes.

4. 16 bits that contain an *identification tag* to help reconstruct the packet from several fragments.

5. 3 bits. The first contains a zero, followed by a flag that says whether the packet is allowed to be *fragmented* or not (DF: Don't fragment), and a flag to state whether more fragments of a packet follow (MF: More Fragments).

6. 13 bits that contain the *fragment offset*, a field to identify position of fragment within original packet.

7. 8 bits that contain the *Time to live* (TTL), which is the number of hops (router, computer or device along a network) the packet is allowed to pass before it dies (for example, a packet with a TTL of 16 will be allowed to go across 16 routers to get to its destination before it is discarded).

8. 8 bits that contain the *protocol* (TCP, UDP, ICMP, etc.)

9. 16 bits that contain the *Header Checksum,* a number used in error detection.

10. 32 bits that contain the *source IP address*.

11. 32 bits that contain the *destination address*.

After those 160 bits, optional flags can be added of varied length, which can change based on the protocol used, then the data that packet carries is added. An IP packet has no trailer. However, an IP packet is often carried as the payload inside an Ethernet frame, which has its own header and trailer.

Many networks do not provide guarantees of delivery, nonduplication of packets, or in-order delivery of packets, e.g., the UDP protocol of the Internet. However, it is possible to layer a transport protocol on top of the packet service that can provide such protection; TCP and UDP are the best examples of layer 4, the Transport Layer, of the seven layered OSI model.

## Example: the NASA Deep Space Network

The Consultative Committee for Space Data Systems (CCSDS) packet telemetry standard defines the protocol used for the transmission of spacecraft instrument data over the deep-space channel. Under this standard, an image or other data sent from a spacecraft instrument is transmitted using one or more packets.

## CCSDS Packet Definition

A packet is a block of data with length that can vary between successive packets, ranging from 7 to 65,542 bytes, including the packet header.

- Packetized data is transmitted via frames, which are fixed-length data blocks. The size of a frame, including frame header and control information, can range up to 2048 bytes.

- Packet sizes are fixed during the development phase.

Because packet lengths are variable but frame lengths are fixed, packet boundaries usually do not coincide with frame boundaries.

## Telecom Processing Notes

Data in a frame is typically protected from channel errors by error-correcting codes.

- Even when the channel errors exceed the correction capability of the error-correcting code, the presence of errors is nearly always detected by the error-correcting code or by a separate error-detecting code.

- Frames for which uncorrectable errors are detected are marked as undecodable and typically are deleted.

## Handling Data Loss

Deleted undecodable whole frames are the principal type of data loss that affects compressed data sets. In general, there would be little to gain from attempting to use compressed data from a frame marked as undecodable.

- When errors are present in a frame, the bits of the subband pixels are already decoded before the first bit error will remain intact, but all subsequent decoded bits in the segment usually will be completely corrupted; a single bit error is often just as disruptive as many bit errors.

- Furthermore, compressed data usually are protected by powerful, long-block-length error-correcting codes, which are the types of codes most likely to yield substantial fractions of bit errors throughout those frames that are undecodable.

Thus, frames with detected errors would be essentially unusable even if they were not deleted by the frame processor.

This data loss can be compensated for with the following mechanisms.

- If an erroneous frame escapes detection, the decompressor will blindly use the frame data as if they were reliable, whereas in the case of detected erroneous frames, the decompressor can base its reconstruction on incomplete, but not misleading, data.

- However, it is extremely rare for an erroneous frame to go undetected.

- For frames coded by the CCSDS Reed–Solomon code, fewer than 1 in 40,000 erroneous frames can escape detection.

- All frames not employing the Reed–Solomon code use a cyclic redundancy check (CRC) error-detecting code, which has an undetected frame-error rate of less than 1 in 32,000.

## Example: Radio and TV broadcasting

### MPEG Packetized Stream

Packetized Elementary Stream (PES) is a specification defined by the MPEG communication protocol that allows an elementary stream to be divided into packets. The elementary stream is packetized by encapsulating sequential data bytes from the elementary stream inside PES packet headers.

A typical method of transmitting elementary stream data from a video or audio encoder is to first create PES packets from the elementary stream data and then to encapsulate these PES packets inside an MPEG transport stream (TS) packets or an MPEG program stream (PS). The TS packets can then be multiplexed and transmitted using broadcasting techniques, such as those used in an ATSC and DVB.

### PES Packet Header

| Name | Size | Description |
|---|---|---|
| Packet start code prefix | 3 bytes | 0x000001 |
| Stream id | 1 byte | Examples: Audio streams (0xC0-0xDF), Video streams (0xE0-0xEF) |
| | | Note: The above 4 bytes is called the 32-bit start code. |
| PES Packet length | 2 bytes | Can be zero as in not specified for video streams in MPEG transport streams |
| Optional PES header | variable length | |
| Stuffing bytes | variable length | |
| Data | | See elementary stream. In the case of private streams the first byte of the payload is the sub-stream number. |

## Optional PES Header

| Name | Number of Bits | Description |
|---|---|---|
| Marker bits | 2 | **10** binary or 0x2 hex |
| Scrambling control | 2 | 00 implies not scrambled |
| Priority | 1 | |
| Data alignment indicator | 1 | 1 indicates that the PES packet header is immediately followed by the video start code or audio syncword |
| Copyright | 1 | 1 implies copyrighted |
| Original or Copy | 1 | 1 implies original |
| PTS DTS indicator | 2 | 11 = both present, 10 = only PTS |
| ESCR flag | 1 | |
| ES rate flag | 1 | |
| DSM trick mode flag | 1 | |
| Additional copy info flag | 1 | |
| CRC flag | 1 | |
| extension flag | 1 | |
| PES header length | 8 | gives the length of the remainder of the PES header |
| Optional fields | variable length | presence is determined by flag bits above |
| Stuffing Bytes | variable length | 0xff |

## NICAM

In order to provide mono "compatibility", the NICAM signal is transmitted on a sub-carrier alongside the sound carrier. This means that the FM or AM regular mono sound carrier is left alone for reception by monaural receivers.

A NICAM-based stereo-TV infrastructure can transmit a stereo TV programme as well as the mono "compatibility" sound at the same time, or can transmit two or three entirely different sound streams. This latter mode could be used to transmit audio in different languages, in a similar manner to that used for in-flight movies on international flights. In this mode, the user can select which soundtrack to listen to when watching the content by operating a "sound-select" control on the receiver.

NICAM offers the following possibilities. The mode is auto-selected by the inclusion of a 3-bit type field in the data-stream.

- One digital stereo sound channel.

- Two completely different digital mono sound channels.

- One digital mono sound channel and a 352 kbit/s data channel.

- One 704 kbit/s data channel.

The four other options could be implemented at a later date. Only the first two of the ones listed are known to be in general use however.

## NICAM Packet Transmission

The NICAM packet (except for the header) is scrambled with a nine-bit pseudo-random bit-generator before transmission.

- The topology of this pseudo-random generator yields a bitstream with a repetition period of 511 bits.

- The pseudo-random generator's polynomial is: $x^9 + x^4 + 1$.

- The pseudo-random generator is initialized with: 111111111.

Making the NICAM bitstream look more like white noise is important because this reduces signal patterning on adjacent TV channels.

- The NICAM header is not subject to scrambling. This is necessary so as to aid in locking on to the NICAM data stream and resynchronisation of the data stream at the receiver.

- At the start of each NICAM packet the pseudo-random bit generator's shift-register is reset to all-ones.

## References

- G. Schneider; J. Evans; K. Pinard. The Internet - Illustrated. published by Cengage Learning 26 Oct 2009, 296 pages, ISBN 0538750987, Available Titles Skills Assessment Manager (SAM) - Office 2010 Series Illustrated (Course Technology). Retrieved 2015-08-15

- Scantlebury, Roger (25 June 2013). "Internet pioneers airbrushed from history". The Guardian. Retrieved 1 August 2015

- L.A Lievrouw - Handbook of New Media: Student Edition (p.253) (edited by L.A Lievrouw, S.M. Livingstone), published by SAGE 2006 (abridged, reprint, revised), 475 pages, ISBN 1412918731 [Retrieved 2015-08-15]

- R. Oppliger. Internet and Intranet Security (p.12). Artech House, 1 Jan 2001, 403 pages, Artech House computer security series, ISBN 1580531660. Retrieved 2015-08-15

- "KDDI to Close VENUS-P International Public Data Communications Service", KDDI, 9 November 2005. Retrieved 3 September 2013

- "TransPAC3 - Asia-US High Performance International Networking", International Research Network Connections Program (IRNC), U.S. National Science Foundation, October 2011. Retrieved 3 September 2013

- Isaacson, Walter (2014). The Innovators: How a Group of Hackers, Geniuses, and Geeks Created the Digital Revolution. Simon & Schuster. p. 237. ISBN 9781476708690

- M. Ziewitz & I. Brown (2013). Research Handbook on Governance of the Internet. Edward Elgar Publishing. p. 7. ISBN 1849805040. Retrieved 2015-08-16

- Martin Weik - Fiber Optics Standard Dictionary Springer Science & Business Media 6 Dec 2012, 1219 pages, ISBN 1461560233 [Retrieved 2015-08-04]

# Information Management: An Integrated Study

Information management is the branch of information technology that deals with the infrastructure used to control the accumulation and transmission of information. A few of the significant topics studied in relation to information management are data modeling, computer data storage, ontology, knowledge organizations, etc. These topics are crucial for a complete understanding of the subject.

## Information Management

Information management (IM) concerns a cycle of organisational activity: the acquisition of information from one or more sources, the custodianship and the distribution of that information to those who need it, and its ultimate disposition through archiving or deletion.

This cycle of organisational involvement with information involves a variety of stakeholders: for example those who are responsible for assuring the quality, accessibility and utility of acquired information, those who are responsible for its safe storage and disposal, and those who need it for decision making. Stakeholders might have rights to originate, change, distribute or delete information according to organisational information management policies.

Information management embraces all the generic concepts of management, including: planning, organizing, structuring, processing, controlling, evaluation and reporting of information activities, all of which is needed in order to meet the needs of those with organisational roles or functions that depend on information.

Information management is closely related to, and overlaps with, the management of data, systems, technology, processes and – where the availability of information is critical to organisational success – strategy. This broad view of the realm of information management contrasts with the earlier, more traditional view, that the life cycle of managing information is an operational matter that requires specific procedures, organisational capabilities and standards that deal with information as a product or a service.

## History

### Emergent Ideas Out of Data Management

In the 1970s the management of information largely concerned matters closer to what would now be called data management: punched cards, magnetic tapes and other re-cord-keeping media, involving a life cycle of such formats requiring origination, distri-bution, backup, maintenance and disposal. At this time the huge potential of informa-tion technology began to be recognised: for example a single chip storing a whole book, or electronic mail moving messages instantly around the world, remarkable ideas at the time. With the proliferation of information technology and the extending reach of information systems in the 1980s and 1990s, information management took on a new form. Progressive businesses such as British Petroleum transformed the vocabulary of what was then "IT management", so that "systems analysts" became "business an-alysts", "monopoly supply" became a mixture of "insourcing" and "outsourcing", and the large IT function was transformed into "lean teams" that began to allow some agil-ity in the processes that harness information for business benefit. The scope of senior management interest in information at British Petroleum extended from the creation of value through improved business processes, based upon the effective management of information, permitting the implementation of appropriate information systems (or "applications") that were operated on IT infrastructure that was outsourced. In this way, information management was no longer a simple job that could be performed by anyone who had nothing else to do, it became highly strategic and a matter for senior management attention. An understanding of the technologies involved, an ability to manage information systems projects and business change well, and a willingness to align technology and business strategies all became necessary.

## Positioning Information Management in the Bigger Picture

In the transitional period leading up to the strategic view of information management, Venkatraman (a strong advocate of this process of transition and transformation, prof-fered a simple arrangement of ideas that succinctly brought data management, informa-tion management and knowledge management together) argued that:

- Data that is maintained in IT infrastructure has to be interpreted in order to render information.

- The information in our information systems has to be understood in order to emerge as knowledge.

- Knowledge allows managers to take effective decisions.

- Effective decisions have to lead to appropriate actions.

- Appropriate actions are expected to deliver meaningful results.

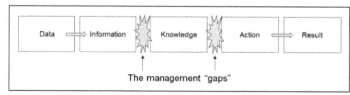

This simple model summarises a presentation by Venkatraman in 1996.

This is often referred to as the DIKAR model: Data, Information, Knowledge, Action and Result, it gives a strong clue as to the layers involved in aligning technology and organisational strategies, and it can be seen as a pivotal moment in changing attitudes to information management. The recognition that information management is an investment that must deliver meaningful results is important to all modern organisations that depend on information and good decision making for their success.

## Some Theoretical Background

## Behavioural and Organisational Theories

Clearly, good information management is crucial to the smooth working of organisations, and although there is no commonly accepted theory of information management per se, behavioural and organisational theories help. Following the behavioural science theory of management, mainly developed at Carnegie Mellon University and prominently supported by March and Simon, most of what goes on in modern organizations is actually information handling and decision making. One crucial factor in information handling and decision making is an individuals' ability to process information and to make decisions under limitations that might derive from the context: a person's age, the situational complexity, or a lack of requisite quality in the information that is at hand – all of which is exacerbated by the rapid advance of technology and the new kinds of system that it enables, especially as the social web emerges as a phenomenon that business cannot ignore. And yet, well before there was any general recognition of the importance of information management in organisations, March and Simon  argued that organizations have to be considered as cooperative systems, with a high level of information processing and a vast need for decision making at various levels. Instead of using the model of the "economic man", as advocated in classical theory  they proposed "administrative man" as an alternative, based on their argumentation about the cognitive limits of rationality. Additionally they proposed the notion of satisficing, which entails searching through the available alternatives until an acceptability threshold is met - another idea that still has currency.

## Economic Theory

In addition to the organisational factors mentioned by March and Simon, there are other issues that stem from economic and environmental dynamics. There is the cost of collecting and evaluating the information needed to take a decision, including the time and effort required. The transaction cost associated with information processes can be high. In particular, established organizational rules and procedures can prevent the taking of the most appropriate decision, leading to sub-optimum outcomes . This is an issue that has been presented as a major problem with bureaucratic organizations that lose the economies of strategic change because of entrenched attitudes.

# Strategic Information Management

## Background

According to the Carnegie Mellon School an organization's ability to process information is at the core of organizational and managerial competency, and an organization's strategies must be designed to improve information processing capability and as information systems that provide that capability became formalised and automated, competencies were severely tested at many levels. It was recognised that organisations needed to be able to learn and adapt in ways that were never so evident before and academics began to organise and publish definitive works concerning the strategic management of information, and information systems. Concurrently, the ideas of business process management and knowledge management although much of the optimistic early thinking about business process redesign has since been discredited in the information management literature.

## Aligning Technology and Business Strategy with Information Management

Venkatraman has provided a simple view of the requisite capabilities of an organisation that wants to manage information well – the DIKAR model. He also worked with others to understand how technology and business strategies could be appropriately aligned in order to identify specific capabilities that are needed. This work was paralleled by other writers in the world of consulting, practice and academia.

## A contemporary Portfolio Model for Information

Bytheway has collected and organised basic tools and techniques for information management in a single volume. At the heart of his view of information management is a portfolio model that takes account of the surging interest in external sources of information and the need to organise un-structured information external so as to make it useful.

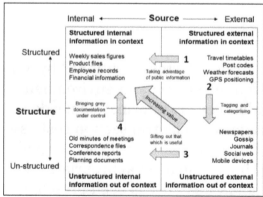

This portfolio model organizes issues of internal and external sourcing and management of information, that may be either structured or unstructured.

Such an information portfolio as this shows how information can be gathered and usefully organised, in four stages:

Stage 1: Taking advantage of public information: recognise and adopt well-structured external schemes of reference data, such as post codes, weather data, GPS positioning data and travel timetables, exemplified in the personal computing press.

Stage 2: Tagging the noise on the world wide web: use existing schemes such as post codes and GPS data or more typically by adding "tags", or construct a formal ontology that provides structure. Shirky provides an overview of these two approaches.

Stage 3: Sifting and analysing: in the wider world the generalised ontologies that are under development extend to hundreds of entities and hundreds of relations between them and provide the means to elicit meaning from large volumes of data. Structured data in databases works best when that structure reflects a higher-level information model – an ontology, or an entity-relationship model.

Stage 4: Structuring and archiving: with the large volume of data available from sources such as the social web and from the miniature telemetry systems used in personal health management, new ways to archive and then trawl data for meaningful information. Map-reduce methods, originating from functional programming, are a more recent way of eliciting information from large archival datasets that is becoming interesting to regular businesses that have very large data resources to work with, but it requires advanced multi-processor resources.

## Competencies to Manage Information Well

The Information Management Body of Knowledge was made available on the world wide web in 2004 and sets out to show that the required management competencies to derive real benefits from an investment in information are complex and multi-layered. The framework model that is the basis for understanding competencies comprises six "knowledge" areas and four "process" areas:

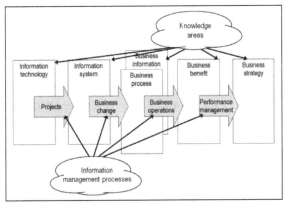

This framework is the basis of organising the "Information Management Body of Knowledge" first made available in 2004.

# The Information Management Knowledge Areas

The IMBOK is based on the argument that there are six areas of required management competency, two of which ("business process management" and "business information management") are very closely related.

- Information technology: The pace of change of technology and the pressure to constantly acquire the newest technological products can undermine the stability of the infrastructure that supports systems, and thereby optimises business processes and delivers benefits. It is necessary to manage the "supply side" and recognise that technology is, increasingly, becoming a commodity.

- Information system: While historically information systems were developed in-house, over the years it has become possible to acquire most of the software systems that an organisation needs from the software package industry. However, there is still the potential for competitive advantage from the implementation of new systems ideas that deliver to the strategic intentions of organisations.

- Business processes and Business information: Information systems are applied to business processes in order to improve them, and they bring data to the business that becomes useful as business information. Business process management is still seen as a relatively new idea because it is not universally adopted, and it has been difficult in many cases; business information management is even more of a challenge.

- Business benefit: What are the benefits that we are seeking? It is necessary not only to be brutally honest about what can be achieved, but also to ensure the active management and assessment of benefit delivery. Since the emergence and popularisation of the Balanced scorecard there has been huge interest in business performance management but not much serious effort has been made to relate business performance management to the benefits of information technology investments and the introduction of new information systems until the turn of the millennium.

- Business strategy: Although a long way from the workaday issues of managing information in organisations, strategy in most organisations simply has to be informed by information technology and information systems opportunities, whether to address poor performance or to improve differentiation and competitiveness. Strategic analysis tools such as the value chain and critical success factor analysis are directly dependent on proper attention to the information that is (or could be) managed.

# The Information Management Processes

Even with full capability and competency within the six knowledge areas, it is argued that things can still go wrong. The problem lies in the migration of ideas and information management value from one area of competency to another. Summarising what

Bytheway explains in some detail (and supported by selected secondary references):

- Projects: Information technology is without value until it is engineered into information systems that meet the needs of the business by means of good project management.

- Business change: The best information systems succeed in delivering benefits through the achievement of change within the business systems, but people do not appreciate change that makes new demands upon their skills in the ways that new information systems often do. Contrary to common expectations, there is some evidence that the public sector has succeeded with information technology induced business change.

- Business operations: With new systems in place, with business processes and business information improved, and with staff finally ready and able to work with new processes, then the business can get to work, even when new systems extend far beyond the boundaries of a single business.

- Performance management: Investments are no longer solely about financial results, financial success must be balanced with internal efficiency, customer satisfaction, and with organisational learning and development.

## Summary

There are always many ways to see a business, and the information management viewpoint is only one way. It is important to remember that other areas of business activity will also contribute to strategy – it is not only good information management that moves a business forwards. Corporate governance, human resource management, product development and marketing will all have an important role to play in strategic ways, and we must not see one domain of activity alone as the sole source of strategic success. On the other hand, corporate governance, human resource management, product development and marketing are all dependent on effective information management, and so in the final analysis our competency to manage information well, on the broad basis that is offered here, can be said to be predominant.

## Operationalising Information Management

### Managing Requisite Change

Organizations are often confronted with many information management challenges and issues at the operational level, especially when organisational change is engendered. The novelty of new systems architectures and a lack of experience with new styles of information management requires a level of organisational change management that is notoriously difficult to deliver. As a result of a general organisational reluctance to change, to enable new forms of information management, there might be (for example): a shortfall in the requisite resources, a failure to acknowledge new classes of information and the new procedures that use them, a lack of support from senior management leading to a loss of strategic vision, and even political manoeuvring that undermines the operation of the whole organisation. However, the implementation of new forms of information management should normally lead to operational benefits.

## The Early Work Of Galbraith

In early work, taking an information processing view of organisation design, Jay Galbraith has identified five tactical areas to increase information processing capacity and reduce the need for information processing.

- Developing, implementing, and monitoring all aspects of the "environment" of an organization.

- Creation of slack resources so as to decrease the load on the overall hierarchy of resources and to reduce information processing relating to overload.

- Creation of self-contained tasks with defined boundaries and that can achieve proper closure, and with all the resources at hand required to perform the task.

- Recognition of lateral relations that cut across functional units, so as to move decision power to the process instead of fragmenting it within the hierarchy.

- Investment in vertical information systems that route information flows for a specific task (or set of tasks) in accordance to the applied business logic.

## The Matrix Organisation

The lateral relations concept leads to an organizational form that is different from the simple hierarchy, the "matrix organization". This brings together the vertical (hierarchical) view of an organisation and the horizontal (product or project) view of the work that it does visible to the outside world. The creation of a matrix organization is one management response to a persistent fluidity of external demand, avoiding multifarious and spurious responses to episodic demands that tend to be dealt with individually.

# IBM Information Management System

IBM Information Management System (IMS) is a joint hierarchical database and information management system with extensive transaction processing capabilities.

## History

IBM designed the IMS with Rockwell and Caterpillar starting in 1966 for the Apollo program, where it was used to inventory the very large bill of materials (BOM) for the Saturn V moon rocket and Apollo space vehicle.

The first "IMS READY" message appeared on an IBM 2740 terminal in Downey, California, on 14 August 1968. In the interim period, IMS has undergone many developments as IBM System/360 technology evolved into the current z/OS and System z9 and z10 technologies. For example, IMS now supports the Java programming language, JDBC, XML, and, since late 2005, web services.

Vern Watts was IMS's chief architect for many years. Watts joined IBM in 1956 and worked at IBM's Silicon Valley development labs until his death on April 4, 2009. He had continuously worked on IMS since the 1960s.

## Database

The IMS Database component stores data using a hierarchical model, which is quite different from IBM's later released relational database, DB2. In IMS, the hierarchical model is implemented using blocks of data known as segments. Each segment can contain several pieces of data, which are called fields. For example, a customer database may have a root segment (or the segment at the top of the hierarchy) with fields such as phone, name, and age. Child segments may be added underneath another segment, for instance, one order segment under each customer segment representing each order a customer has placed with a company. Likewise, each order segment may have many children segments for each item on the order. Unlike other databases, you do not need to define all of the data in a segment to IMS. A segment may be defined with a size of 40 bytes but only define one field that is six bytes long as a key field that you can use to find the segment when performing queries. IMS will retrieve and save all 40 bytes as directed by a program but may not understand (or care) what the other bytes represent. In practice, often all data in a segment may map to a COBOL copybook. Besides DL/I query usage, a field may be defined in IMS so that the data can be hidden from certain applications for security reasons. The database component of IMS can be purchased standalone, without the transaction manager component, and used by systems such as CICS.

There are three basic forms of IMS hierarchical databases:

### "Full Function" Databases

- Directly descended from the Data Language Interface (DL/I) databases originally developed for Apollo, full function databases can have primary and secondary indexes, accessed using DL/I calls from an application program, like SQL calls to DB2 or Oracle.

- Full function databases can be accessed by a variety of methods, although Hierarchical Direct (HDAM) and Hierarchical Indexed Direct (HIDAM) dominate. The other formats are Simple Hierarchical Indexed Sequential (SHISAM), Hierarchical Sequential (HSAM), and Hierarchical Indexed Sequential (HISAM).

- Full function databases store data using VSAM, a native z/OS access method, or Overflow Sequential (OSAM), an IMS-specific access method that optimizes the I/O channel program for IMS access patterns. In particular, OSAM performance benefits from sequential access of IMS databases (OSAM Sequential Buffering).

## "Fast Path" Databases

- Fast Path databases are optimized for extremely high transaction rates. Data Entry Databases (DEDBs) and Main Storage Databases (MSDBs) are the two types of Fast Path databases. DEDBs use a direct (randomizer) access technique similar to Full Function HDAM and IMS V12 provided a DEDB Secondary Index function. MSDBs do not support secondary indexing. Virtual Storage Option (VSO) DEDBs can replace MSDBs in modern IMS releases, so MSDBs are gradually disappearing.

DEDB performance comes from use of high performance (Media Manager) access method, asynchronous write after commit, and optimized code paths. Logging is minimized because no data is updated on disk until commit, so UNDO (before image) logging is not needed, nor is a backout function. Uncommitted changes can simply be discarded. Starting with IMS Version 11, DEDBs can use z/OS 64-bit storage for database buffers. DEDBs architecture includes a Unit of Work (UOW) concept which made an effective online reorganization utility simple to implement. This function is included in the base product.

## High Availability Large Databases (HALDBs)

- IMS V7 introduced HALDBs, an extension of IMS full function databases to provide better availability, better handling of extremely large data volumes, and, with IMS V9, online reorganization to support continuous availability. (Third party tools exclusively provided online reorganization prior to IMS V9.) A HALDB can store in excess of 40 terabytes of data.

Fast path DEDBs can only be built atop VSAM. DL/I databases can be built atop either VSAM or OSAM, with some restrictions depending on database organization. Although the maximum size of a z/OS VSAM dataset increased to 128 TB a few years ago, IMS still limits a VSAM dataset to 4 GB (and OSAM to 8 GB). This "limitation" simply means that IMS customers will use multiple datasets for large amounts of data. VSAM and OSAM are usually referred to as the access methods, and the IMS "logical" view of the database is referred to as the database "organization" (HDAM, HIDAM, HISAM, etc.) Internally the data are linked using 4-byte pointers or addresses. In the database datasets (DBDSs) the pointers are referred to as RBAs (relative byte addresses).

Collectively the database-related IMS capabilities are often called IMS DB. IMS DB has grown and evolved over nearly four decades to support myriad business needs. IMS, with assistance from z/OS hardware - the Coupling Facility - supports N-way inter-IMS sharing of databases. Many large configurations involve multiple IMS systems managing common databases, a technique providing for scalable growth and system redundancy in the event of hardware or software failures.

## Transaction Manager

IMS is also a robust transaction manager (IMS TM, also known as IMS DC) — one of the "big three" classic transaction managers along with CICS and BEA (now Oracle) Tuxedo. A transaction manager interacts with an end user (connected through VTAM or TCP/IP, including 3270 and Web user interfaces) or another application, processes a business function (such as a banking account withdrawal), and maintains state throughout the process, making sure that the system records the business function correctly to a data store. Thus IMS TM is quite like a Web application, operating through a CGI program (for example), to provide an interface to query or update a database. IMS TM typically uses either IMS DB or DB2 as its backend database. When used alone with DB2 the IMS TM component can be purchased without the IMS DB component.

IMS TM uses a messaging and queuing paradigm. An IMS control program receives a transaction entered from a terminal (or Web browser or other application) and then stores the transaction on a message queue (in memory or in a dataset). IMS then invokes its scheduler on the queued transaction to start the business application program in a message processing region. The message processing region retrieves the transaction from the IMS message queue and processes it, reading and updating IMS and/or DB2 databases, assuring proper recording of the transaction. Then, if required, IMS enqueues a response message back onto the IMS message queue. Once the output message is complete and available the IMS control program sends it back to the originating terminal. IMS TM can handle this whole process thousands (or even tens of thousands) of times per second. A recently completed[year missing] IBM benchmark demonstrated the ability to process 100,000 transactions per second on a single IMS system.

## Application

Prior to IMS, businesses and governments had to write their own transaction processing environments. IMS TM provides a straightforward, easy-to-use, reliable, standard environment for high performance transaction execution. In fact, much of the world's banking industry relies on IMS, including the U.S. Federal Reserve. For example, chances are that withdrawing money from an automated teller machine (ATM) will trigger an IMS transaction. Several Chinese banks have recently purchased IMS to support that country's burgeoning financial industry.

Today IMS complements DB2, IBM's relational database system, introduced in 1982. In general, IMS performs faster than DB2 for the common tasks but may require more programming effort to design and maintain for non-primary duties. Relational data-bases have generally proven superior in cases where the requirements, especially reporting requirements, change frequently or require a variety of viewpoint "angles" outside the primary or original function.

A relational "data warehouse" may be used to supplement an IMS database. For example, IMS may provide primary ATM transactions because it performs well for such a specific task. However, nightly copies of the IMS data may be copied to relational systems such that a variety of reports and processing tasks may be performed on the data. This allows each kind of database to focus best on its relative strength.

# Data Modeling

Data modeling in software engineering is the process of creating a data model for an information system by applying formal data modeling techniques.

## Overview

Data modeling is a process used to define and analyze data requirements needed to support the business processes within the scope of corresponding information systems in organizations. Therefore, the process of data modeling involves professional data modelers working closely with business stakeholders, as well as potential users of the information system.

There are three different types of data models produced while progressing from requirements to the actual database to be used for the information system. The data requirements are initially recorded as a conceptual data model which is essentially a set of technology independent specifications about the data and is used to discuss initial requirements with the business stakeholders. The conceptual model is then translated into a logical data model, which documents structures of the data that can be implemented in databases. Implementation of one conceptual data model may require multiple logical data models. The last step in data modeling is transforming the logical data model to a physical data model that organizes the data into tables, and accounts for access, performance and storage details. Data modeling defines not just data elements, but also their structures and the relationships between them.

Data modeling techniques and methodologies are used to model data in a standard, consistent, predictable manner in order to manage it as a resource. The use of data modeling standards is strongly recommended for all projects requiring a standard means of defining and analyzing data within an organization, e.g., using data modeling:

- to assist business analysts, programmers, testers, manual writers, IT package selectors, engineers, managers, related organizations and clients to understand and use an agreed semi-formal model the concepts of the organization and how they relate to one another.

- To manage data as a resource.

- For the integration of information systems.

- For designing databases/data warehouses (aka data repositories).

Data modeling may be performed during various types of projects and in multiple phases of projects. Data models are progressive; there is no such thing as the final data model for a business or application. Instead a data model should be considered a living document that will change in response to a changing business. The data models should ideally be stored in a repository so that they can be retrieved, expanded, and edited over time. Whitten et al. (2004) determined two types of data modeling:

- Strategic data modeling: This is part of the creation of an information systems strategy, which defines an overall vision and architecture for information systems is defined. Information engineering is a methodology that embraces this approach.

- Data modeling during systems analysis: In systems analysis logical data models are created as part of the development of new databases.

Data modeling is also used as a technique for detailing business requirements for specific databases. It is sometimes called database modeling because a data model is eventually implemented in a database.

## Data Modeling Topics

## Data Models

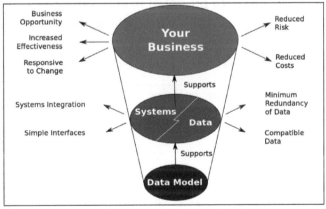

How data models deliver benefit.

Data models provide a structure for data used within information systems by providing specific definition and format. If a data model is used consistently across systems then compatibility of data can be achieved. If the same data structures are used to store and access data then different applications can share data seamlessly. The results of this are indicated in the diagram. However, systems and interfaces often cost more than they should, to build, operate, and maintain. They may also constrain the business rather than support it. This may occur when the quality of the data models implemented in systems and interfaces is poor.

- Business rules, specific to how things are done in a particular place, are often fixed in the structure of a data model. This means that small changes in the way business is conducted lead to large changes in computer systems and interfaces. So, business rules need to be implemented in a flexible way that does not result in complicated dependencies, rather the data model should be flexible enough so that changes in the business can be implemented within the data model in a relatively quick and efficient way.

- Entity types are often not identified, or are identified incorrectly. This can lead to replication of data, data structure and functionality, together with the attendant costs of that duplication in development and maintenance.Therefore, data definitions should be made as explicit and easy to understand as possible to minimize misinterpretation and duplication.

- Data models for different systems are arbitrarily different. The result of this is that complex interfaces are required between systems that share data. These interfaces can account for between 25-70% of the cost of current systems. Required interfaces should be considered inherently while designing a data model, as a data model on its own would not be usable without interfaces within different systems.

- Data cannot be shared electronically with customers and suppliers, because the structure and meaning of data has not been standardised. To obtain optimal value from an implemented data model, it is very important to define standards that will ensure that data models will both meet business needs and be consistent.

## Conceptual, Logical and Physical Schemas

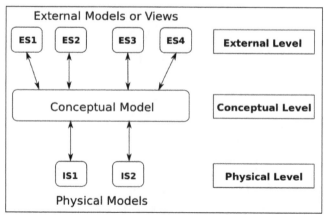

The ANSI/SPARC three level architecture. This shows that a data model can be an external model (or view), a conceptual model, or a physical model. This is not the only way to look at data models, but it is a useful way, particularly when comparing models.

In 1975 ANSI described three kinds of data-model instance:

- Conceptual schema: describes the semantics of a domain (the scope of the model). For example, it may be a model of the interest area of an organization or of an industry. This consists of entity classes, representing kinds of things of significance in the domain, and relationships assertions about associations between pairs of entity classes. A conceptual schema specifies the kinds of facts or propositions that can be expressed using the model. In that sense, it defines the allowed expressions in an artificial "language" with a scope that is limited by the scope of the model. Simply described, a conceptual schema is the first step in organizing the data requirements.

- Logical schema: describes the structure of some domain of information. This consists of descriptions of (for example) tables, columns, object-oriented classes, and XML tags. The logical schema and conceptual schema are sometimes implemented as one and the same.

- Physical schema: describes the physical means used to store data. This is concerned with partitions, CPUs, tablespaces, and the like.

According to ANSI, this approach allows the three perspectives to be relatively independent of each other. Storage technology can change without affecting either the logical or the conceptual schema. The table/column structure can change without (necessarily) affecting the conceptual schema. In each case, of course, the structures must remain consistent across all schemas of the same data model.

## Data Modeling Process

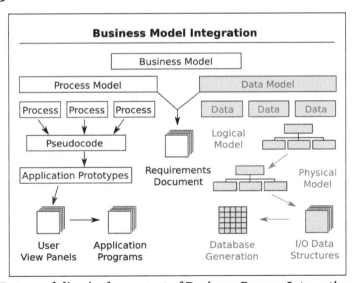

Data modeling in the context of Business Process Integration.

In the context of business process integration, data modeling complements business process modeling, and ultimately results in database generation.

The process of designing a database involves producing the previously described three types of schemas - conceptual, logical, and physical. The database design documented in these schemas are converted through a Data Definition Language, which can then be used to generate a database. A fully attributed data model contains detailed attributes (descriptions) for every entity within it. The term "database design" can describe many different parts of the design of an overall database system. Principally, and most correctly, it can be thought of as the logical design of the base data structures used to store the data. In the relational model these are the tables and views. In an object database the entities and relationships map directly to object classes and named relationships. However, the term "database design" could also be used to apply to the overall process of designing, not just the base data structures, but also the forms and queries used as part of the overall database application within the Database Management System or DBMS.

In the process, system interfaces account for 25% to 70% of the development and support costs of current systems. The primary reason for this cost is that these systems do not share a common data model. If data models are developed on a system by system basis, then not only is the same analysis repeated in overlapping areas, but further analysis must be performed to create the interfaces between them. Most systems within an organization contain the same basic data, redeveloped for a specific purpose. Therefore, an efficiently designed basic data model can minimize rework with minimal modifications for the purposes of different systems within the organization

## Modeling Methodologies

Data models represent information areas of interest. While there are many ways to create data models, according to Len Silverston (1997) only two modeling methodologies stand out, top-down and bottom-up:

- Bottom-up models or View Integration models are often the result of a reengineering effort. They usually start with existing data structures forms, fields on application screens, or reports. These models are usually physical, application-specific, and incomplete from an enterprise perspective. They may not promote data sharing, especially if they are built without reference to other parts of the organization.

- Top-down logical data models, on the other hand, are created in an abstract way by getting information from people who know the subject area. A system may not implement all the entities in a logical model, but the model serves as a reference point or template.

Sometimes models are created in a mixture of the two methods: by considering the data needs and structure of an application and by consistently referencing a subject-area model. Unfortunately, in many environments the distinction between a logical data model and a physical data model is blurred. In addition, some CASE tools don't make a distinction between logical and physical data models.

## Entity Relationship Diagrams

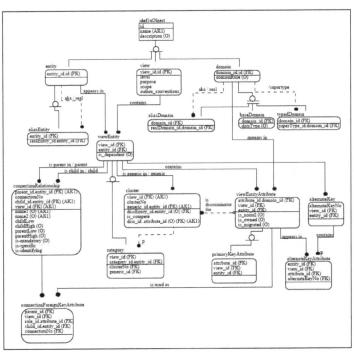

Example of an IDEF1X Entity relationship diagrams used to model IDEF1X itself. The name of the view is mm. The domain hierarchy and constraints are also given. The constraints are expressed as sentences in the formal theory of the meta model.

There are several notations for data modeling. The actual model is frequently called "Entity relationship model", because it depicts data in terms of the entities and relationships described in the data. An entity-relationship model (ERM) is an abstract conceptual representation of structured data. Entity-relationship modeling is a relational schema database modeling method, used in software engineering to produce a type of conceptual data model (or semantic data model) of a system, often a relational database, and its requirements in a top-down fashion.

These models are being used in the first stage of information system design during the requirements analysis to describe information needs or the type of information that is to be stored in a database. The data modeling technique can be used to describe any ontology (i.e. an overview and classifications of used terms and their relationships) for a certain universe of discourse i.e. area of interest.

Several techniques have been developed for the design of data models. While these methodologies guide data modelers in their work, two different people using the same methodology will often come up with very different results. Most notable are:

- Bachman diagrams

- Barker's notation

- Chen's Notation

- Data Vault Modeling

- Extended Backus–Naur form

- IDEF1X

- Object-relational mapping

- Object-Role Modeling

- Relational Model

- Relational Model/Tasmania

## Generic Data Modeling

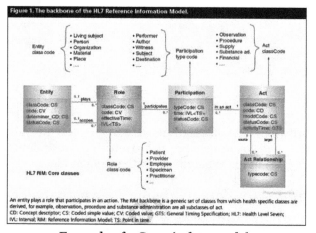

Example of a Generic data model.

Generic data models are generalizations of conventional data models. They define standardized general relation types, together with the kinds of things that may be related by such a relation type. The definition of generic data model is similar to the definition of a natural language. For example, a generic data model may define relation types such as a 'classification relation', being a binary relation between an individual thing and a kind of thing (a class) and a 'part-whole relation', being a binary relation between two things, one with the role of part, the other with the role of whole, regardless the kind of things that are related.

Given an extensible list of classes, this allows the classification of any individual thing and to specify part-whole relations for any individual object. By standardization of an extensible list of relation types, a generic data model enables the expression of an unlimited number of kinds of facts and will approach the capabilities of natural languages.

Conventional data models, on the other hand, have a fixed and limited domain scope, because the instantiation (usage) of such a model only allows expressions of kinds of facts that are predefined in the model.

## Semantic Data Modeling

The logical data structure of a DBMS, whether hierarchical, network, or relational, cannot totally satisfy the requirements for a conceptual definition of data because it is limited in scope and biased toward the implementation strategy employed by the DBMS.

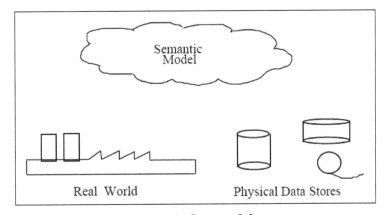

Semantic data models.

Therefore, the need to define data from a conceptual view has led to the development of semantic data modeling techniques. That is, techniques to define the meaning of data within the context of its interrelationships with other data. As illustrated in the figure the real world, in terms of resources, ideas, events, etc., are symbolically defined within physical data stores. A semantic data model is an abstraction which defines how the stored symbols relate to the real world. Thus, the model must be a true representation of the real world.

A semantic data model can be used to serve many purposes, such as:

- Planning of data resources.

- Building of shareable databases.

- Evaluation of vendor software.

- Integration of existing databases.

The overall goal of semantic data models is to capture more meaning of data by integrating relational concepts with more powerful abstraction concepts known from the Artificial Intelligence field. The idea is to provide high level modeling primitives as integral part of a data model in order to facilitate the representation of real world situations.

# Computer Data Storage

Computer data storage, often called storage or memory, is a technology consisting of computer components and recording media used to retain digital data. It is a core function and fundamental component of computers.

The central processing unit (CPU) of a computer is what manipulates data by performing computations. In practice, almost all computers use a storage hierarchy, which puts fast but expensive and small storage options close to the CPU and slower but larger and cheaper options farther away. Generally the fast volatile technologies (which lose data when off power) are referred to as "memory", while slower persistent technologies are referred to as "storage"; however, "memory" is sometimes also used when referring to persistent storage.

In the Von Neumann architecture, the CPU consists of two main parts: The control unit and the arithmetic / logic unit (ALU). The former controls the flow of data between the CPU and memory, while the latter performs arithmetic and logical operations on data.

## Functionality

Without a significant amount of memory, a computer would merely be able to perform fixed operations and immediately output the result. It would have to be reconfigured to change its behavior. This is acceptable for devices such as desk calculators, digital signal processors, and other specialized devices. Von Neumann machines differ in having a memory in which they store their operating instructions and data. Such computers are more versatile in that they do not need to have their hardware reconfigured for each new program, but can simply be reprogrammed with new in-memory instructions; they also tend to be simpler to design, in that a relatively simple processor may keep state between successive computations to build up complex procedural results. Most modern computers are von Neumann machines.

## Data Organization and Representation

A modern digital computer represents data using the binary numeral system. Text, numbers, pictures, audio, and nearly any other form of information can be converted into a string of bits, or binary digits, each of which has a value of 1 or 0. The most common unit of storage is the byte, equal to 8 bits. A piece of information can be handled by any computer or device whose storage space is large enough to accommodate the binary representation of the piece of information, or simply data. For example, the complete works of Shakespeare, about 1250 pages in print, can be stored in about five megabytes (40 million bits) with one byte per character.

Data is encoded by assigning a bit pattern to each character, digit, or multimedia object. Many standards exist for encoding (e.g., character encodings like ASCII, image encodings like JPEG, video encodings like MPEG-4).

By adding bits to each encoded unit, redundancy allows the computer to both detect errors in coded data and correct them based on mathematical algorithms. Errors generally occur in low probabilities due to random bit value flipping, or "physical bit fatigue", loss of the physical bit in storage its ability to maintain distinguishable value (0 or 1), or due to errors in inter or intra-computer communication. A random bit flip (e.g., due to random radiation) is typically corrected upon detection. A bit, or a group of malfunctioning physical bits (not always the specific defective bit is known; group definition depends on specific storage device) is typically automatically fenced-out, taken out of use by the device, and replaced with another functioning equivalent group in the device, where the corrected bit values are restored (if possible). The cyclic redundancy check (CRC) method is typically used in communications and storage for error detection. A detected error is then retried.

Data compression methods allow in many cases (such as a database) to represent a string of bits by a shorter bit string ("compress") and reconstruct the original string ("decompress") when needed. This utilizes substantially less storage (tens of percents) for many types of data at the cost of more computation (compress and decompress when needed). Analysis of trade-off between storage cost saving and costs of related computations and possible delays in data availability is done before deciding whether to keep certain data compressed or not.

For security reasons certain types of data (e.g., credit-card information) may be kept encrypted in storage to prevent the possibility of unauthorized information reconstruction from chunks of storage snapshots.

## Hierarchy of Storage

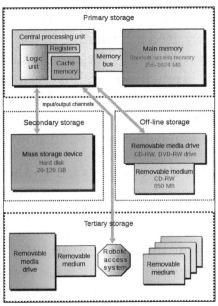

Various forms of storage, divided according to their distance from the central processing unit. The fundamental components of a general-purpose computer are arithmetic and logic unit, control circuitry, storage space, and input/output devices. Technology and capacity as in common home computers around 2005.

## Primary Storage

Primary storage (also known as main memory or internal memory), often referred to simply as memory, is the only one directly accessible to the CPU. The CPU continuously reads instructions stored there and executes them as required. Any data actively operated on is also stored there in uniform manner.

Historically, early computers used delay lines, Williams tubes, or rotating magnetic drums as primary storage. By 1954, those unreliable methods were mostly replaced by magnetic core memory. Core memory remained dominant until the 1970s, when advances in integrated circuit technology allowed semiconductor memory to become economically competitive.

This led to modern random-access memory (RAM). It is small-sized, light, but quite expensive at the same time. (The particular types of RAM used for primary storage are also volatile, i.e. they lose the information when not powered).

Traditionally there are two more sub-layers of the primary storage, besides main large-capacity RAM:

- Processor registers are located inside the processor. Each register typically holds a word of data (often 32 or 64 bits). CPU instructions instruct the arithmetic logic unit to perform various calculations or other operations on this data (or with the help of it). Registers are the fastest of all forms of computer data storage.

- Processor cache is an intermediate stage between ultra-fast registers and much slower main memory. It was introduced solely to improve the performance of computers. Most actively used information in the main memory is just duplicated in the cache memory, which is faster, but of much lesser capacity. On the other hand, main memory is much slower, but has a much greater storage capacity than processor registers. Multi-level hierarchical cache setup is also commonly used—primary cache being smallest, fastest and located inside the processor; secondary cache being somewhat larger and slower.

Main memory is directly or indirectly connected to the central processing unit via a memory bus. It is actually two buses (not on the diagram): an address bus and a data bus. The CPU firstly sends a number through an address bus, a number called memory address, that indicates the desired location of data. Then it reads or writes the data in the memory cells using the data bus. Additionally, a memory management unit (MMU) is a small device between CPU and RAM recalculating the actual memory address, for example to provide an abstraction of virtual memory or other tasks.

As the RAM types used for primary storage are volatile (uninitialized at start up), a computer containing only such storage would not have a source to read instructions from, in order to start the computer. Hence, non-volatile primary storage containing a small startup program (BIOS) is used to bootstrap the computer, that is, to read a larger program from non-volatile secondary storage to RAM and start to execute it. A non-volatile technology used for this purpose is called ROM, for read-only memory (the terminology may be somewhat confusing as most ROM types are also capable of random access).

Many types of "ROM" are not literally read only, as updates to them are possible; however it is slow and memory must be erased in large portions before it can be re-written. Some embedded systems run programs directly from ROM (or similar), because such programs are rarely changed. Standard computers do not store non-rudimentary programs in ROM, and rather, use large capacities of secondary storage, which is non-volatile as well, and not as costly.

Recently, primary storage and secondary storage in some uses refer to what was historically called, respectively, secondary storage and tertiary storage.

## Secondary Storage

A hard disk drive with protective cover removed.

Secondary storage (also known as external memory or auxiliary storage), differs from primary storage in that it is not directly accessible by the CPU. The computer usually uses its input/output channels to access secondary storage and transfers the desired data using intermediate area in primary storage. Secondary storage does not lose the data when the device is powered down—it is non-volatile. Per unit, it is typically also two orders of magnitude less expensive than primary storage. Modern computer systems typically have two orders of magnitude more secondary storage than primary storage and data are kept for a longer time there.

In modern computers, hard disk drives are usually used as secondary storage. The time taken to access a given byte of information stored on a hard disk is typically a few thousandths of a second, or milliseconds. By contrast, the time taken to access a given byte of information stored in random-access memory is measured in billionths of a second, or nanoseconds. This illustrates the significant access-time difference which distinguishes solid-state memory from rotating magnetic storage devices: hard disks are typically about a million times slower than memory. Rotating optical storage devices, such as CD and DVD drives, have even longer access times. With disk drives, once the disk read/write head reaches the proper placement and the data of interest rotates under it, subsequent data on the track are very fast to access. To reduce the seek time and rotational latency, data are transferred to and from disks in large contiguous blocks.

When data reside on disk, blocking access to hide latency offers an opportunity to design efficient external memory algorithms. Sequential or block access on disks is orders of magnitude faster than random access, and many sophisticated paradigms have been developed to design efficient algorithms based upon sequential and block access. Another way to reduce the I/O bottleneck is to use multiple disks in parallel in order to increase the bandwidth between primary and secondary memory.

Some other examples of secondary storage technologies are flash memory (e.g. USB flash drives or keys), floppy disks, magnetic tape, paper tape, punched cards, standalone RAM disks, and Iomega Zip drives.

The secondary storage is often formatted according to a file system format, which provides the abstraction necessary to organize data into files and directories, providing also additional information (called metadata) describing the owner of a certain file, the access time, the access permissions, and other information.

Most computer operating systems use the concept of virtual memory, allowing utilization of more primary storage capacity than is physically available in the system. As the primary memory fills up, the system moves the least-used chunks (pages) to secondary storage devices (to a swap file or page file), retrieving them later when they are needed. As more of these retrievals from slower secondary storage are necessary, the more the overall system performance is degraded.

## Tertiary Storage

A large tape library, with tape cartridges placed on shelves in the front, and a robotic arm moving in the back. Visible height of the library is about 180 cm.

Tertiary storage or tertiary memory provides a third level of storage. Typically, it involves a robotic mechanism which will mount (insert) and dismount removable mass storage media into a storage device according to the system's demands; this data is often copied to secondary storage before use. It is primarily used for archiving rarely accessed information since it is much slower than secondary storage (e.g. 5–60 seconds vs. 1–10 milliseconds). This is primarily useful for extraordinarily large data stores, accessed without human operators. Typical examples include tape libraries and optical jukeboxes.

When a computer needs to read information from the tertiary storage, it will first consult a catalog database to determine which tape or disc contains the information. Next, the computer will instruct a robotic arm to fetch the medium and place it in a drive. When the computer has finished reading the information, the robotic arm will return the medium to its place in the library.

Tertiary storage is also known as nearline storage because it is "near to online". The formal distinction between online, nearline, and offline storage is:

- Online storage is immediately available for I/O.

- Nearline storage is not immediately available, but can be made online quickly without human intervention.

- Offline storage is not immediately available, and requires some human intervention to become online.

For example, always-on spinning hard disk drives are online storage, while spinning drives that spin down automatically, such as in massive arrays of idle disks (MAID), are nearline storage. Removable media such as tape cartridges that can be automatically loaded, as in tape libraries, are nearline storage, while tape cartridges that must be manually loaded are offline storage.

## Off-line Storage

Off-line storage is a computer data storage on a medium or a device that is not under the control of a processing unit. The medium is recorded, usually in a secondary or tertiary storage device, and then physically removed or disconnected. It must be inserted or connected by a human operator before a computer can access it again. Unlike tertiary storage, it cannot be accessed without human interaction.

Off-line storage is used to transfer information, since the detached medium can be easily physically transported. Additionally, in case a disaster, for example a fire, destroys the original data, a medium in a remote location will probably be unaffected, enabling disaster recovery. Off-line storage increases general information security, since it is physically inaccessible from a computer, and data confidentiality or integrity cannot be affected by computer-based attack techniques. Also, if the information stored for archival purposes is rarely accessed, off-line storage is less expensive than tertiary storage.

In modern personal computers, most secondary and tertiary storage media are also used for off-line storage. Optical discs and flash memory devices are most popular, and to much lesser extent removable hard disk drives. In enterprise uses, magnetic tape is predominant. Older examples are floppy disks, Zip disks, or punched cards.

## Characteristics of Storage

A 1GB DDR RAM module (detail).

Storage technologies at all levels of the storage hierarchy can be differentiated by evaluating certain core characteristics as well as measuring characteristics specific to a particular implementation. These core characteristics are volatility, mutability, accessibility, and addressability. For any particular implementation of any storage technology, the characteristics worth measuring are capacity and performance.

## Storage Media

As of 2011, the most commonly used data storage technologies are semiconductor, magnetic, and optical, while paper still sees some limited usage. Media is a common name for what actually holds the data in the storage device. Some other fundamental storage technologies have also been used in the past or are proposed for development.

## Semiconductor

Semiconductor memory uses semiconductor-based integrated circuits to store information. A semiconductor memory chip may contain millions of tiny transistors or capacitors. Both volatile and non-volatile forms of semiconductor memory exist. In modern computers, primary storage almost exclusively consists of dynamic volatile semiconductor memory or dynamic random-access memory. Since the turn of the century, a type of non-volatile semiconductor memory known as flash memory has steadily gained share as off-line storage for home computers. Non-volatile semiconductor memory is also used for secondary storage in various advanced electronic devices and specialized computers.

As early as 2006, notebook and desktop computer manufacturers started using flash-based solid-state drives (SSDs) as default configuration options for the secondary storage either in addition to or instead of the more traditional HDD.

## Magnetic

Magnetic storage uses different patterns of magnetization on a magnetically coated surface to store information. Magnetic storage is non-volatile. The information is accessed using one or more read/write heads which may contain one or more recording transducers. A read/write head only covers a part of the surface so that the head or medium or both must be moved relative to another in order to access data. In modern computers, magnetic storage will take these forms:

- Magnetic disk:

    o  Floppy disk, used for off-line storage.

    o  Hard disk drive, used for secondary storage.

- Magnetic tape, used for tertiary and off-line storage.

- Carousel memory (magnetic rolls).

In early computers, magnetic storage was also used as:

- Primary storage in a form of magnetic memory, or core memory, core rope memory, thin-film memory and/or twistor memory.

- Tertiary (e.g. NCR CRAM) or off line storage in the form of magnetic cards.

- Magnetic tape was then often used for secondary storage.

## Optical

Optical storage, the typical optical disc, stores information in deformities on the surface of a circular disc and reads this information by illuminating the surface with a laser diode and observing the reflection. Optical disc storage is non-volatile. The deformities may be permanent (read only media), formed once (write once media) or reversible (recordable or read/write media). The following forms are currently in common use:

- CD, CD-ROM, DVD, BD-ROM: Read only storage, used for mass distribution of digital information (music, video, computer programs).

- CD-R, DVD-R, DVD+R, BD-R: Write once storage, used for tertiary and off-line storage.

- CD-RW, DVD-RW, DVD+RW, DVD-RAM, BD-RE: Slow write, fast read storage, used for tertiary and off-line storage.

- Ultra Density Optical or UDO is similar in capacity to BD-R or BD-RE and is slow write, fast read storage used for tertiary and off-line storage.

Magneto-optical disc storage is optical disc storage where the magnetic state on a ferromagnetic surface stores information. The information is read optically and written by combining magnetic and optical methods. Magneto-optical disc storage is non-volatile, sequential access, slow write, fast read storage used for tertiary and off-line storage.

3D optical data storage has also been proposed.

## Paper

Paper data storage, typically in the form of paper tape or punched cards, has long been used to store information for automatic processing, particularly before general-purpose computers existed. Information was recorded by punching holes into the paper or cardboard medium and was read mechanically (or later optically) to determine whether a particular location on the medium was solid or contained a hole. A few technologies allow people to make marks on paper that are easily read by machine—these are widely used for tabulating votes and grading standardized tests. Barcodes made it possible for any object that was to be sold or transported to have some computer readable information securely attached to it.

## Other Storage Media or Substrates

Vacuum tube memory:

> A Williams tube used a cathode ray tube, and a Selectron tube used a large vacuum tube to store information. These primary storage devices were short-lived in the market, since Williams tube was unreliable and the Selectron tube was expensive.

Electro-acoustic memory:

> Delay line memory used sound waves in a substance such as mercury to store information. Delay line memory was dynamic volatile, cycle sequential read/write storage, and was used for primary storage.

Optical tape:

> Is a medium for optical storage generally consisting of a long and narrow strip of plastic onto which patterns can be written and from which the patterns can

be read back. It shares some technologies with cinema film stock and optical discs, but is compatible with neither. The motivation behind developing this technology was the possibility of far greater storage capacities than either magnetic tape or optical discs.

Phase-change memory:

Uses different mechanical phases of Phase Change Material to store information in an X-Y addressable matrix, and reads the information by observing the varying electrical resistance of the material. Phase-change memory would be non-volatile, random-access read/write storage, and might be used for primary, secondary and off-line storage. Most rewritable and many write once optical disks already use phase change material to store information.

Holographic data storage:

Stores information optically inside crystals or photopolymers. Holographic storage can utilize the whole volume of the storage medium, unlike optical disc storage which is limited to a small number of surface layers. Holographic storage would be non-volatile, sequential access, and either write once or read/write storage. It might be used for secondary and off-line storage.

Molecular memory:

Stores information in polymer that can store electric charge. Molecular memory might be especially suited for primary storage. The theoretical storage capacity of molecular memory is 10 terabits per square inch.

## Related Technologies

## Redundancy

While a group of bits malfunction may be resolved by error detection and correction mechanisms, storage device malfunction requires different solutions. The following solutions are commonly used and valid for most storage devices:

- Device mirroring (replication) – A common solution to the problem is constantly maintaining an identical copy of device content on another device (typically of a same type). The downside is that this doubles the storage, and both devices (copies) need to be updated simultaneously with some overhead and possibly some delays. The upside is possible concurrent read of a same data group by two independent processes, which increases performance. When one of the replicated devices is detected to be defective, the other copy is still operational, and is being utilized to generate a new copy on another device (usually available operational in a pool of stand-by devices for this purpose).

- Redundant array of independent disks (RAID) – This method generalizes the device mirroring above by allowing one device in a group of N devices to fail and be replaced with the content restored (Device mirroring is RAID with N=2). RAID groups of N=5 or N=6 are common. N>2 saves storage, when comparing with N=2, at the cost of more processing during both regular operation (with often reduced performance) and defective device replacement.

Device mirroring and typical RAID are designed to handle a single device failure in the RAID group of devices. However, if a second failure occurs before the RAID group is completely repaired from the first failure, then data can be lost. The probability of a single failure is typically small. Thus the probability of two failures in a same RAID group in time proximity is much smaller (approximately the probability squared, i.e., multiplied by itself). If a database cannot tolerate even such smaller probability of data loss, then the RAID group itself is replicated (mirrored). In many cases such mirroring is done geographically remotely, in a different storage array, to handle also recovery from disasters.

## Network Connectivity

A secondary or tertiary storage may connect to a computer utilizing computer networks. This concept does not pertain to the primary storage, which is shared between multiple processors to a lesser degree.

- Direct-attached storage (DAS) is a traditional mass storage, that does not use any network. This is still a most popular approach. This retronym was coined recently, together with NAS and SAN.

- Network-attached storage (NAS) is mass storage attached to a computer which another computer can access at file level over a local area network, a private wide area network, or in the case of online file storage, over the Internet. NAS is commonly associated with the NFS and CIFS/SMB protocols.

- Storage area network (SAN) is a specialized network, that provides other computers with storage capacity. The crucial difference between NAS and SAN is the former presents and manages file systems to client computers, whilst the latter provides access at block-addressing (raw) level, leaving it to attaching systems to manage data or file systems within the provided capacity. SAN is commonly associated with Fibre Channel networks.

## Robotic Storage

Large quantities of individual magnetic tapes, and optical or magneto-optical discs may be stored in robotic tertiary storage devices. In tape storage field they are known as tape libraries, and in optical storage field optical jukeboxes, or optical disk libraries per analogy. Smallest forms of either technology containing just one drive device are referred to as autoloaders or autochangers.

Robotic-access storage devices may have a number of slots, each holding individual media, and usually one or more picking robots that traverse the slots and load media to built-in drives. The arrangement of the slots and picking devices affects performance. Important characteristics of such storage are possible expansion options: adding slots, modules, drives, robots. Tape libraries may have from 10 to more than 100,000 slots, and provide terabytes or petabytes of near-line information. Optical jukeboxes are somewhat smaller solutions, up to 1,000 slots.

Robotic storage is used for backups, and for high-capacity archives in imaging, medical, and video industries. Hierarchical storage management is a most known archiving strategy of automatically migrating long-unused files from fast hard disk storage to libraries or jukeboxes. If the files are needed, they are retrieved back to disk.

# Ontology

In computer science and information science, an ontology is a formal naming and definition of the types, properties, and interrelationships of the entities that really or fundamentally exist for a particular domain of discourse. It is thus a practical application of philosophical ontology, with a taxonomy.

An ontology compartmentalizes the variables needed for some set of computations and establishes the relationships between them.

The fields of artificial intelligence, the Semantic Web, systems engineering, software engineering, biomedical informatics, library science, enterprise bookmarking, and information architecture all create ontologies to limit complexity and to organize information. The ontology can then be applied to problem solving.

## Etymology and Definition

The term ontology has its origin in philosophy and has been applied in many different ways. The core meaning within computer science is a model for describing the world that consists of a set of types, properties, and relationship types. There is also generally an expectation that the features of the model in an ontology should closely resemble the real world (related to the object).

## Overview

What many ontologies have in common in both computer science and in philosophy is the representation of entities, ideas, and events, along with their properties and relations, according to a system of categories. In both fields, there is considerable work on problems of ontological relativity (e.g., Quine and Kripke in philosophy, Sowa and Guarino in computer science), and debates concerning whether a normative ontology is viable (e.g., debates over foundationalism in philosophy, and over the Cyc project in AI). Differences between the two are largely matters of focus. Computer scientists are more concerned with establishing fixed, controlled vocabularies, while philosophers are more concerned with first principles, such as whether there are such things as fixed essences or whether enduring objects must be ontologically more primary than processes.

Other fields make ontological assumptions that are sometimes explicitly elaborated and explored. For instance, the definition and ontology of economics (also sometimes called the political economy) is hotly debated especially in Marxist economics where it is a primary concern, but also in other subfields. Such concerns intersect with those of information science when a simulation or model is intended to enable decisions in the economic realm; for example, to determine what capital assets are at risk and if so by how much. Some claim all social sciences have explicit ontology issues because they do not have hard falsifiability criteria like most models in physical sciences and that indeed the lack of such widely accepted hard falsification criteria is what defines a social or soft science.

## History

Historically, ontologies arise out of the branch of philosophy known as metaphysics, which deals with the nature of reality – of what exists. This fundamental branch is concerned with analyzing various types or modes of existence, often with special attention to the relations between particulars and universals, between intrinsic and extrinsic properties, and between essence and existence. The traditional goal of ontological inquiry in particular is to divide the world "at its joints" to discover those fundamental categories or kinds into which the world's objects naturally fall.

During the second half of the 20th century, philosophers extensively debated the possible methods or approaches to building ontologies without actually building any very elaborate ontologies themselves. By contrast, computer scientists were building some large and robust ontologies, such as WordNet and Cyc, with comparatively little debate over how they were built.

Since the mid-1970s, researchers in the field of artificial intelligence (AI) have recognized that capturing knowledge is the key to building large and powerful AI systems. AI researchers argued that they could create new ontologies as computational models that enable certain kinds of automated reasoning. In the 1980s, the AI community began to use the term ontology to refer to both a theory of a modeled world and a component of knowledge systems. Some researchers, drawing inspiration from philosophical ontologies, viewed computational ontology as a kind of applied philosophy.

In the early 1990s, the widely cited Web page and paper "Toward Principles for the Design of Ontologies Used for Knowledge Sharing" by Tom Gruber is credited with a deliberate definition of ontology as a technical term in computer science. Gruber introduced the term to mean a specification of a conceptualization:

An ontology is a description (like a formal specification of a program) of the concepts and relationships that can formally exist for an agent or a community of agents. This definition is consistent with the usage of ontology as set of concept definitions, but more general. And it is a different sense of the word than its use in philosophy.

According to Gruber (1993):

Ontologies are often equated with taxonomic hierarchies of classes, class definitions, and the subsumption relation, but ontologies need not be limited to these forms. Ontologies are also not limited to conservative definitions — that is, definitions in the traditional logic sense that only introduce terminology and do not add any knowledge about the world. To specify a conceptualization, one needs to state axioms that do constrain the possible interpretations for the defined terms.

## Components

Contemporary ontologies share many structural similarities, regardless of the language in which they are expressed. As mentioned above, most ontologies describe individuals (instances), classes (concepts), attributes, and relations. In this section each of these components is discussed in turn.

Common components of ontologies include:

- Individuals: instances or objects (the basic or "ground level" objects).

- Classes: sets, collections, concepts, classes in programming, types of objects, or kinds of things.

- Attributes: aspects, properties, features, characteristics, or parameters that objects (and classes) can have.

- Relations: ways in which classes and individuals can be related to one another.

- Function terms: complex structures formed from certain relations that can be used in place of an individual term in a statement.

- Restrictions: formally stated descriptions of what must be true in order for some assertion to be accepted as input.

- Rules: statements in the form of an if-then (antecedent-consequent) sentence that describe the logical inferences that can be drawn from an assertion in a particular form.

- Axioms: assertions (including rules) in a logical form that together comprise the overall theory that the ontology describes in its domain of application. This definition differs from that of "axioms" in generative grammar and formal logic. In those disciplines, axioms include only statements asserted as a priori knowledge. As used here, "axioms" also include the theory derived from axiomatic statements.

- Events: the changing of attributes or relations.

Ontologies are commonly encoded using ontology languages.

## Types

## Domain Ontology

A domain ontology (or domain-specific ontology) represents concepts which belong to part of the world. Particular meanings of terms applied to that domain are provided by domain ontology. For example, the word card has many different meanings. An ontology about the domain of poker would model the "playing card" meaning of the word, while an ontology about the domain of computer hardware would model the "punched card" and "video card" meanings.

Since domain ontologies represent concepts in very specific and often eclectic ways, they are often incompatible. As systems that rely on domain ontologies expand, they often need to merge domain ontologies into a more general representation. This presents a challenge to the ontology designer. Different ontologies in the same domain arise due to different languages, different intended usage of the ontologies, and different perceptions of the domain (based on cultural background, education, ideology, etc.).

At present, merging ontologies that are not developed from a common foundation ontology is a largely manual process and therefore time-consuming and expensive. Domain ontologies that use the same foundation ontology to provide a set of basic elements with which to specify the meanings of the domain ontology elements can be merged automatically. There are studies on generalized techniques for merging ontologies, but this area of research is still largely theoretical.

## Upper Ontology

An upper ontology (or foundation ontology) is a model of the common objects that are generally applicable across a wide range of domain ontologies. It usually employs a core glossary that contains the terms and associated object descriptions as they are used in various relevant domain sets.

There are several standardized upper ontologies available for use, including BFO, BORO method, Dublin Core, GFO, OpenCyc/ResearchCyc, SUMO, the Unified Foundational Ontology (UFO), and DOLCE. WordNet, while considered an upper ontology by some, is not strictly an ontology. However, it has been employed as a linguistic tool for learning domain ontologies.

## Hybrid Ontology

The Gellish ontology is an example of a combination of an upper and a domain ontology.

## Visualization

A survey of ontology visualization techniques is presented by Katifori et al. An evaluation of two most established ontology visualization techniques: indented tree and graph is discussed in. A visual language for ontologies represented in OWL is specified by the Visual Notation for OWL Ontologies (VOWL).

## Engineering

Ontology engineering (or ontology building) is a subfield of knowledge engineering. It studies the ontology development process, the ontology life cycle, the methods and methodologies for building ontologies, and the tool suites and languages that support them.

Ontology engineering aims to make explicit the knowledge contained within software applications, and within enterprises and business procedures for a particular domain. Ontology engineering offers a direction towards solving the interoperability problems brought about by semantic obstacles, such as the obstacles related to the definitions of business terms and software classes. Ontology engineering is a set of tasks related to the development of ontologies for a particular domain.

## Editor

Ontology editors are applications designed to assist in the creation or manipulation of ontologies. They often express ontologies in one of many ontology languages. Some provide export to other ontology languages however.

Among the most relevant criteria for choosing an ontology editor are the degree to which the editor abstracts from the actual ontology representation language used for persistence and the visual navigation possibilities within the knowledge model. Next come built-in inference engines and information extraction facilities, and the support of meta-ontologies such as OWL-S, Dublin Core, etc. Another important feature is the ability to import & export foreign knowledge representation languages for ontology matching. Ontologies are developed for a specific purpose and application.

- a.k.a. software (Ontology, taxonomy and thesaurus management software available from The Synercon Group).

- Anzo for Excel (Includes an RDFS and OWL ontology editor within Excel; generates ontologies from Excel spreadsheets).

- Chimaera (Other web service by Stanford).

- CmapTools Ontology Editor (COE) (Java based ontology editor from the Florida Institute for Human and Machine Cognition. Supports numerous formats).

- dot15926 Editor (Open source ontology editor for data compliant to engineering ontology standard ISO 15926. Allows Python scripting and pattern-based data analysis. Supports extensions.)

- EMFText OWL2 Manchester Editor, Eclipse-based, open-source, Pellet integration.

- Enterprise Architect, along with UML modeling, supports OMG's Ontology Definition MetaModel which includes OWL and RDF.

- Fluent Editor, a comprehensive ontology editor for OWL and SWRL with Controlled Natural Language (Controlled English). Supports OWL, RDF, DL and Functional rendering, unlimited imports and built-in reasoning services.

- HOZO (Java-based graphical editor especially created to produce heavy-weight and well thought out ontologies, from Osaka University and Enegate Co, ltd.)

- Java Ontology Editor (JOE) (1998).

- KAON (single user and server based solutions possible, open source, from FZI/ AIFB Karlsruhe).

- KMgen (Ontology editor for the KM language. km: The Knowledge Machine).

- Knoodl (Free web application/service that is an ontology editor, wiki, and ontology registry. Supports creation of communities where members can collaboratively import, create, discuss, document and publish ontologies. Supports OWL, RDF, RDFS, and SPARQL queries. Available since early Nov 2006 from Revelytix, Inc..)

- Model Futures IDEAS AddIn (free) A plug-in for Sparx Systems Enterprise Architect that allows IDEAS Group 4D ontologies to be developed using a UML profile.

- Model Futures OWL Editor (Free) Able to work with very large OWL files (e.g. Cyc) and has extensive import and export capabilities (inc. UML, Thesaurus Descriptor, MS Word, CA ERwin Data Modeler, CSV, etc.)

- myWeb (Java-based, mySQL connection, bundled with applet that allows online browsing of ontologies (including OBO)).

- Neologism (Web-based, open source, supports RDFS and a subset of OWL, built on Drupal).

- NeOn Toolkit (Eclipse-based, open source, OWL support, several import mechanisms, support for reuse and management of networked ontologies, visualization, etc....from NeOn Project).

- OBO-Edit (Java-based, downloadable, open source, developed by the Gene Ontology Consortium for editing biological ontologies).

- OntoStudio (Eclipse-based, downloadable, support for RDF(S), OWL and F-Logic, graphical rule editor, visualizations, from ontoprise).

- Ontolingua (Web service offered by Stanford University).

- Open Semantic Framework (OSF), an integrated software stack using semantic technologies for knowledge management, which includes an ontology editor·

- OWLGrEd (A graphical ontology editor, easy-to-use).

- PoolParty Thesaurus Server (Commercial ontology, taxonomy and thesaurus management software available from Semantic Web Company, fully based on standards like RDFS, SKOS and SPARQL, integrated with Virtuoso Universal Server).

- Protégé (Java-based, downloadable, Supports OWL, open source, many sample ontologies, from Stanford University).

- ScholOnto (net-centric representations of research).

- Semantic Turkey (Firefox extension - also based on Java - for managing ontologies and acquiring new knowledge from the Web; developed at University of Rome, Tor Vergata ).

- Sigma knowledge engineering environment is a system primarily for development of the Suggested Upper Merged Ontology.

- Swoop (Java-based, downloadable, open source, OWL Ontology browser and editor from the University of Maryland).

- Semaphore Ontology Manager (Commercial ontology, taxonomy and thesaurus management software available from Smartlogic Semaphore Limited. Intuitive tool to manage the entire "build - enhance - review - maintain" ontology lifecycle.)

- Synaptica (Ontology, taxonomy and thesaurus management software available from Synaptica, LLC. Web based, supports OWL and SKOS.)

- TopBraid Composer (Eclipse-based, downloadable, full support for RDFS and OWL, built-in inference engine, SWRL editor and SPARQL queries, visualization, import of XML and UML, from TopQuadrant).

- Transinsight (The editor is especially designed for creating text mining ontologies and part of GoPubMed.org).

- WebODE (Web service offered by the Technical University of Madrid).

- TwoUse Toolkit (Eclipse-based, open source, model-driven ontology editing environment especially designed for software engineers).

- Be Informed Suite (Commercial tool for building large ontology based applications. Includes visual editors, inference engines, export to standard formats).

- Thesaurus Master (Manages creation and use of ontologies for use in data management and semantic enrichment by enterprise, government, and scholarly publishers.)

- TODE (A Dot Net-based Tool for Ontology Development and Editing).

- VocBench (Collaborative Web Application for SKOS/SKOS-XL Thesauri Management - developed on a joint effort between University of Rome, Tor Vergata and the Food and Agriculture Organization of the United Nations: FAO ).

- OBIS (Web based user interface that allows to input ontology instances in a user friendly way that can be accessed via SPARQL endpoint).

- Menthor Editor (An ontology engineering tool for dealing with OntoUML. It also includes OntoUML syntax validation, Alloy simulation, Anti-Pattern verification, and transformations from OntoUML to OWL, SBVR and Natural Language (Brazilian Portuguese)).

## Learning

Ontology learning is the automatic or semi-automatic creation of ontologies, including extracting a domain's terms from natural language text. As building ontologies manually is extremely labor-intensive and time consuming, there is great motivation to automate the process. Information extraction and text mining methods have been explored to automatically link ontologies to documents, e.g. in the context of the BioCreative challenges.

## Languages

An ontology language is a formal language used to encode the ontology. There are a number of such languages for ontologies, both proprietary and standards-based:

- Common Algebraic Specification Language is a general logic-based specification language developed within the IFIP working group 1.3 "Foundations of System Specifications" and functions as a de facto standard in the area of software specifications. It is now being applied to ontology specifications in order to provide modularity and structuring mechanisms.

- Common logic is ISO standard 24707, a specification for a family of ontology languages that can be accurately translated into each other.

- The Cyc project has its own ontology language called CycL, based on first-order predicate calculus with some higher-order extensions.

- DOGMA (Developing Ontology-Grounded Methods and Applications) adopts the fact-oriented modeling approach to provide a higher level of semantic stability.

- The Gellish language includes rules for its own extension and thus integrates an ontology with an ontology language.

- IDEF5 is a software engineering method to develop and maintain usable, accurate, domain ontologies.

- KIF is a syntax for first-order logic that is based on S-expressions. SUO-KIF is a derivative version supporting the Suggested Upper Merged Ontology.

- MOF and UML are standards of the OMG

- Olog is a category theoretic approach to ontologies, emphasizing translations between ontologies using functors.

- OBO, a language used for biological and biomedical ontologies.

- OntoUML is an ontologically well-founded profile of UML for conceptual modeling of domain ontologies.

- OWL is a language for making ontological statements, developed as a follow-on from RDF and RDFS, as well as earlier ontology language projects including OIL, DAML, and DAML+OIL. OWL is intended to be used over the World Wide Web, and all its elements (classes, properties and individuals) are defined as RDF resources, and identified by URIs.

- Rule Interchange Format (RIF) and F-Logic combine ontologies and rules.

- Semantic Application Design Language (SADL) captures a subset of the expressiveness of OWL, using an English-like language entered via an Eclipse Plug-in.

- SBVR (Semantics of Business Vocabularies and Rules) is an OMG standard adopted in industry to build ontologies.

- TOVE Project, TOronto Virtual Enterprise project.

## Published Examples

- AURUM - Information Security Ontology, An ontology for information security knowledge sharing, enabling users to collaboratively understand and extend the domain knowledge body. It may serve as a basis for automated information security risk and compliance management.

- BabelNet, a very large multilingual semantic network and ontology, lexicalized in many languages.

- Basic Formal Ontology, a formal upper ontology designed to support scientific research.

- BioPAX, an ontology for the exchange and interoperability of biological pathway (cellular processes) data.

- BMO, an e-Business Model Ontology based on a review of enterprise ontologies and business model literature.

- CCO and GexKB, Application Ontologies (APO) that integrate diverse types of knowledge with the Cell Cycle Ontology (CCO) and the Gene Expression Knowledge Base (GexKB).

- CContology (Customer Complaint Ontology), an e-business ontology to support online customer complaint management.

- CIDOC Conceptual Reference Model, an ontology for cultural heritage.

- COSMO, a Foundation Ontology (current version in OWL) that is designed to contain representations of all of the primitive concepts needed to logically specify the meanings of any domain entity. It is intended to serve as a basic ontology that can be used to translate among the representations in other ontologies or databases. It started as a merger of the basic elements of the OpenCyc and SUMO ontologies, and has been supplemented with other ontology elements (types, relations) so as to include representations of all of the words in the Longman dictionary defining vocabulary.

- Cyc, a large Foundation Ontology for formal representation of the universe of discourse.

- Disease Ontology, designed to facilitate the mapping of diseases and associated conditions to particular medical codes.

- DOLCE, a Descriptive Ontology for Linguistic and Cognitive Engineering.

- Dublin Core, a simple ontology for documents and publishing.

- Foundational, Core and Linguistic Ontologies.

- Foundational Model of Anatomy, an ontology for human anatomy.

- Friend of a Friend, an ontology for describing persons, their activities and their relations to other people and objects.

- Gene Ontology for genomics.

- Gellish English dictionary, an ontology that includes a dictionary and taxonomy that includes an upper ontology and a lower ontology that focusses on industrial and business applications in engineering, technology and procurement.

- Geopolitical ontology, an ontology describing geopolitical information created by Food and Agriculture Organization(FAO). The geopolitical ontology includes names in multiple languages (English, French, Spanish, Arabic, Chinese, Russian and Italian); maps standard coding systems (UN, ISO, FAOSTAT, AGROVOC, etc.); provides relations among territories (land borders, group membership, etc.); and tracks historical changes. In addition, FAO provides web services.

- <http://www.fao.org/countryprofiles/webservices.asp?lang=en> of geopolitical ontology and a module maker.

- <http://www.fao.org/countryprofiles/geoinfo/modulemaker/index.html> to download modules of the geopolitical ontology into different formats (RDF, XML, and EXCEL).

- <http://www.fao.org/countryprofiles/geoinfo.asp?lang=en>.

- GOLD, General Ontology for Linguistic Description.

- GUM (Generalized Upper Model), a linguistically motivated ontology for mediating between clients systems and natural language technology.

- IDEAS Group, a formal ontology for enterprise architecture being developed by the Australian, Canadian, UK and U.S. Defence Depts.

- Linkbase, a formal representation of the biomedical domain, founded upon Basic Formal Ontology.

- LPL, Lawson Pattern Language.

- NCBO Bioportal, biological and biomedical ontologies and associated tools to search, browse and visualise.

- NIFSTD Ontologies from the Neuroscience Information Framework: a modular set of ontologies for the neuroscience domain.

- OBO-Edit, an ontology browser for most of the Open Biological and Biomedical Ontologies.

- OBO Foundry, a suite of interoperable reference ontologies in biology and biomedicine.

- OMNIBUS Ontology, an ontology of learning, instruction, and instructional design.

- Ontology for Biomedical Investigations, an open access, integrated ontology for the description of biological and clinical investigations.

- ONSTR, Ontology for Newborn Screening Follow-up and Translational Research, Newborn Screening Follow-up Data Integration Collaborative, Emory University, Atlanta, GA.

- Plant Ontology for plant structures and growth/development stages, etc.

- POPE, Purdue Ontology for Pharmaceutical Engineering.

- PRO, the Protein Ontology of the Protein Information Resource, Georgetown University.

- Program abstraction taxonomy program abstraction taxonomy.

- Protein Ontology for proteomics.

- RXNO Ontology, for name reactions in chemistry.

- SNOMED CT (Systematized Nomenclature of Medicine -- Clinical Terms).

- Suggested Upper Merged Ontology, a formal upper ontology.

- Systems Biology Ontology (SBO), for computational models in biology.

- SWEET, Semantic Web for Earth and Environmental Terminology.

- ThoughtTreasure ontology.

- TIME-ITEM, Topics for Indexing Medical Education.

- Uberon, representing animal anatomical structures.

- UMBEL, a lightweight reference structure of 20,000 subject concept classes and their relationships derived from OpenCyc.

- WordNet, a lexical reference system·

- YAMATO, Yet Another More Advanced Top-level Ontology.

The W3C Linking Open Data community project coordinates attempts to converge different ontologies into worldwide Semantic Web.

## Libraries

The development of ontologies for the Web has led to the emergence of services providing lists or directories of ontologies with search facility. Such directories have been called ontology libraries.

The following are libraries of human-selected ontologies.

- COLORE is an open repository of first-order ontologies in Common Logic with formal links between ontologies in the repository.

- DAML Ontology Library maintains a legacy of ontologies in DAML.

- Ontology Design Patterns portal is a wiki repository of reusable components and practices for ontology design, and also maintains a list of exemplary ontologies. Started within the NeOn EU project.

- Protégé Ontology Library contains a set of OWL, Frame-based and other format ontologies.

- SchemaWeb is a directory of RDF schemata expressed in RDFS, OWL and DAML+OIL.

The following are both directories and search engines. They include crawlers searching the Web for well-formed ontologies:

- OBO Foundry is a suite of interoperable reference ontologies in biology and biomedicine.

- Bioportal (ontology repository of NCBO).

- OntoSelect Ontology Library offers similar services for RDF/S, DAML and OWL ontologies.

- Ontaria is a "searchable and browsable directory of semantic web data" with a focus on RDF vocabularies with OWL ontologies. (NB Project "on hold" since 2004).

- Swoogle is a directory and search engine for all RDF resources available on the Web, including ontologies.

- OOR - the Open Ontology Repository initiative - http://oor.net.

- ROMULUS is a foundational ontology repository aimed at improving semantic interoperability. Currently there are three foundational ontologies in the repository: DOLCE, BFO and GFO.

## Examples of Applications

In general, ontologies can be used beneficially in:

- enterprise applications. A more concrete example is SAPPHIRE (Health care) or Situational Awareness and Preparedness for Public Health Incidences and Reasoning Engines which is a semantics-based health information system capable of tracking and evaluating situations and occurrences that may affect public health.

- geographic information systems bring together data from different sources and benefit therefore from ontological metadata which helps to connect the semantics of the data.

## Criticisms

Werner Ceusters has noted the confusion caused by the significant differences in the meaning of word ontology when used by philosophy compared with the use of the word ontology in computer science, and advocates for greater precision in use of the word ontology so that members of the various disciplines using various definitions of the word ontology can communicate. He writes 'before one is able to answer the question 'what is an ontology?', one must provide first an answer to the question 'what does the word ontology mean?'.

It's also not clear how ontology fits with Schema on Read (NoSQL) databases.

# Knowledge Organization

Knowledge organization (KO) (or "organization of knowledge", "organization of information" or "information organization") is a branch of Library and Information Science (LIS) concerned with activities such as document description, indexing and classification performed in libraries, databases, archives, etc. These activities are done by librarians, archivists, subject specialists as well as by computer algorithms. KO as a field of study is concerned with the nature and quality of such knowledge organizing processes (KOP) (such as taxonomy and ontology) as well as the knowledge organizing systems (KOS) used to organize documents, document representations and concepts.

There exist different historical and theoretical approaches to and theories about organizing knowledge, which are related to different views of knowledge, cognition, language, and social organization. Each of these approaches tends to answer the question: "What is knowledge organization?" differently.

Traditional human-based activities are increasingly challenged by computer-based retrieval techniques. It is appropriate to investigate the relative contributions of different approaches; the current challenges make it imperative to reconsider this understanding.

The leading journal in this field is Knowledge Organization published by the International Society for Knowledge Organization (ISKO).

## Theoretical Approaches

One widely-used analysis of organizational principles summarizes them as by Location, Alphabet, Time, Category, Hierarchy (LATCH).

## Traditional Approaches

Among the major figures in the history of KO, which can be classified as "traditional", are Melvil Dewey (1851-1931) and Henry Bliss (1870-1955).

Dewey's goal was an efficient way to manage library collections; not an optimal system to support users of libraries. His system was meant to be used in many libraries as a standardized way to manage collections.

An important characteristic in Henry Bliss' (and many contemporary thinkers of KO) was that the sciences tend to reflect the order of Nature and that library classification should reflect the order of knowledge as uncovered by science:

Natural order --> Scientific Classification --> Library classification (KO)

The implication is that librarians, in order to classify books, should know about scientific developments. This should also be reflected in their education: "Again from the standpoint of the higher education of librarians, the teaching of systems of classification . . . would be perhaps better conducted by including courses in the systematic encyclopedia and methodology of all the sciences, that is to say, outlines which try to summarize the most recent results in the relation to one another in which they are now studied together. . . ." (Ernest Cushing Richardson, quoted from Bliss, 1935, p. 2).

Among the other principles, which may be attributed to the traditional approach to KO are:

- Principle of controlled vocabulary.

- Cutter's rule about specificity.

- Hulme's principle of literary warrant (1911).

- Principle of organizing from the general to the specific.

Today, after more than 100 years of research and development in LIS, the "traditional" approach still has a strong position in KO and in many ways its principles still dominate.

## Facet Analytic Approaches

The date of the foundation of this approach may be chosen as the publication of S. R. Ranganathan's Colon Classification in 1933. The approach has been further developed by, in particular, the British Classification Research Group. In many ways this approach has dominated what might be termed "modern classification theory."

The best way to explain this approach is probably to explain its analytico-synthetic methodology. The meaning of the term "analysis" is: Breaking down each subject into its basic concepts. The meaning of the term synthesis is: Combining the relevant units and concepts to describe the subject matter of the information package in hand.

Given subjects (as they appear in, for example, book titles) are first analyzed into a few common categories, which are termed "facets". Ranganathan proposed his PMEST formula: Personality, Matter, Energy, Space and Time:

## The Information Retrieval Tradition (IR)

Important in the IR-tradition have been, among others, the Cranfield experiments, which were founded in the 1950s, and the TREC experiments (Text Retrieval Conferences) starting in 1992. It was the Cranfield experiments, which introduced the famous measures "recall" and "precision" as evaluation criteria for systems efficiency. The Cranfield experiments found that classification systems like UDC and facet-analytic systems were less efficient compared to free-text searches or low level indexing systems ("UNITERM"). The Cranfield I test found according to Ellis (1996, 3-6) the following results.

| system | recall |
|---|---|
| UNITERM | 82,0% |
| Alphabetical subject headings | 81,5% |
| UDC | 75,6% |
| Facet classification scheme | 73,8% |

Although these results have been criticized and questioned, the IR-tradition became much more influential while library classification research lost influence. The dominant trend has been to regard only statistical averages. What has largely been neglected is to ask: Are there certain kinds of questions in relation to which other kinds of representation, for example, controlled vocabularies, may improve recall and precision?

## User-oriented and Cognitive Views

The best way to define this approach is probably by method: Systems based upon user-oriented approaches must specify how the design of a system is made on the basis of empirical studies of users.

User studies demonstrated very early that users prefer verbal search systems as opposed to systems based on classification notations. This is one example of a principle derived from empirical studies of users. Adherents of classification notations may, of course, still have an argument: That notations are well-defined and that users may miss important information by not considering them.

Folksonomies is a recent kind of KO based on users' rather than on librarians' or subject specialists' indexing.

# Bibliometric Approaches

These approaches are primarily based on using bibliographical references to organize networks of papers, mainly by bibliographic coupling (introduced by Kessler 1963) or co-citation analysis ( independently suggested by Marshakova 1973 and Small 1973). In recent years it has become a popular activity to construe bibliometric maps as structures of research fields.

Two considerations are important in considering bibliometric approaches to KO:

1. The level of indexing depth is partly determined by the number of terms assigned to each document. In citation indexing this corresponds to the number of references in a given paper. On the average, scientific papers contain 10-15 references, which provide quite a high level of depth.

2. The references, which function as access points, are provided by the highest subject-expertise: The experts writing in the leading journals. This expertise is much higher than that which library catalogs or bibliographical databases typically are able to draw on.

# The Domain Analytic Approach

Domain analysis is a sociological-epistemological standpoint. The indexing of a given document should reflect the needs of a given group of users or a given ideal purpose. In other words, any description or representation of a given document is more or less suited to the fulfillment of certain tasks. A description is never objective or neutral, and the goal is not to standardize descriptions or make one description once and for all for different target groups.

The development of the Danish library "KVINFO" may serve as an example that explains the domain-analytic point of view.

KVINFO was founded by the librarian and writer Nynne Koch and its history goes back to 1965. Nynne Koch was employed at the Royal Library in Copenhagen in a position without influence on book selection. She was interested in women's' studies and began personally to collect printed catalog cards of books in the Royal Library, which were considered relevant for women's studies. She developed a classification system for this subject. Later she became the head of KVINFO and got a budget for buying books and journals, and still later, KVINFO became an independent library. The important theoretical point of view is that the Royal Library had an official systematic catalog of a high standard. Normally it is assumed that such a catalog is able to identify relevant books for users whatever their theoretical orientation. This example demonstrates, however, that for a specific user group (feminist scholars), an alternative way of organizing catalog cards was important. In other words: Different points of view need different systems of organization.

DA is the only approach to KO which has seriously examined epistemological issues in the field, i.e. comparing the assumptions made in different approaches to KO and examining the questions regarding subjectivity and objectivity in KO. Subjectivity is not just about individual differences. Such differences are of minor interest because they cannot be used as guidelines for KO. What seems important are collective views shared by many users. A kind of subjectivity about many users is related to philosophical positions. In any field of knowledge different views are always at play. In arts, for example, different views of art are always present. Such views determine views on art works, writing on art works, how art works are organized in exhibitions and how writings on art are organized in libraries. In general it can be stated that different philosophical positions on any issue have implications for relevance criteria, information needs and for criteria of organizing knowledge.

## References

- Umeh, Jude (October 2007). The World Beyond Digital Rights Management. British Computer Society. p. 320. ISBN 978-1902505879

- J. S. Vitter, Algorithms and Data Structures for External Memory, Series on Foundations and Trends in Theoretical Computer Science, now Publishers, Hanover, MA, 2008, ISBN 978-1-60198-106-6

- Gruber, T. (2008). Liu, Ling; Özsu, M. Tamer, eds. Ontology. Encyclopedia of Database Systems (Springer-Verlag). ISBN 978-0-387-49616-0

- D'Atri A., De Marco M., Casalino N. (2008). "Interdisciplinary Aspects of Information Systems Studies", Physica-Verlag, Springer, Germany, pp. 1–416, doi:10.1007/978-3-7908-2010-2 ISBN 978-3-7908-2009-6

- Schumacher, E.F. Small is Beautiful: a Study of Economics as if People Mattered, ISBN 0-06-131778-0 (also ISBN 0-88179-169-5)

- Levinson, J.C. Guerrilla Marketing, Secrets for making big profits from your small business, Houghton Muffin Co. New York, 1984, ISBN 0-618-78591-4

- Umeh, Jude (October 2007). The World Beyond Digital Rights Management. British Computer Society. p. 320. ISBN 978-1902505879

- Aram, Michael; Neumann, Gustaf (2015-07-01). "Multilayered analysis of co-development of business information systems" (PDF). Journal of Internet Services and Applications 6 (1). doi:10.1186/s13174-015-0030-8

# Permissions

# Index

Printed in the USA
CPSIA information can be obtained
at www.ICGtesting.com
JSHW051418221024
72173JS00006B/1376